World Facts

The Earth

AREA: 196,951,900 sq mi (510,066,000 sq km)

LAND: 57,313,000 sq mi (148,647,000 sq km)—29.1%

WATER: 139,638,900 sq mi (361,419,000 sq km)— 70.9%

POPULATION: 6,314,000,000 people

The Continents

	AREA (sq mi)	(sq km)	Percent of Earth's Land
Asia	17,213,300	44,579,000	30.0
Africa	11,609,000	30,065,000	20.2
North America	9,449,500	24,474,000	16.5
South America	6,880,500	17,819,000	12.0
Antarctica	5,100,400	13,209,000	8.9
Europe	3,837,400	9,938,000	6.7
Australia	2,968,000	7,687,000	5.2

Highest Point On Each Continent

	feet	meters
Everest, Asia	29,035	8,850
Aconcagua, South America	22,834	6,960
McKinley (Denali), N. America	20,320	6,194
Kilimanjaro, Africa	19,340	5,895
El'brus, Europe	18,510	5,642
Vinson Massif, Antarctica	16,067	4,897
Kosciuszko, Australia	7,310	2,228

Lowest Point On Each Continent

	feet	meters
Dead Sea, Asia	-1,365	-416
Lake Assal, Africa	-512	-156
Death Valley, N. America	-282	-86
Valdés Peninsula, S. America	-131	-40
Caspian Sea, Europe	-92	-28
Lake Eyre, Australia	-52	-16
Antarctica (ice covered)	-8,366	-2,550

Ten Longest Rivers

	LENGTH miles	kilometers
Nile, Africa	4,241	6,825
Amazon, South America	4,000	6,437
Chang Jiang (Yangtze), Asia	3,964	6,380
Mississippi-Missouri, N. America	3,710	5,971
Yenisey-Angara, Asia	3,440	5,536
Yellow (Huang), Asia	3,395	5,464
Ob-Irtysh, Asia	3,361	5,410
Amur, Asia	2,744	4,416
Lena, Asia	2,734	4,400
Congo, Africa	2,715	4,370

Ten Largest Lakes

	AREA (Sq mi)	(Sq km)	Greatest Depth (feet)	(meters)
Caspian Sea, Europe-Asia	143,254	371,000	3,363	1,025
Superior, N. America	31,701	82,100	1,332	406
Victoria, Africa	26,836	69,500	269	82
Huron, N. America	23,013	59,600	751	229
Michigan, N. America	22,318	57,800	922	281
Tanganyika, Africa	12,587	32,600	4,823	1,470
Baikal, Asia	12,163	31,500	5,371	1,637
Great Bear, N. America	12,086	31,300	1,463	446
Malawi, Africa	11,159	28,900	2,280	695
Great Slave, N. America	11,100	28,750	2,014	614

Ten Largest Islands

	AREA (Sq mi)	(Sq km)
Greenland	840,065	2,175,600
New Guinea	306,008	792,500
Borneo	280,137	725,500
Madagascar	226,658	587,000
Baffin	195,961	507,500
Sumatra	164,993	427,300
Honshu	87,806	227,400
Great Britain	84,215	218,100
Victoria	83,906	217,300
Ellesmere	75,759	196,200

Oceans

	AREA (Sq mi)	(Sq km)	Percent of Earth's Water Area
Pacific	65,436,246	169,479,100	46.8
Atlantic	35,338,040	91,526,400	25.3
Indian	29,829,823	74,694,800	20.6
Arctic	5,390,024	13,960,100	3.9

Deepest Point In Each Ocean

	feet	meters
Challenger Deep, Mariana Trench, Pacific	35,827	10,920
Puerto Rico Trench, Atlantic	28,232	8,605
Java Trench, Indian	23,376	7,125
Molloy Hole, Arctic	18,599	5,669

Ten Largest Seas

	AREA (Sq mi)	(Sq km)	Average Depth (feet)	(meters)
Coral	1,615,262	4,183,510	8,106	2,471
South China	1,388,573	3,596,390	3,841	1,180
Caribbean	1,094,325	2,834,290	8,517	2,596
Bering	972,815	2,519,580	6,010	1,832
Mediterranean	953,324	2,469,100	5,147	1,572
Sea of Okhotsk	627,489	1,627,519	2,670	814
Gulf of Mexico	591,435	1,531,810	5,065	1,544
Norwegian	550,303	1,425,380	5,800	1,768
Greenland	447,048	1,157,850	4,734	1,443
Sea of Japan (East Sea)	389,291	1,008,260	5,403	1,647

Earth's Extremes

HOTTEST PLACE: Dalol, Denakil Depression, Ethiopia; annual average temperature— 93°F (34°C)

COLDEST PLACE: Plateau Station, Antarctica; annual average temperature— -134°F (-56.7°C)

WETTEST PLACE: Mawsynram, Assam, India; annual average rainfall— 467 in (1,187.3 cm)

DRIEST PLACE: Atacama Desert, Chile; rainfall barely measurable

HIGHEST WATERFALL: Angel, Venezuela— 3,212ft (979 m)

LARGEST DESERT: Sahara, Africa— 3,475,000 sq mi (9,000,000 sq km)

LARGEST CANYON: Grand Canyon, Colorado River, Arizona; 275 mi (443 km) long along river; 590 ft (180 m) to 18 mi (29 km) wide, about 1 mi (1.6 km) deep

LONGEST REEF: Great Barrier Reef, Australia— 1,429 mi (2,300 km)

GREATEST TIDES: Bay of Fundy, Nova Scotia— 55 ft (17 m)

ABBREVIATIONS

COUNTRY NAMES

ARM.	Armenia
AZERB.	Azerbaijan
B. & H.; BOSN. & HERZ.	Bosnia and Herzegovina
BELG.	Belgium
CRO.	Croatia
EST.	Estonia
HUNG.	Hungary
LATV.	Latvia
LIECH.	Liechtenstein
LITH.	Lithuania
LUX.	Luxembourg
MACED.	Macedonia
MOLD.	Moldova
N.Z.	New Zealand
NETH.	Netherlands
SERB. & MONT.	Serbia and Montenegro
SLOV.	Slovenia
SWITZ.	Switzerland
U.A.E.	United Arab Emirates
U.K.	United Kingdom
U.S.	United States

PHYSICAL FEATURES

I.-s.	Island-s
L.	Lake
Mt.-s.	Mont, Mount-ain-s
R.	River

OTHER

Eq.	Equatorial
Pop.	Population
Rep.	Republic
St.	Saint
&	and

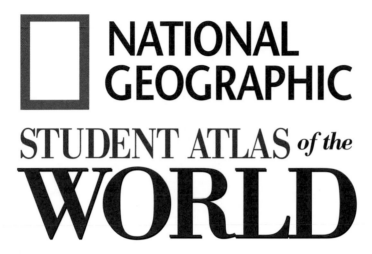

STUDENT ATLAS *of the* WORLD

NATIONAL GEOGRAPHIC
Washington, D.C.

About the Earth

The Continents

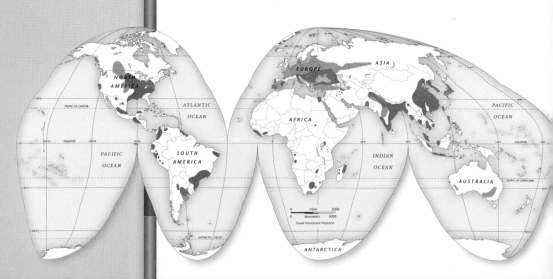

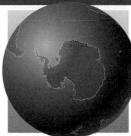

MERCURY

VENUS

EARTH

MARS

SUN

JUPITER

SATURN

URANUS

NEPTUNE

PLUTO

▲ *Nine planets* orbit the sun, held in place by its gravitational field. Mercury's orbit (below) is the shortest: 88 Earth days; Pluto's is the longest: 248 Earth years.

SUN
PLUTO
MERCURY
NEPTUNE
URANUS
SATURN
VENUS
EARTH
MARS
JUPITER

The Earth in Space

A t the center of our solar system is the sun, a huge mass of hot gas that is the source of both light and warmth for Earth. Third in a group of nine planets that revolve around the sun, Earth is a terrestrial, or mostly rocky, planet. So are Mercury, Venus, and Mars. Earth is about 93 million miles (150 million kilometers) from the sun, and its journey, or revolution, around the sun takes 365¼ days. Farther away from the sun, five more planets—Jupiter, Saturn, Uranus, and Neptune (all made up primarily of gases) plus tiny, mostly icy Pluto—complete the major heavenly bodies that make up our solar system. The solar system, in turn, is part of the Milky Way galaxy.

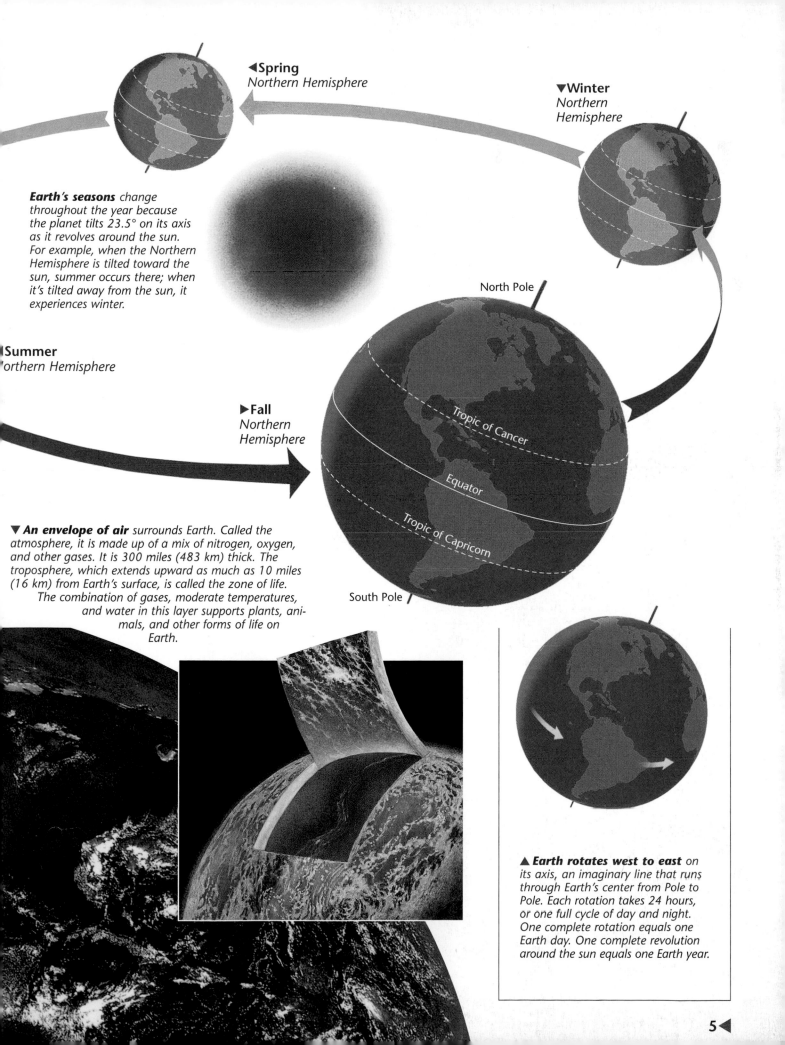

◀**Spring**
Northern Hemisphere

▼**Winter**
*Northern
Hemisphere*

Earth's seasons *change throughout the year because the planet tilts 23.5° on its axis as it revolves around the sun. For example, when the Northern Hemisphere is tilted toward the sun, summer occurs there; when it's tilted away from the sun, it experiences winter.*

◀**Summer**
Northern Hemisphere

▶**Fall**
*Northern
Hemisphere*

North Pole

Tropic of Cancer

Equator

Tropic of Capricorn

South Pole

▼ **An envelope of air** *surrounds Earth. Called the atmosphere, it is made up of a mix of nitrogen, oxygen, and other gases. It is 300 miles (483 km) thick. The troposphere, which extends upward as much as 10 miles (16 km) from Earth's surface, is called the zone of life. The combination of gases, moderate temperatures, and water in this layer supports plants, animals, and other forms of life on Earth.*

▲ **Earth rotates west to east** *on its axis, an imaginary line that runs through Earth's center from Pole to Pole. Each rotation takes 24 hours, or one full cycle of day and night. One complete rotation equals one Earth day. One complete revolution around the sun equals one Earth year.*

Learning About Maps

MAP PROJECTIONS

Maps tell a story about physical and human systems, places and regions, patterns and relationships. This atlas is a collection of maps that tell a story about Earth.

Understanding that story requires a knowledge of how maps are made and a familiarity with the special language used by cartographers, the people who create maps.

Globes present a model of Earth as it is—a sphere—but they are bulky and can be difficult to use and store. Flat maps are much more convenient, but certain problems result from transferring Earth's curved surface to a flat piece of paper, a process called projection. There are many different types of projections, all of which involve some form of distortion: area, distance, direction, or shape.

Web Link

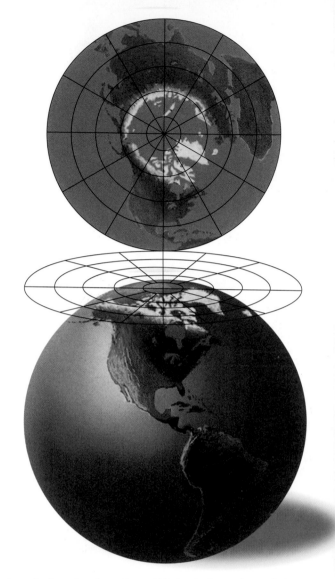

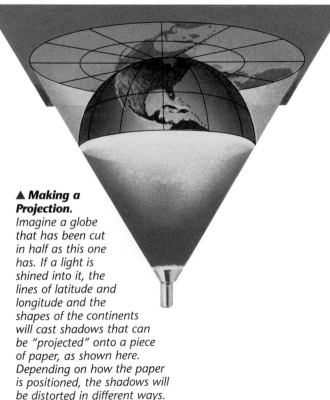

▲ **Making a Projection.** Imagine a globe that has been cut in half as this one has. If a light is shined into it, the lines of latitude and longitude and the shapes of the continents will cast shadows that can be "projected" onto a piece of paper, as shown here. Depending on how the paper is positioned, the shadows will be distorted in different ways.

▲ **Azimuthal Projection Map.** This kind of map is made by projecting a globe onto a flat surface that touches the globe at a single point, such as the North Pole. These maps accurately represent direction along any straight line extending from the point of contact. Away from the point of contact, shape is increasingly distorted.

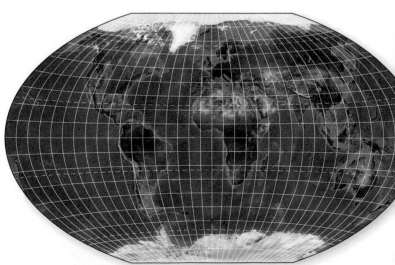

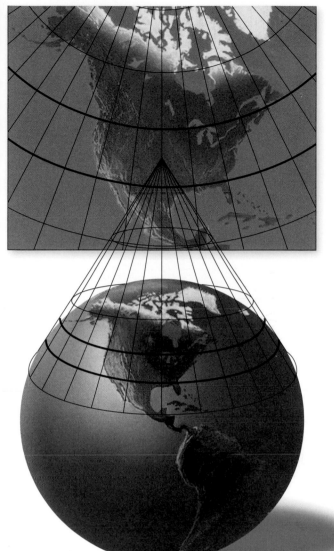

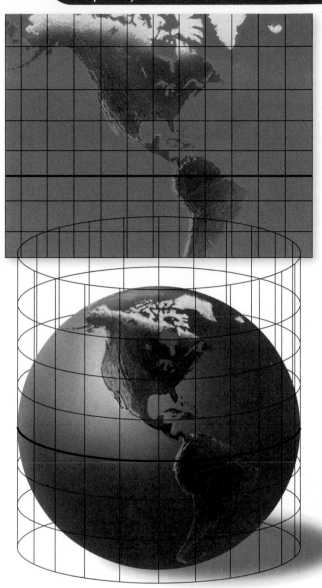

▲**Conic Projection Map.** This kind of map is made by projecting a globe onto a cone. The part of Earth being mapped touches the sides of the cone. Lines of longitude appear as straight lines; lines of latitude appear as parallel arcs. Conic projections are often used to map mid-latitude areas with great east-west extent, such as North America.

▲**Cylindrical Projection Map.** A cylindrical projection map is made by projecting a globe onto a cylinder that touches Earth's surface along the Equator. Latitude and longitude lines on this kind of map show true compass directions, which makes it useful for navigation. But there is great distortion in the size of high-latitude landmasses.

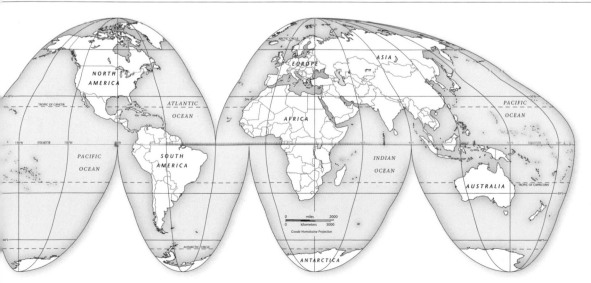

◄ **Other Projections.** Sometimes cartographers create general purpose world projections, such as the Winkel Tripel (far left), in which distortion of both size and shape is minimized. This creates a reasonably accurate image of Earth. Another general purpose projection is the Goode's Interrupted Homolosine (left), which interrupts ocean areas to preserve the relative size and shape of land areas.

READING MAPS

People can use maps to find locations, to determine direction or distance, and to understand information about places. Cartographers rely on a special graphic language to communicate through maps.

An imaginary system of lines, called the global grid, helps us locate particular points on Earth's surface. The global grid is made up of lines of latitude and longitude that are measured in degrees, minutes, and seconds. The point where these lines intersect identifies the absolute location of a place. No other place has the exact same address. Web Link

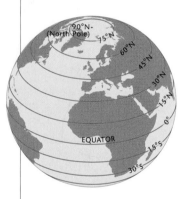

◀ **Latitude.** Lines of latitude—also called parallels because they are parallel to the Equator—run east to west around the globe and measure location north or south of the Equator. The Equator is 0° latitude.

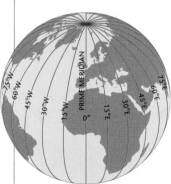

◀ **Longitude.** Lines of longitude, also called meridians, run from Pole to Pole and measure location east or west of the prime meridian. The prime meridian is 0° longitude, and it runs through Greenwich, near London, England.

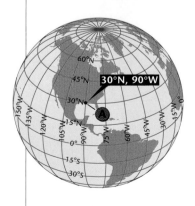

◀ **Global Grid.** When used together, latitude and longitude form a grid that provides a system for determining the exact, or absolute, location of every place on Earth. For example, the absolute location of point A is 30°N, 90°W.

▲ **Direction.** Cartographers put a north arrow or a compass rose, which shows the four cardinal directions—north, south, east, and west—on a map. On this map, point B is northwest (NW) of point A. Northwest is an example of an intermediate direction, which means it is between two cardinal directions. Grid lines can also be used to indicate north.

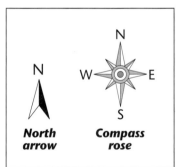

North arrow   **Compass rose**

▶ **Scale.** A map represents a part of Earth's surface, but that part is greatly reduced. Cartographers include a map scale to show what distance on Earth is represented by a given length on the map. Scale can be graphic (a bar), verbal, or a ratio.

To determine how many miles point A is from point B, place a piece of paper on the map above and mark the distance between A and B. Then compare the marks on the paper with the bar scale on the map.

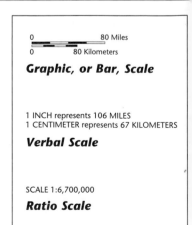

Graphic, or Bar, Scale

1 INCH represents 106 MILES
1 CENTIMETER represents 67 KILOMETERS

Verbal Scale

SCALE 1:6,700,000

Ratio Scale

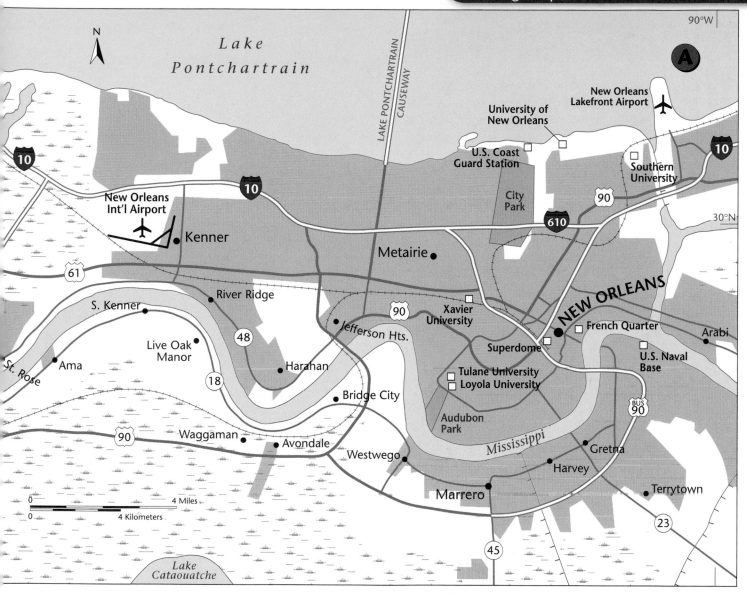

▼ **Symbols.** *Finally, cartographers use a variety of symbols, which are identified in a map key or legend, to tell us more about the places represented on the map. There are three general types of symbols:*

Point symbols show exact location of places (such as cities) or quantity (a large dot can mean a more populous city).

Line symbols show boundaries or connections (such as roads, canals, and other trade links).

Area symbols show the form and extent of a feature (such as a lake, park, or swamp).

Additional information may be coded in color, size, and shape.

▲ **Putting It All Together.** *We already know from the map on page 8 which states A and B are located in. But to find out more about city A, we need a larger scale map—one that shows a smaller area in more detail (see above).*

▨ Metropolitan area		━━━ Road	
▨ Lake or river		┼┼┼┼ Railroad	
▨ Park		╲╱ Runway	
▨ Swamp		✈ Airport	
┼┼┼ Canal		□ Point of interest	
══ Highway		●●● Town	

TYPES OF MAPS

This atlas includes many different types of maps so that a wide variety of information about Earth can be presented. Three of the most commonly used types of maps are physical, political, and thematic.

A **physical map** identifies natural features, such as mountains, deserts, oceans, and lakes. Area symbols of various colors and shadings may indicate height above sea level or, as in the example here, ecosystems. Similar symbols could also show water depth.

A **political map** shows how people have divided the world into countries. Political maps can also show states, counties, or cities within a country. Line symbols indicate boundaries, and point symbols show the locations and sometimes sizes of cities.

Thematic maps use a variety of symbols to show distributions and patterns on Earth. For example, a choropleth map uses shades of color to represent different values. The example here shows the amount of energy consumed each year by various countries. Thematic maps can show many different things, such as patterns of vegetation, land use, and religions.

A **cartogram** is a special kind of thematic map in which the size of a country is based on some statistic other than land area. In the cartogram at far right, population size determines the size of each country. This is why Nigeria—the most populous country in Africa—appears much larger than Sudan, which has more than double the land area of Nigeria (see the political map). Cartograms allow for a quick visual comparison of countries in terms of a selected statistic.

Web Link

This globe is useful for showing Africa's position and size relative to other landmasses, but very little detail is possible at this scale. By using different kinds of maps, mapmakers can show a variety of information in more detail.

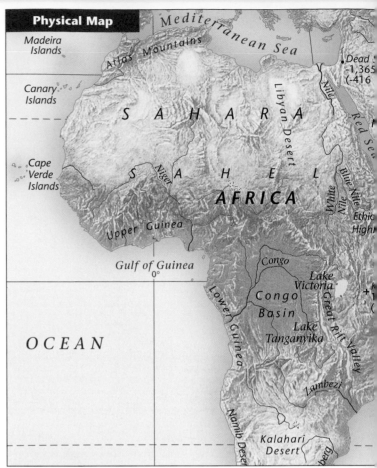

Physical Map

Madeira Islands
Canary Islands
Cape Verde Islands
Mediterranean Sea
Atlas Mountains
Nile
Dead
-1,365
(-416
S A H A R A
Libyan Desert
Red Sea
S A H E L
AFRICA
White Nile
Blue Nile
Ethiopic High
Niger
Upper Guinea
Gulf of Guinea
0°
Congo
Lake Victoria
Congo Basin
Great Rift Valley
Lake Tanganyika
Lower Guinea
OCEAN
Zambezi
Namib Desert
Kalahari Desert
berg

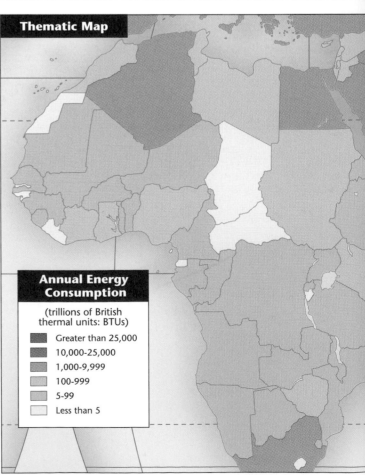

Thematic Map

Annual Energy Consumption

(trillions of British thermal units: BTUs)

■	Greater than 25,000
■	10,000-25,000
■	1,000-9,999
■	100-999
■	5-99
□	Less than 5

Political Map

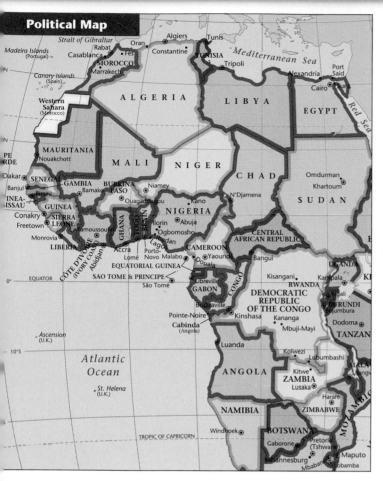

Cartogram

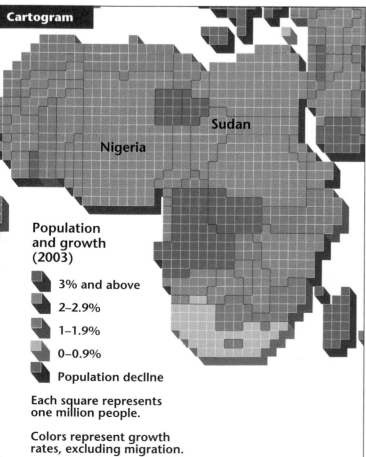

Population and growth (2003)

- 3% and above
- 2–2.9%
- 1–1.9%
- 0–0.9%
- Population decline

Each square represents one million people.

Colors represent growth rates, excluding migration.

Satellite Image Maps

Satellites orbiting Earth transmit images of the surface to computers on the ground. These computers translate the information into special maps (below) that use colors to show various characteristics. Such maps are valuable tools for identifying patterns or comparing changes over time.

▼ **Cloud Coverage**

▼ **Topography/Bathymetry**

▼ **Sea Level Variability**

▼ **Sea Surface Temperature**

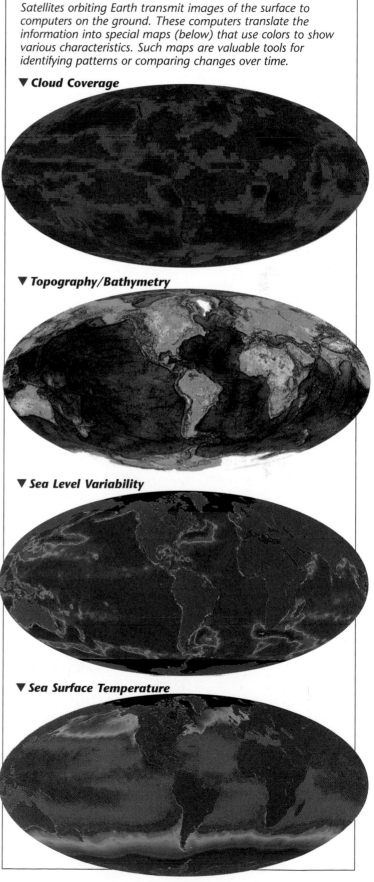

Physical Systems

THE PHYSICAL WORLD

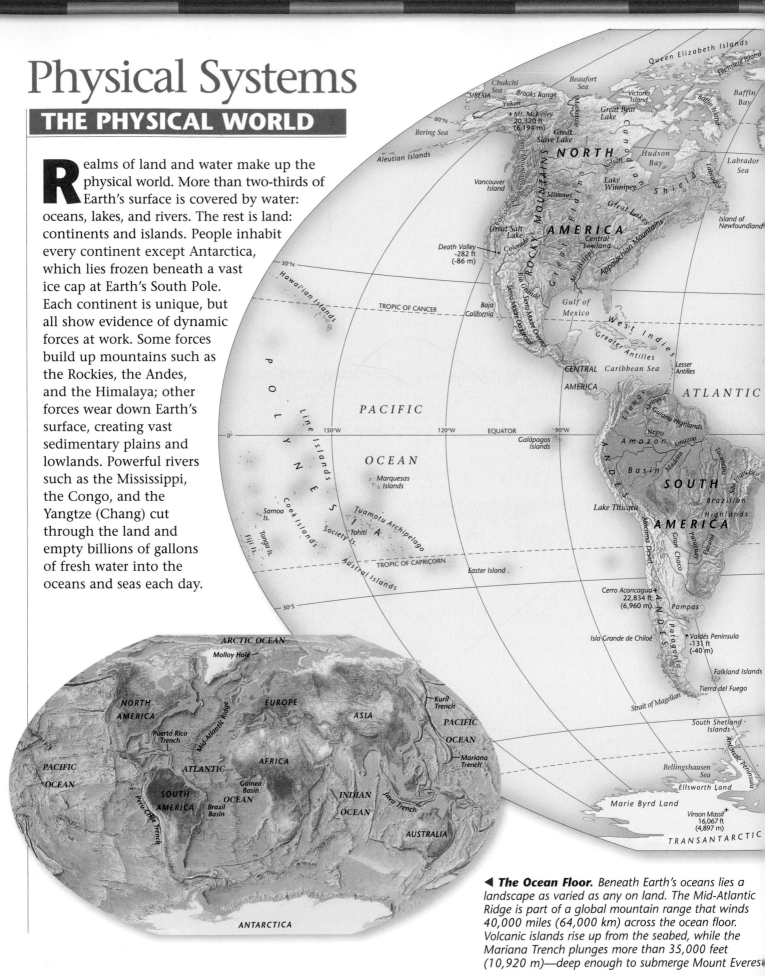

Realms of land and water make up the physical world. More than two-thirds of Earth's surface is covered by water: oceans, lakes, and rivers. The rest is land: continents and islands. People inhabit every continent except Antarctica, which lies frozen beneath a vast ice cap at Earth's South Pole. Each continent is unique, but all show evidence of dynamic forces at work. Some forces build up mountains such as the Rockies, the Andes, and the Himalaya; other forces wear down Earth's surface, creating vast sedimentary plains and lowlands. Powerful rivers such as the Mississippi, the Congo, and the Yangtze (Chang) cut through the land and empty billions of gallons of fresh water into the oceans and seas each day.

◀ **The Ocean Floor.** Beneath Earth's oceans lies a landscape as varied as any on land. The Mid-Atlantic Ridge is part of a global mountain range that winds 40,000 miles (64,000 km) across the ocean floor. Volcanic islands rise up from the seabed, while the Mariana Trench plunges more than 35,000 feet (10,920 m)—deep enough to submerge Mount Everest

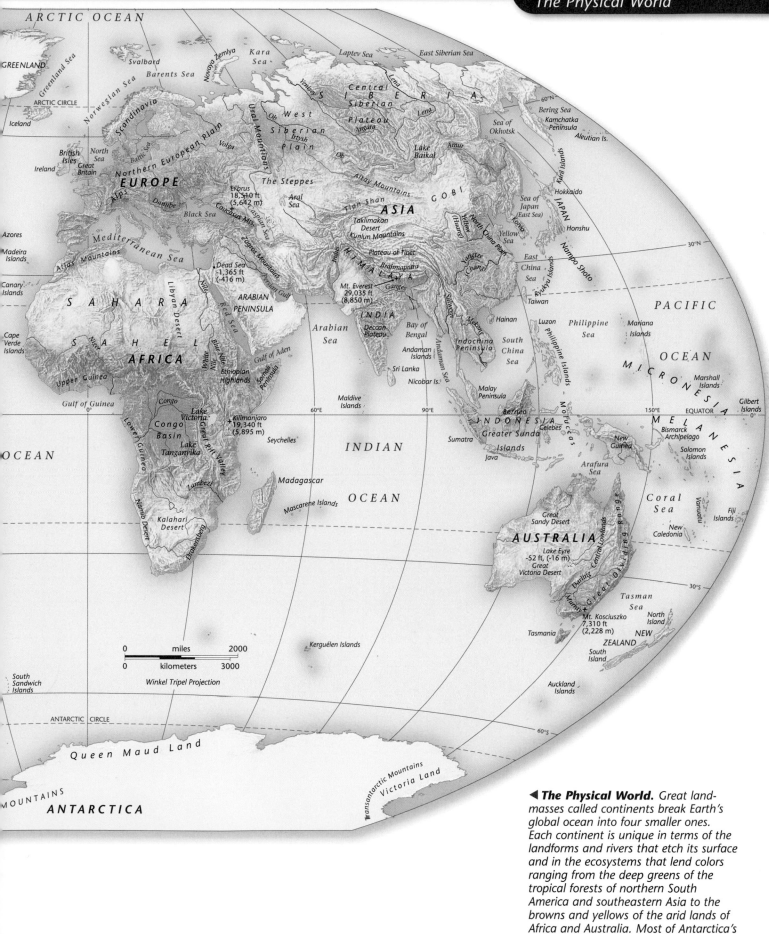

ARCTIC OCEAN

GREENLAND

Greenland Sea

ARCTIC CIRCLE

Iceland

Norwegian Sea

Svalbard

Barents Sea

Novaya Zemlya

Kara Sea

Laptev Sea

East Siberian Sea

Lena

Central Siberian Plateau

60°N

Bering Sea

Kamchatka Peninsula

Aleutian Is.

British Isles

Ireland

North Sea

Great Britain

Baltic Sea

Scandinavia

Northern European Plain

Ural Mountains

West Siberian Plain

Ob

Irtysh

Yenisey

Angara

Lena

Amur

Lake Baikal

Sea of Okhotsk

Kuril Islands

Hokkaido

EUROPE

Alps

Danube

Volga

The Steppes

Altay Mountains

GOBI

Sea of Japan (East Sea)

JAPAN

Honshu

Azores

Madeira Islands

Canary Islands

Cape Verde Islands

Mediterranean Sea

Atlas Mountains

Black Sea

Caucasus Mts.

Elbrus 18,510 ft (5,642 m)

Caspian Sea

Aral Sea

Tian Shan

ASIA

Taklimakan Desert

Kunlun Mountains

Plateau of Tibet

Korea

Yellow (Huang)

North China Plain

Yellow Sea

East China Sea

Ryukyu Islands

Taiwan

Nampo Shoto

30°N

PACIFIC

SAHARA

SAHEL

AFRICA

Libyan Desert

Nile

Red Sea

Dead Sea -1,365 ft (-416 m)

Zagros Mountains

Persian Gulf

ARABIAN PENINSULA

Arabian Sea

Tigris

HIMALAYA

Mt. Everest 29,035 ft (8,850 m)

Brahmaputra

Ganges

INDIA

Deccan Plateau

Yangtze (Chang)

Mekong

Salween

Hainan

Luzon

Philippine Sea

Mariana Islands

OCEAN

Upper Guinea

Niger

Gulf of Guinea

0°

White Nile

Blue Nile

Ethiopian Highlands

Somali Peninsula

Gulf of Aden

Bay of Bengal

Andaman Islands

Sri Lanka

Nicobar Is.

Andaman Sea

Indochina Peninsula

South China Sea

Philippine Islands

MICRONESIA

Marshall Islands

Gilbert Islands

0°

Congo

Lake Victoria

Great Rift Valley

Kilimanjaro 19,340 ft (5,895 m)

60°E

Maldive Islands

90°E

Malay Peninsula

Borneo

INDONESIA

Greater Sunda Islands

Celebes

Moluccas

150°E

EQUATOR

MELANESIA

Bismarck Archipelago

Lower Guinea

Congo Basin

Lake Tanganyika

Seychelles

INDIAN

Sumatra

Java

New Guinea

Solomon Islands

OCEAN

Zambezi

Madagascar

Mascarene Islands

OCEAN

Arafura Sea

Vanuatu

Fiji Islands

Namib Desert

Kalahari Desert

Drakensberg

Coral Sea

New Caledonia

South Sandwich Islands

0 miles 2000

0 kilometers 3000

Winkel Tripel Projection

Kerguélen Islands

Great Sandy Desert

AUSTRALIA

Lake Eyre -52 ft, (-16 m)

Great Victoria Desert

Darling

Murray

Central Lowlands

Great Dividing Range

Tasman Sea

North Island

30°S

Mt. Kosciuszko 7,310 ft (2,228 m)

Tasmania

NEW ZEALAND

South Island

Auckland Islands

60°S

ANTARCTIC CIRCLE

Queen Maud Land

Transantarctic Mountains

Victoria Land

MOUNTAINS

ANTARCTICA

◀ **The Physical World.** *Great land-masses called continents break Earth's global ocean into four smaller ones. Each continent is unique in terms of the landforms and rivers that etch its surface and in the ecosystems that lend colors ranging from the deep greens of the tropical forests of northern South America and southeastern Asia to the browns and yellows of the arid lands of Africa and Australia. Most of Antarctica's features are hidden beneath its ice cap.*

EARTH'S GEOLOGIC HISTORY

Earth is a dynamic planet. Its outer shell, or crust, is broken into huge pieces called plates. These plates ride on the slowly moving molten rock, or magma, that lies beneath the crust. Their movement constantly changes Earth's surface. For instance, along one convergent boundary—a place where two plates meet—the Indian Plate moves northward, colliding with the Eurasian Plate and heaving up the still growing mountains of the Himalaya. Along another convergent boundary, the Nazca Plate dives beneath the South American Plate in a process called subduction. Volcanoes and underwater earthquakes may occur along subduction zones, sometimes triggering giant waves called tsunamis. Along transform zones, such as California's San Andreas Fault, plates grind past each other, resulting in destructive earthquakes. The Mid-Atlantic Ridge is a divergent boundary where plates are pulling apart, allowing rising molten rock to form new ocean floor. `Web Link`

▼ **Our Changing Planet.** The Latin phrase terra firma implies planet Earth is solid and unchanging. However, Earth's surface has been anything but unchanging. Geologic evidence suggests that moving plates have collided and moved apart more than once over the course of the planet's long history. As the main map shows, the forces of change show no signs of stopping.

JUAN DE FUCA PLATE

NORTH AMERICAN PLATE

ROCKY MOUNTAINS

MID-ATLANTIC RIDGE

San Andreas Fault

Hawaiian Islands

PACIFIC PLATE

PACIFIC OCEAN

EQUATOR

EAST PACIFIC RISE

COCOS PLATE

CARIBBEAN PLATE

ATLANTIC

NAZCA PLATE

ANDES

SOUTH AMERICAN PLATE

ANTARCTIC PLATE

SCOTIA PLATE

▶ **Pangaea.**
About 240 million years ago, all of Earth's continents collided to form a vast landmass (now called Pangaea) that stretched from Pole to Pole.

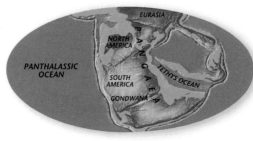

EURASIA

NORTH AMERICA

PANGAEA

PANTHALASSIC OCEAN

SOUTH AMERICA

TETHYS OCEAN

GONDWANA

▶ **Drifting Apart.**
By 94 million years ago, Pangaea had been pulled apart into smaller landmasses. In the warm global climate, dinosaurs evolved into Earth's dominant animal group.

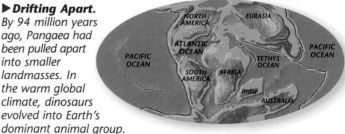

NORTH AMERICA

EURASIA

ATLANTIC OCEAN

PACIFIC OCEAN

PACIFIC OCEAN

SOUTH AMERICA

AFRICA

TETHYS OCEAN

India

AUSTRALIA

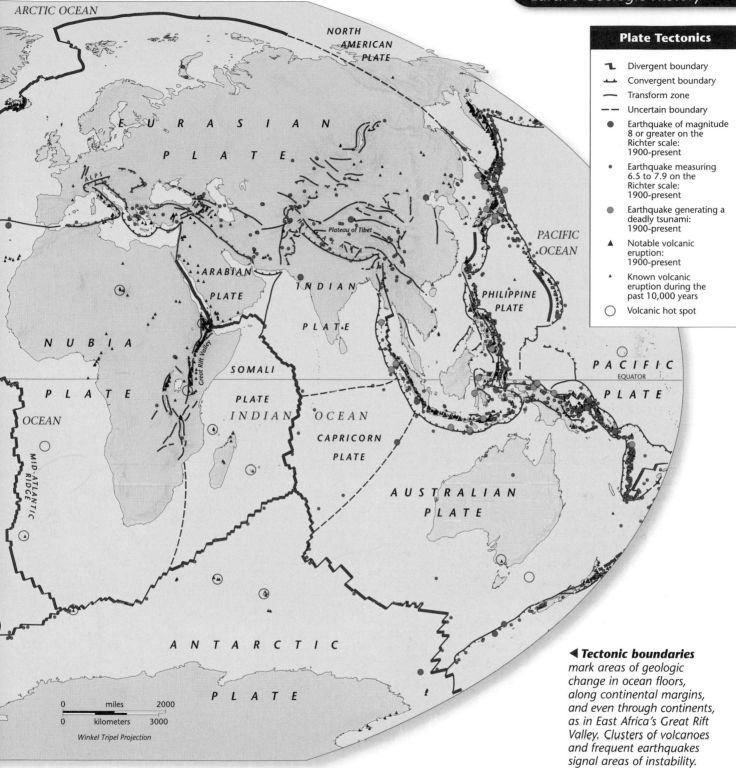

ARCTIC OCEAN

NORTH AMERICAN PLATE

E U R A S I A N   P L A T E

ALPS

ARABIAN PLATE

Plateau of Tibet

PACIFIC OCEAN

PHILIPPINE PLATE

N U B I A   P L A T E

OCEAN

Great Rift Valley

SOMALI PLATE

INDIAN PLATE

INDIAN OCEAN

CAPRICORN PLATE

PACIFIC PLATE

EQUATOR

MID-ATLANTIC RIDGE

A U S T R A L I A N   P L A T E

A N T A R C T I C   P L A T E

0 miles 2000
0 kilometers 3000
Winkel Tripel Projection

Plate Tectonics

⊿	Divergent boundary
⊿⊿	Convergent boundary
—	Transform zone
- - -	Uncertain boundary
●	Earthquake of magnitude 8 or greater on the Richter scale: 1900-present
•	Earthquake measuring 6.5 to 7.9 on the Richter scale: 1900-present
●	Earthquake generating a deadly tsunami: 1900-present
▲	Notable volcanic eruption: 1900-present
▴	Known volcanic eruption during the past 10,000 years
○	Volcanic hot spot

◀ **Tectonic boundaries**
mark areas of geologic
change in ocean floors,
along continental margins,
and even through continents,
as in East Africa's Great Rift
Valley. Clusters of volcanoes
and frequent earthquakes
signal areas of instability.

▶ **Eve of Destruction.**
By 65 million years
ago, continents were
moving toward their
current positions.
The impact (✱) of an
asteroid in the Gulf
of Mexico probably
extinguished the
dinosaurs and many
other species.

▶ **Deep Freeze.**
By 18,000 years
ago, the continents
resembled their
current shapes.
A great ice age
had the far
northern and
southern regions
locked under huge
ice sheets.

EARTH'S LAND & WATER FEATURES

The largest land and water features on Earth are the continents and the oceans, but many other features—large and small—make each place unique. Mountains, plateaus, and plains give texture to the land. The Rockies and the Andes rise high above the lowlands of North and South America. In Asia, the Himalaya and the Plateau of Tibet form the rugged core of Earth's largest continent. These features are the result of powerful forces within Earth pushing up the land. Other landforms, such as canyons and valleys, are created when weathering and erosion wear down parts of Earth's surface.

Dramatic features are not limited to the land. Submarine mountains, appearing like pale blue threads against the deep blue on the satellite map, rise from the seafloor and trace zones of underwater geologic activity. Deep trenches form where plates collide, causing one to dive beneath the other. **Web Link**

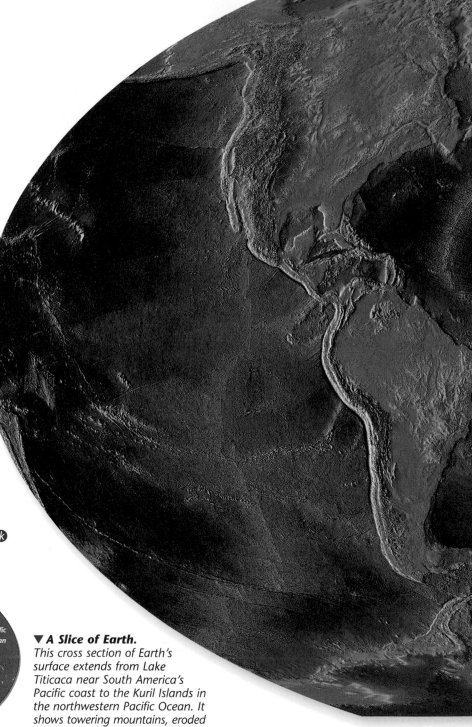

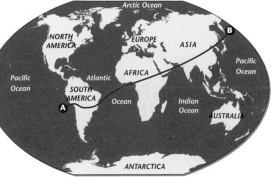

▼ A Slice of Earth.
This cross section of Earth's surface extends from Lake Titicaca near South America's Pacific coast to the Kuril Islands in the northwestern Pacific Ocean. It shows towering mountains, eroded highlands, broad coastal plains, and deep ocean basins.

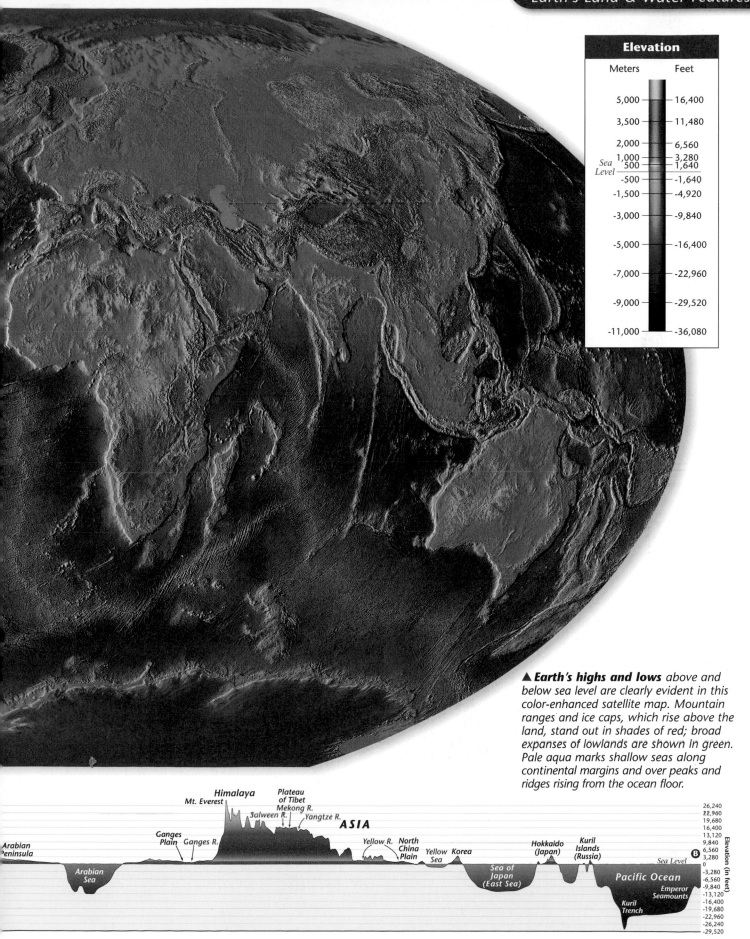

Elevation

Meters	Feet
5,000	16,400
3,500	11,480
2,000	6,560
1,000	3,280
500	1,640
Sea Level	
-500	-1,640
-1,500	-4,920
-3,000	-9,840
-5,000	-16,400
-7,000	-22,960
-9,000	-29,520
-11,000	-36,080

▲ **Earth's highs and lows** above and below sea level are clearly evident in this color-enhanced satellite map. Mountain ranges and ice caps, which rise above the land, stand out in shades of red; broad expanses of lowlands are shown in green. Pale aqua marks shallow seas along continental margins and over peaks and ridges rising from the ocean floor.

EARTH'S CLIMATES

Climate is not the same as weather. Climate is the long-term average of conditions in the atmosphere at a particular location on Earth's surface. Weather refers to the momentary conditions of the atmosphere. Climate is important because it influences vegetation and soil development. It also influences people's choices about how and where to live.

There are many different systems for classifying climates. One commonly used system was developed by Russian-born climatologist Wladimir Köppen and later modified by American climatologist Glenn Trewartha. Köppen's system identifies five major climate zones based on average precipitation and temperature, and a sixth zone for highland, or high elevation, areas. Except for continental climate, all climate zones occur in mirror image north and south of the Equator. Web Link

▼ *Climate Graphs. A climate graph is a combination bar and line graph that shows monthly averages of precipitation and temperature for a particular place. The bar graph shows precipitation in inches and centimeters; the line graph shows temperature in degrees Fahrenheit and Celsius. The graphs below are typical for places in the climate zone represented by their background color. The seeming inversion of the temperature lines for Alice Springs and McMurdo reflects the reversal of seasons south of the Equator, where January is midsummer.*

NORTH AMERICA

Resolute

Fairbanks

60°N

Subarctic Current

North Pacific Drift

Des Moines

30°N

Gulf Stream

North Atlantic Drift

Labrador Current

TROPIC OF CANCER

Monterrey

PACIFIC OCEAN

Equatorial Countercurrent

150°W   120°W   EQUATOR   90°W

0°

South Equatorial Current

ATLANTIC

Belém

SOUTH AMERICA

Peru Current

Brazil Current

TROPIC OF CAPRICORN

30°S

0   miles   2000
0   kilometers   3000

Winkel Tripel Projection

Falkland Current

60°S

West Wind Drift

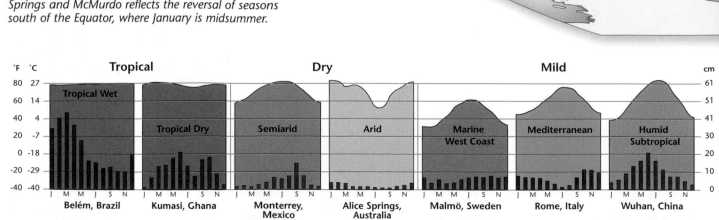

	Tropical		Dry		Mild		
Tropical Wet	Tropical Dry	Semiarid	Arid	Marine West Coast	Mediterranean	Humid Subtropical	
Belém, Brazil	Kumasi, Ghana	Monterrey, Mexico	Alice Springs, Australia	Malmö, Sweden	Rome, Italy	Wuhan, China	

°F °C
80 27
60 14
40 4
20 -7
0 -18
-20 -29
-40 -40

cm
61
51
41
30
20
10
0

Climatic Zones

(based on Köppen System)

Tropical
- Tropical wet
- Tropical dry

Dry
- Semiarid
- Arid

Mild
- Marine west coast
- Mediterranean
- Humid subtropical

Continental
- Warm summer
- Cool Summer
- Subarctic

Polar
- Tundra
- Ice cap

High Elevations
- Highlands
- Uplands

→ Warm ocean current
→ Cool ocean current
→ Prevailing wind

ARCTIC OCEAN

North Atlantic Drift

ARCTIC CIRCLE

Malmö

Minsk

EUROPE

Rome

AFRICA

Kumasi

Kampala

ASIA

Lhasa

Wuhan

Kuroshio

North Equatorial Current

PACIFIC

60°N

OCEAN

Equatorial Countercurrent

EQUATOR

150°E

OCEAN

Benguela Current

Agulhas Current

60°E

90°E

South Equatorial Current

INDIAN

OCEAN

AUSTRALIA

Alice Springs

30°S

West Australia Current

West Wind Drift

60°S

ANTARCTIC CIRCLE

McMurdo

ANTARCTICA

0°

▲**Climate patterns** become apparent when viewed at the global level. A band of tropical wet climate hugs the Equator, and continental climates are present only in the Northern Hemisphere. Tundra and ice caps are found in the high latitudes near both Poles.

°F	°C	Continental	Polar	High Elevations	cm	in
80	27				61	24
60	14				51	20
40	4				41	16
20	-7				30	12
0	-18	Warm Summer · Cool Summer · Subarctic	Tundra · Ice Cap	Highlands · Uplands	20	8
-20	-29				10	4
-40	-40				0	0

J M M J S N   J M M J S N   J M M J S N   J M M J S N   J M M J S N   J M M J S N   J M M J S N

Des Moines, Iowa, U.S.A.   Minsk, Belarus   Fairbanks, Alaska, U.S.A.   Resolute, Nunavut, Canada   McMurdo, Antarctica   Lhasa, China   Kampala, Uganda

CLIMATE CONTROLS

The patterns of climate vary widely. Some climates, such as those near the Equator and the Poles, are nearly constant year-round. Others experience great seasonal variations, such as the wet and dry patterns of the tropical dry zone and the monthly average temperature extremes of the subarctic.

Climate patterns are not random. They are the result of complex interactions of basic climate controls: **latitude, elevation, prevailing winds, ocean currents, landforms,** and **location.**

These controls combine in various ways to create the bands of climate that can be seen on the world climate map on pages 18–19 and on the climate maps in the individual continent sections of this atlas. At the local level, however, special conditions may create microclimates that differ from those that are more typical of the region.

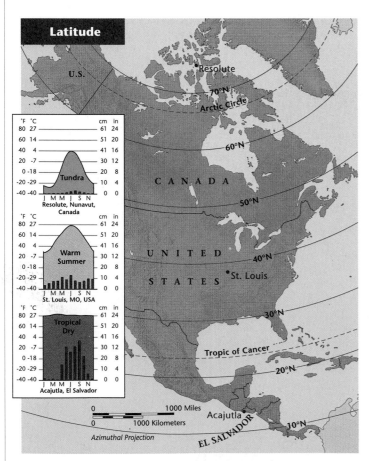

▲ **Latitude.** *Energy from the sun strikes the Equator at a right angle. As latitude (distance north or south of the Equator) increases, the angle becomes increasingly oblique, or slanted. Less energy is received from the sun, and annual average temperatures fall. Therefore, the annual average temperature decreases as latitude increases from Acajutla, El Salvador, to St. Louis, Missouri, to Resolute, Canada.*

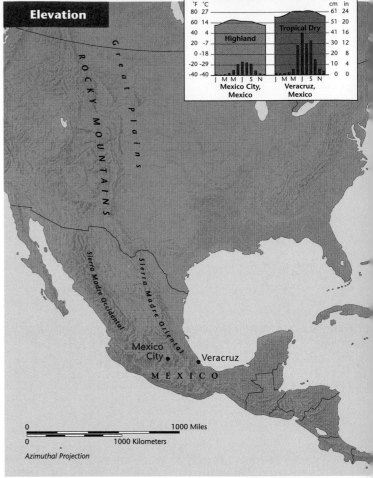

▲ **Elevation.** *Not all locations at the same latitude experience similar climates. Air at higher elevations is cooler and holds less moisture than air at lower elevations. This explains why the climate at Veracruz, Mexico, which is near sea level, is warm and wet, and the climate at Mexico City, which is more than 7,000 feet (2,100 m) above sea level, is cooler and drier.*

▶ **Landforms.** *Air carried by prevailing winds blowing off the ocean is full of moisture. If that air encounters a mountain when it reaches land, it is forced to rise. It becomes cooler, causing precipitation on the windward side of the mountain (see Portland graph). When air descends on the side away from the wind—the leeward side— the air warms and absorbs available moisture. This creates a dry condition known as rain shadow (see Wallowa graph).*

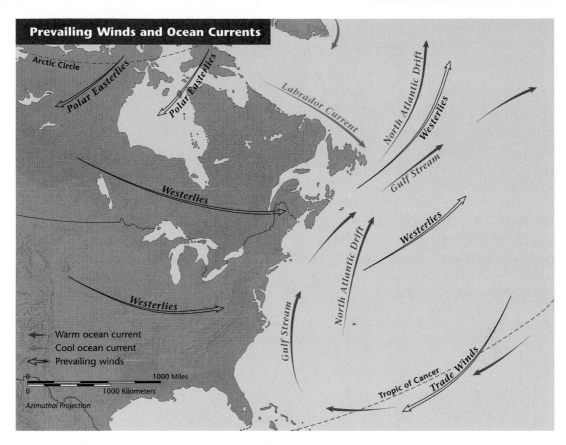

Prevailing Winds and Ocean Currents. Earth's rotation combined with heat energy from the sun creates patterns of movement in Earth's atmosphere called prevailing winds. In the oceans, similar movements of water are called currents. Prevailing winds and ocean currents bring warm and cold temperatures to land areas. They also bring moisture or take it away. The Gulf Stream and the North Atlantic Drift, for example, are warm-water currents that influence average temperatures in eastern North America and northern Europe. Prevailing winds—trade winds, polar easterlies, and westerlies—also affect temperature and precipitation averages.

Location. Marine locations—places near large bodies of water—have mild climates with little temperature variation because water gains and loses heat slowly (see San Francisco graph). Interior locations—places far from large water bodies—have much more extreme climates. There are great temperature variations because land gains and loses heat rapidly (see Wichita graph). Richmond, which is relatively near the Atlantic Ocean but which is also influenced by prevailing westerly winds blowing across the land, has moderate characteristics of both conditions.

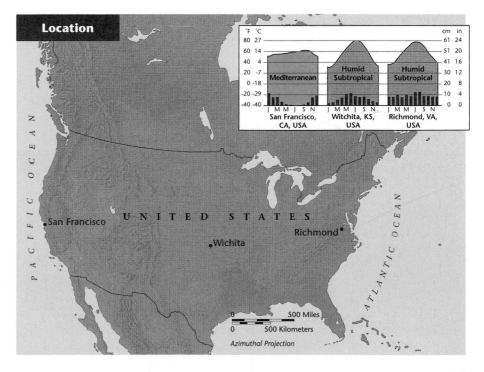

EARTH'S NATURAL VEGETATION

Natural vegetation is the plant life that would be found in an area if it were undisturbed by human activity. Natural vegetation varies widely depending on climate and soil conditions. In the rain forest, trees tower as much as 200 feet (60 m) above the forest floor. In the tundra, dwarf species of shrubs and flowers are adaptations to harsh conditions at high latitudes and high elevations.

Vegetation is important to human life. It provides oxygen, food, fuel, products with economic value, even lifesaving medicines. Human activities, however, have greatly affected natural vegetation (see pages 24–25). Huge forests have been cut to provide fuel and lumber. Grasslands have yielded to the plow as people extend agricultural lands. As many as one in eight plants may become extinct as a result of human interference.

Web Link

▼ **Types of Vegetation.** *Vegetation creates a mosaic of colors and textures across Earth's surface. Grasslands dominate in places where there is too little precipitation to support trees. In the wet conditions of the tropics, rain forests and mangroves flourish. Desert shrubs are adapted to dry climates, and tundra plants survive a short growing season. These photographs show some of the plants found in various vegetation regions. Each is keyed to the map by color and number.*

▲ **Tundra**

▲ **Northern coniferous forest**

▲ **Temperate broadleaf forest**

▲ **Desert and dry shrub**

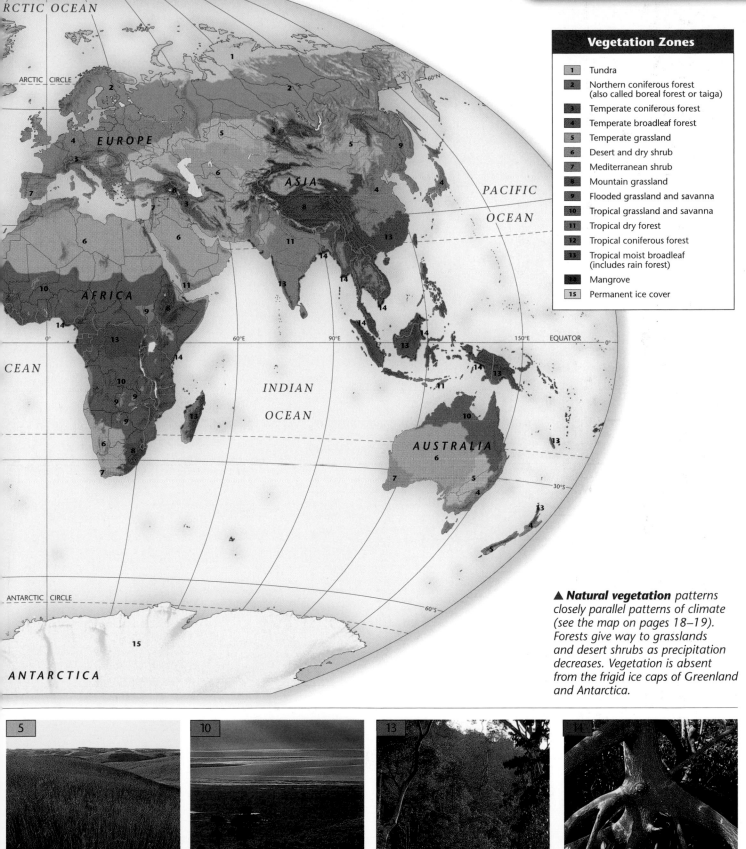

ARCTIC OCEAN

ARCTIC CIRCLE

EUROPE

ASIA

PACIFIC

OCEAN

AFRICA

CEAN

INDIAN

OCEAN

AUSTRALIA

EQUATOR

ANTARCTIC CIRCLE

ANTARCTICA

Vegetation Zones

1	Tundra
2	Northern coniferous forest (also called boreal forest or taiga)
3	Temperate coniferous forest
4	Temperate broadleaf forest
5	Temperate grassland
6	Desert and dry shrub
7	Mediterranean shrub
8	Mountain grassland
9	Flooded grassland and savanna
10	Tropical grassland and savanna
11	Tropical dry forest
12	Tropical coniferous forest
13	Tropical moist broadleaf (includes rain forest)
14	Mangrove
15	Permanent ice cover

▲ **Natural vegetation** patterns closely parallel patterns of climate (see the map on pages 18–19). Forests give way to grasslands and desert shrubs as precipitation decreases. Vegetation is absent from the frigid ice caps of Greenland and Antarctica.

5	10	13	14
▲ **Temperate grassland**	▲ **Tropical grassland/savanna**	▲ **Tropical moist broadleaf**	▲ **Mangrove**

ENVIRONMENTAL HOT SPOTS

As Earth's human populations increase, pressures on the natural environment also increase.

In industrialized countries, landfills overflow with the volume of trash produced. Industries generate waste and pollution that foul the air and water. Farmers use chemical fertilizers and pesticides that run off into streams and groundwater. Cars release exhaust fumes that pollute the air and perhaps also contribute to global climate change.

In less developed countries, forests are cut, making the land vulnerable to erosion. Fragile grasslands turn to deserts as farmers and herders move onto marginal land as they try to make a living. And cities struggle with issues such as water safety, sanitation, and basic services that accompany the explosive urban growth that characterizes many less developed countries. **Web Link**

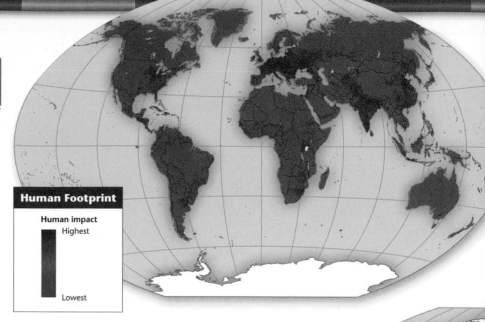

Human Footprint

Human impact

Highest

Lowest

▲ **Human activity** has altered nearly 75 percent of Earth's habitable surface. Referred to as the "human footprint," this disturbance is greatest in areas of high population.

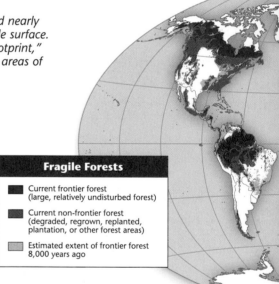

▶ **Forests play** a critical role in Earth's natural systems. They regulate water flow, release oxygen and retain carbon, cycle nutrients, and build soils. But humans have cut, burned, altered, and replaced half of all forests that stood 8,000 years ago.

Fragile Forests

■ Current frontier forest (large, relatively undisturbed forest)

■ Current non-frontier forest (degraded, regrown, replanted, plantation, or other forest areas)

▢ Estimated extent of frontier forest 8,000 years ago

▼ **Polluted water** is part of everyday life for these people who live along a contaminated waterway in Kolkata (Calcutta), India. Home to more than 14 million people, the city doesn't have the resources to provide for many of its residents.

▼ **Deforestation** and heavy monsoon rains trigger landslides near Pokhara, Nepal, putting people, their homes, and their livestock at risk.

DANGER BEACH CLOSED

▲ **An oil spill** off the coast of California closed this beach. Clean-up workers are attempting to reduce the amount of damage to the environment.

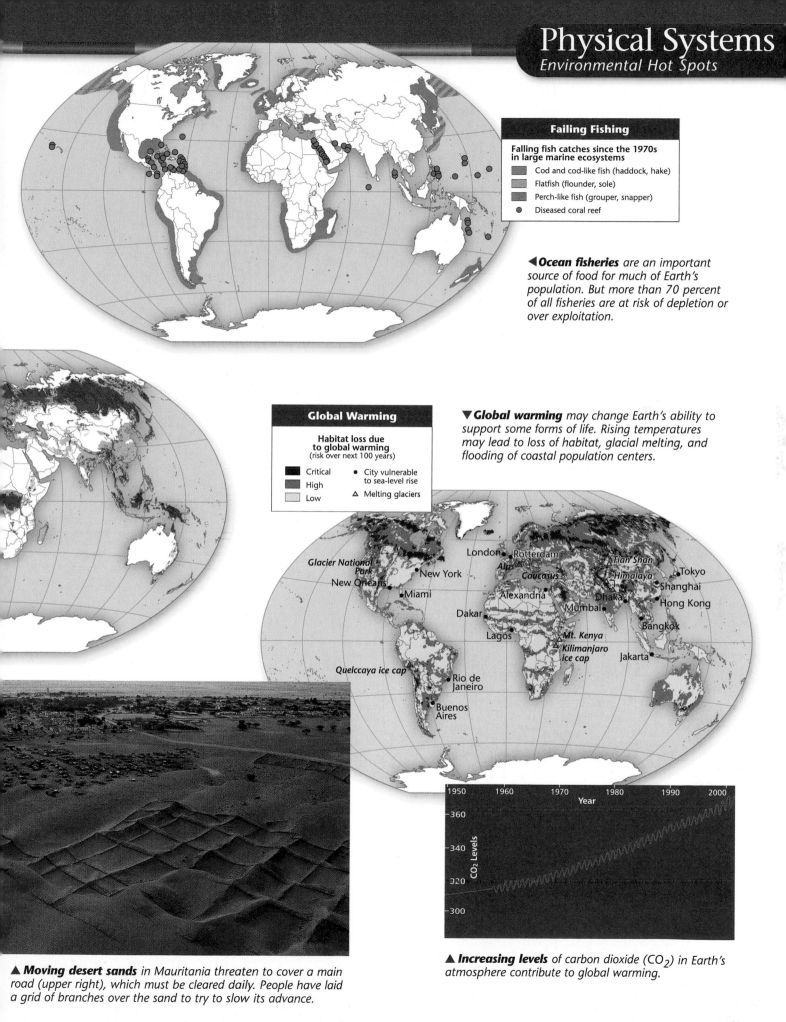

Failing Fishing

Falling fish catches since the 1970s in large marine ecosystems

- Cod and cod-like fish (haddock, hake)
- Flatfish (flounder, sole)
- Perch-like fish (grouper, snapper)
- ● Diseased coral reef

◄ **Ocean fisheries** are an important source of food for much of Earth's population. But more than 70 percent of all fisheries are at risk of depletion or over exploitation.

Global Warming

Habitat loss due to global warming
(risk over next 100 years)

- Critical
- High
- Low
- ● City vulnerable to sea-level rise
- △ Melting glaciers

▼ **Global warming** may change Earth's ability to support some forms of life. Rising temperatures may lead to loss of habitat, glacial melting, and flooding of coastal population centers.

Glacier National Park
London
Rotterdam
Tian Shan
Alps
Caucasus
Himalaya
Tokyo
New York
Shanghai
New Orleans
Alexandria
Dhaka
Hong Kong
Miami
Mumbai
Dakar
Bangkok
Mt. Kenya
Lagos
Kilimanjaro
ice cap
Jakarta
Quelccaya ice cap
Rio de Janeiro
Buenos Aires

▲ **Moving desert sands** in Mauritania threaten to cover a main road (upper right), which must be cleared daily. People have laid a grid of branches over the sand to try to slow its advance.

▲ **Increasing levels** of carbon dioxide (CO_2) in Earth's atmosphere contribute to global warming.

Year
1950 1960 1970 1980 1990 2000
CO_2 Levels
360
340
320
300

THE POLITICAL WORLD

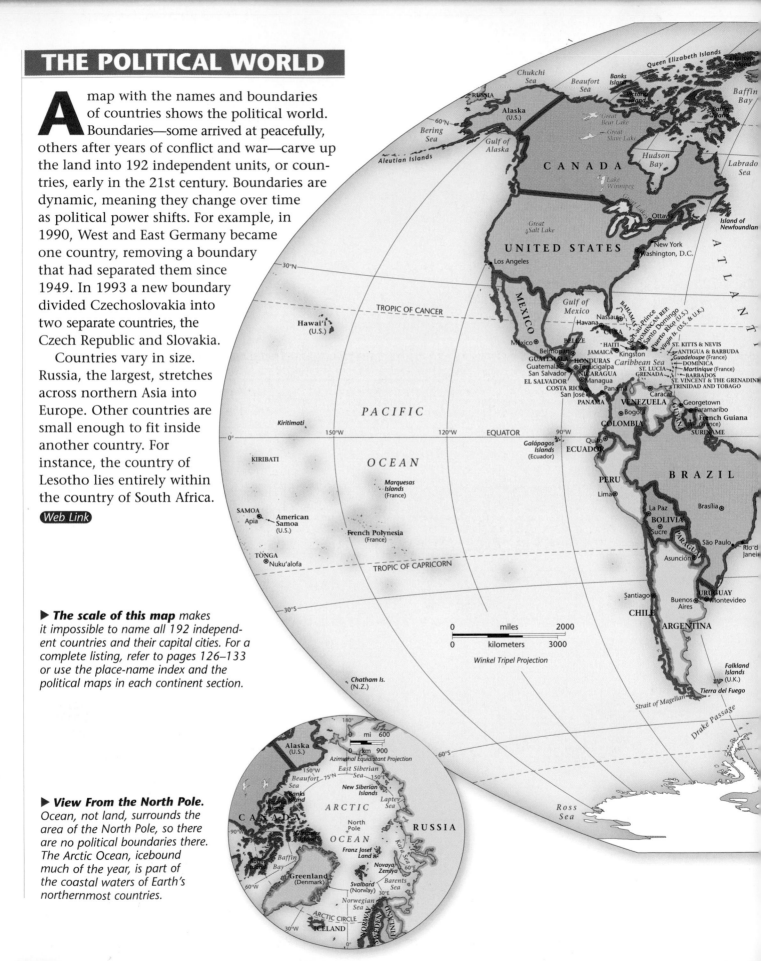

A map with the names and boundaries of countries shows the political world. Boundaries—some arrived at peacefully, others after years of conflict and war—carve up the land into 192 independent units, or countries, early in the 21st century. Boundaries are dynamic, meaning they change over time as political power shifts. For example, in 1990, West and East Germany became one country, removing a boundary that had separated them since 1949. In 1993 a new boundary divided Czechoslovakia into two separate countries, the Czech Republic and Slovakia.

Countries vary in size. Russia, the largest, stretches across northern Asia into Europe. Other countries are small enough to fit inside another country. For instance, the country of Lesotho lies entirely within the country of South Africa.

Web Link

▶ **The scale of this map** makes it impossible to name all 192 independent countries and their capital cities. For a complete listing, refer to pages 126–133 or use the place-name index and the political maps in each continent section.

▶ **View From the North Pole.** Ocean, not land, surrounds the area of the North Pole, so there are no political boundaries there. The Arctic Ocean, icebound much of the year, is part of the coastal waters of Earth's northernmost countries.

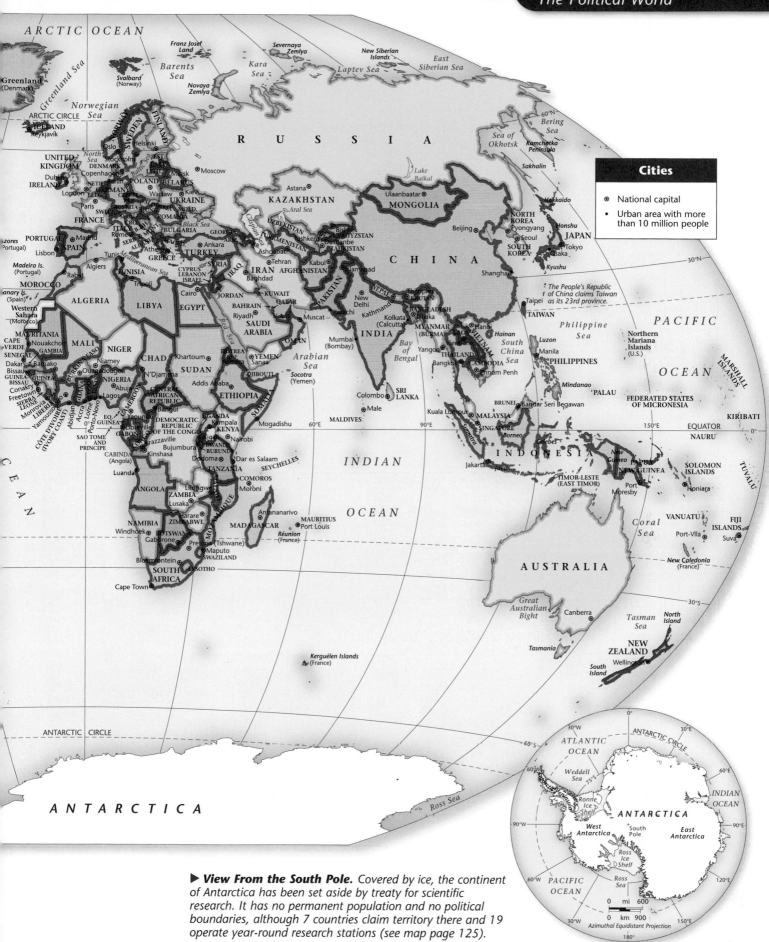

Cities

⊙ National capital

• Urban area with more than 10 million people

The People's Republic of China claims Taiwan as its 23rd province.

ARCTIC OCEAN

Greenland (Denmark)

Greenland Sea

Norwegian Sea

Barents Sea

Franz Josef Land

Severnaya Zemlya

Kara Sea

New Siberian Islands

Laptev Sea

East Siberian Sea

ARCTIC CIRCLE

ICELAND Reykjavík

Svalbard (Norway)

Novaya Zemlya

Bering Sea

Kamchatka Peninsula

60°N

R U S S I A

UNITED KINGDOM

Dublin IRELAND

London

Paris

Oslo

Stockholm

Helsinki

SWEDEN

FINLAND

North Sea

DENMARK

Copenhagen

NETH. Berlin

BEL. GERMANY

POLAND Warsaw

Baltic Sea

EST.

LAT.

LITH. Minsk

BELARUS

Kiev

UKRAINE

Moscow

Astana

KAZAKHSTAN

Aral Sea

Lake Baikal

Ulaanbaatar

MONGOLIA

Sea of Okhotsk

Sakhalin

Hokkaido

NORTH KOREA

Pyongyang

Seoul

SOUTH KOREA

Honshu

JAPAN

Tokyo

Osaka

Kyushu

Beijing

FRANCE

PORTUGAL

Azores (Portugal)

Lisbon

SPAIN

Madrid

Madeira Is. (Portugal)

Canary Is. (Spain)

MOROCCO

Rabat

Western Sahara (Morocco)

AUSTRIA

SWITZ.

ITALY

Rome

SLOVENIA

CROATIA

SERB.

MONT.

ALB.

GREECE

Athens

BULGARIA

ROMANIA

MOLD.

Black Sea

GEORGIA

ARM.

AZER.

Tunis

TUNISIA

Algiers

Mediterranean Sea

ALGERIA

LIBYA

EGYPT

MAURITANIA

Nouakchott

CAPE VERDE

GAMBIA

SENEGAL

Dakar

GUINEA-BISSAU

Bissau

GUINEA

Conakry

SIERRA LEONE

Freetown

LIBERIA

Monrovia

CÔTE D'IVOIRE (IVORY COAST)

Yamoussoukro

Abidjan

MALI

Bamako

BURKINA FASO

Ouagadougou

NIGER

Niamey

GHANA

Accra

TOGO

BENIN

Lomé

Porto-Novo

NIGERIA

Abuja

Lagos

CHAD

N'Djamena

CAMEROON

Yaoundé

EQ. GUINEA

SAO TOME AND PRINCIPE

GABON

Libreville

CABINDA (Angola)

CONGO

Brazzaville

CENTRAL AFRICAN REPUBLIC

Bangui

DEMOCRATIC REPUBLIC OF THE CONGO

Kinshasa

ANGOLA

Luanda

NAMIBIA

Windhoek

BOTSWANA

Gaborone

SOUTH AFRICA

Cape Town

Bloemfontein

Pretoria (Tshwane)

Maputo

SWAZILAND

LESOTHO

ZIMBABWE

Harare

ZAMBIA

Lusaka

MALAWI

Lilongwe

MOZAMBIQUE

TANZANIA

Dodoma

Dar es Salaam

BURUNDI

Bujumbura

RWANDA

UGANDA

Kampala

KENYA

Nairobi

SUDAN

Khartoum

ETHIOPIA

Addis Ababa

ERITREA

Asmara

DJIBOUTI

SOMALIA

Mogadishu

SUDAN

COMOROS

Moroni

SEYCHELLES

MADAGASCAR

Antananarivo

MAURITIUS

Port Louis

Réunion (France)

TURKEY

Ankara

CYPRUS

LEBANON

ISRAEL

SYRIA

IRAQ

Baghdad

Cairo

JORDAN

KUWAIT

QATAR

BAHRAIN

SAUDI ARABIA

Riyadh

YEMEN

Sanaa

Red Sea

OMAN

Muscat

U.A.E.

IRAN

Tehran

AFGHANISTAN

Kabul

TURKMENISTAN

Ashgabat

UZBEKISTAN

Tashkent

Caspian Sea

TAJIKISTAN

Dushanbe

KYRGYZSTAN

Bishkek

PAKISTAN

Islamabad

Karachi

New Delhi

Kathmandu

NEPAL

BHUTAN

Thimphu

INDIA

Mumbai (Bombay)

Kolkata (Calcutta)

BANGLADESH

Dhaka

MYANMAR (BURMA)

Yangon

Arabian Sea

Socotra (Yemen)

SRI LANKA

Colombo

Male

MALDIVES

Bay of Bengal

C H I N A

Shanghai

Hainan

TAIWAN

Taipei

Philippine Sea

PACIFIC OCEAN

Northern Mariana Islands (U.S.)

Luzon

Manila

PHILIPPINES

Mindanao

PALAU

FEDERATED STATES OF MICRONESIA

MARSHALL ISLANDS

KIRIBATI

NAURU

EQUATOR

VIETNAM

Hanoi

LAOS

THAILAND

Bangkok

CAMBODIA

Phnom Penh

South China Sea

BRUNEI

Bandar Seri Begawan

MALAYSIA

SINGAPORE

Kuala Lumpur

Sumatra

Borneo

Celebes

I N D O N E S I A

Jakarta

Java

TIMOR-LESTE (EAST TIMOR)

New Guinea

PAPUA NEW GUINEA

Port Moresby

SOLOMON ISLANDS

Honiara

TUVALU

VANUATU

Port-Vila

FIJI ISLANDS

Suva

New Caledonia (France)

Coral Sea

AUSTRALIA

Great Australian Bight

Canberra

Tasman Sea

North Island

NEW ZEALAND

Wellington

South Island

Tasmania

30°N

30°E

60°E

90°E

150°E

30°S

150°E

0°

INDIAN OCEAN

Kerguélen Islands (France)

ANTARCTIC CIRCLE

A N T A R C T I C A

Ross Sea

▶ **View From the South Pole.** *Covered by ice, the continent of Antarctica has been set aside by treaty for scientific research. It has no permanent population and no political boundaries, although 7 countries claim territory there and 19 operate year-round research stations (see map page 125).*

ATLANTIC OCEAN

ANTARCTIC CIRCLE

30°W

30°E

60°W

60°E

90°W

90°E

Weddell Sea

Ronne Ice Shelf

West Antarctica

South Pole

East Antarctica

A N T A R C T I C A

Ross Ice Shelf

Ross Sea

PACIFIC OCEAN

INDIAN OCEAN

120°E

150°E

180°

0 mi 600

0 km 900

Azimuthal Equidistant Projection

WORLD POPULATION

Late in 1999 the United Nations announced that Earth's population had surpassed six billion. Although more than 80 million people are added each year, the rate, or annual percent, at which the population is growing is gradually decreasing. Earth's population has very uneven distribution, with huge clusters in Asia and in Europe. Population density, the number of people living in each square mile (or square kilometer) on average, is high in these regions. For example, there are more than 2,000 people per square mile (800 people per sq km) in Bangladesh. Other areas, such as deserts and Arctic tundra, have less than 2 people per square mile (1 person per sq km). **Web Link**

▼ **Crowded streets,** *like this one in Shanghai, may become commonplace as Earth's population continues to increase and as more people move to urban areas.*

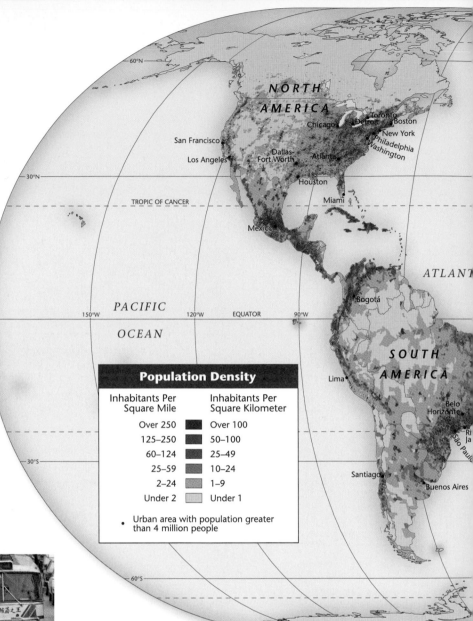

Population Density

Inhabitants Per Square Mile		Inhabitants Per Square Kilometer
Over 250		Over 100
125–250		50–100
60–124		25–49
25–59		10–24
2–24		1–9
Under 2		Under 1

• Urban area with population greater than 4 million people

Population Growth Over Time

The population's rate of increase—the percent by which it changes each year—was slow until industrial and scientific discoveries in the 1800s brought improved health, a more reliable food supply, and other changes that improved the quality of life. Earth's population began to increase rapidly. Although the rate of increase has begun to slow, the United Nations projects that Earth's population will reach almost 9 billion by 2050.

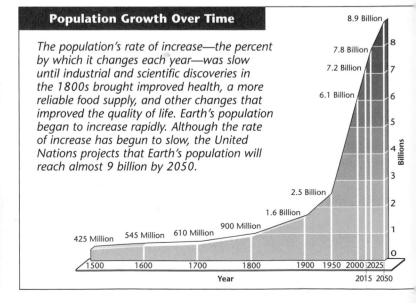

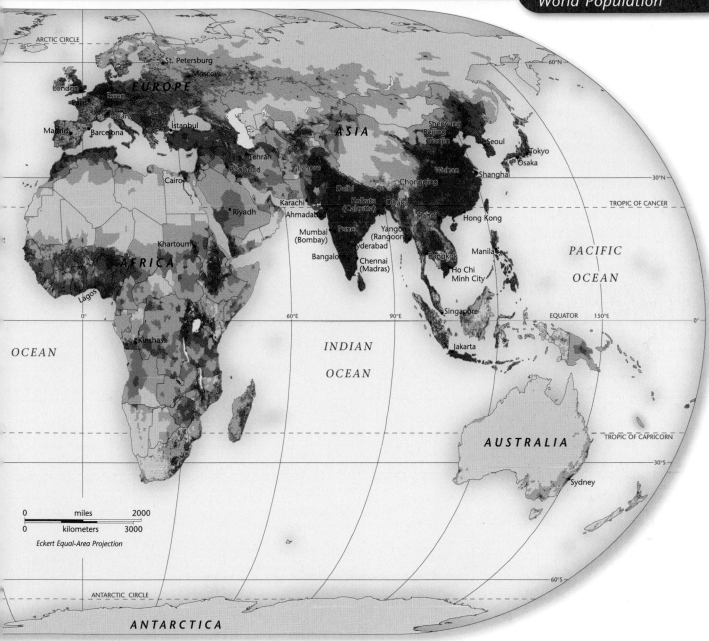

Three Population Pyramids

A population pyramid is a special type of bar graph that shows the distribution of a country's population by sex and age. Italy has a very narrow pyramid, which shows that most people are in middle age. Its population is said to be aging, meaning the median age is increasing. The United States also has a narrow pyramid, but one that shows some growth due to a median age of about 35 years and a young immigrant population. By contrast, Nigeria's pyramid has a broad base, showing it has a young population. More than a third of its people are younger than 15 years.

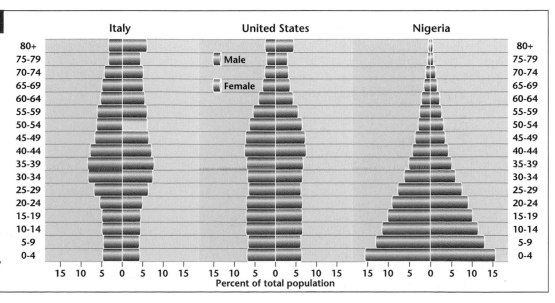

Italy · United States · Nigeria

Male / Female

Percent of total population

WORLD CITIES

Throughout most of history, people have lived spread across the land, first as hunters and gatherers, later as farmers. But urban geographers—people who study cities—predict that sometime in the next decade more people will be living in urban areas than in rural areas. Urban areas include one or more cities and their surrounding suburbs. People living there are employed primarily in industry or in service-related jobs. Large urban areas are sometimes called metropolitan areas. In some countries, such as Belgium, almost all the population lives in cities. But throughout much of Africa south of the Sahara, less than one-third of the people live in urban areas. Even so, some of the world's fastest growing urban areas are towns and small cities in Africa and Asia.

Web Link

Most Populous Urban Areas

In 1950 New York topped a list of only 8 cities with populations of 5 million or more. In 2003 New York had dropped to third behind Tokyo and Mexico City in a list of 46 cities with populations of at least 5 million. By 2015, the list is projected to include 61 cities.

Cities with populations of at least five million for the years:

- 1950
- 1975
- 2003
- 2015

US/Canada	Latin America	Europe	Africa	Asia	Australia/ Oceania
1	1				
2	2	4 4		4	
5	8	6 6	3	24	
8	8	6 6	4	35	0 0 0 0

Urban and Rural Populations

These graphs show the percentages of people living in urban and rural areas in the world and its various regions. Only Asia and Africa are predominantly rural, although both are experiencing rapid urban growth. Asia, which had only 2 cities of five million or more people in 1950, now has 24.

United States & Cana•

79%   21%

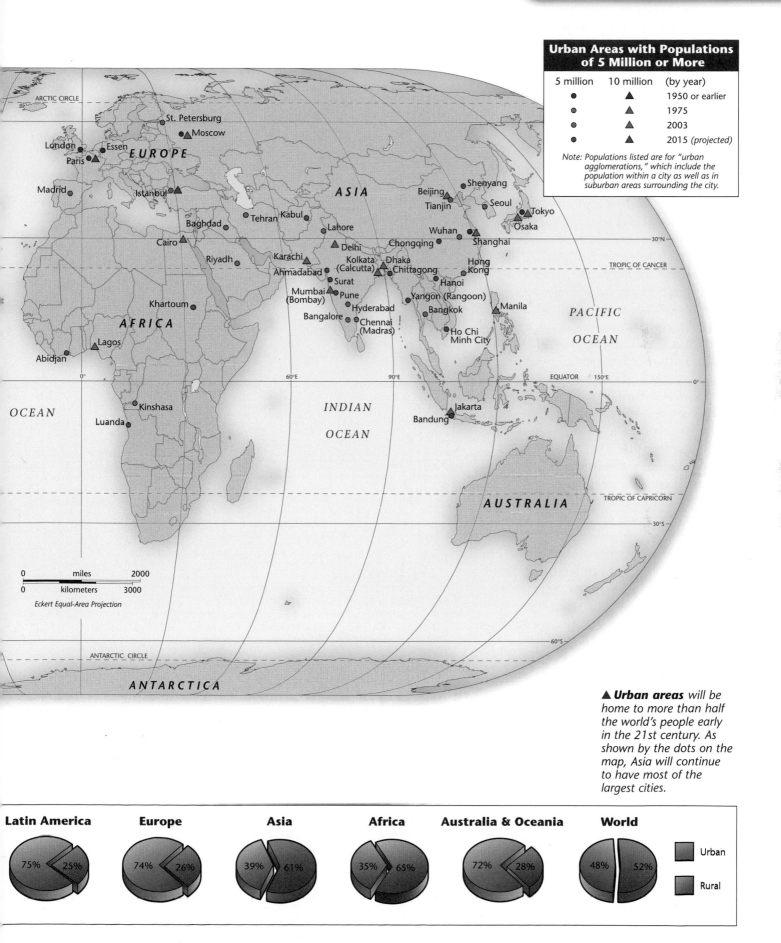

Urban Areas with Populations of 5 Million or More

5 million	10 million	(by year)
●	▲	1950 or earlier
●	▲	1975
●	▲	2003
●	▲	2015 (projected)

Note: Populations listed are for "urban agglomerations," which include the population within a city as well as in suburban areas surrounding the city.

ARCTIC CIRCLE

St. Petersburg
Moscow
London
Essen
EUROPE
Paris
Madrid
Istanbul
Baghdad
Tehran
Kabul
ASIA
Beijing
Shenyang
Tianjin
Seoul
Cairo
Lahore
Wuhan
Tokyo
Osaka
Delhi
Chongqing
Shanghai
30°N
Riyadh
Karachi
Kolkata (Calcutta)
Dhaka
Hong Kong
TROPIC OF CANCER
Ahmadabad
Chittagong
Surat
Hanoi
Mumbai (Bombay)
Pune
Yangon (Rangoon)
Khartoum
Hyderabad
Bangkok
Manila
PACIFIC OCEAN
AFRICA
Bangalore
Chennai (Madras)
Lagos
Ho Chi Minh City
Abidjan
0°
60°E
90°E
EQUATOR
150°E
0°
OCEAN
Kinshasa
INDIAN
Jakarta
Luanda
Bandung
OCEAN
AUSTRALIA
TROPIC OF CAPRICORN
30°S

0 miles 2000
0 kilometers 3000
Eckert Equal-Area Projection

60°S

ANTARCTIC CIRCLE

ANTARCTICA

▲ **Urban areas** will be home to more than half the world's people early in the 21st century. As shown by the dots on the map, Asia will continue to have most of the largest cities.

Latin America	Europe	Asia	Africa	Australia & Oceania	World
75% 25%	74% 26%	39% 61%	35% 65%	72% 28%	48% 52%

Urban
Rural

WORLD LANGUAGES

Culture is all the shared traits that make different groups of people around the world unique. For example, customs and symbols, food and clothing preferences, housing styles and ways of making a living, and music and art forms are all a part of each group's culture.

Language is one of the most defining characteristics of culture. Language reflects what people value and the way they understand the world. It also reveals how certain groups of people may have common roots at some point in history. For example, English and German are two very different languages, but both are part of the same Indo-European language family. This means that these two languages share certain characteristics that suggest they have evolved from a common ancestor language. Other languages, such as Hungarian, are completely different and seem to be related to almost no other languages.

Patterns on the world language families map (right) also offer clues to the diffusion, or movement, of groups of people. For example, the large area in Africa where Niger-Congo languages are spoken can be explained by the migration of the Bantu people from north-central Africa all the way into southern Africa, beginning around 100 BC. The widespread use of English, extending from the United States to India, reflects the far-reaching effects of British colonial empires. Today, English has become the major language of the Internet.

About 6,000 languages are spoken in the world, but experts think many may become extinct as more people become involved in global trade, communications, and travel.

Web Link

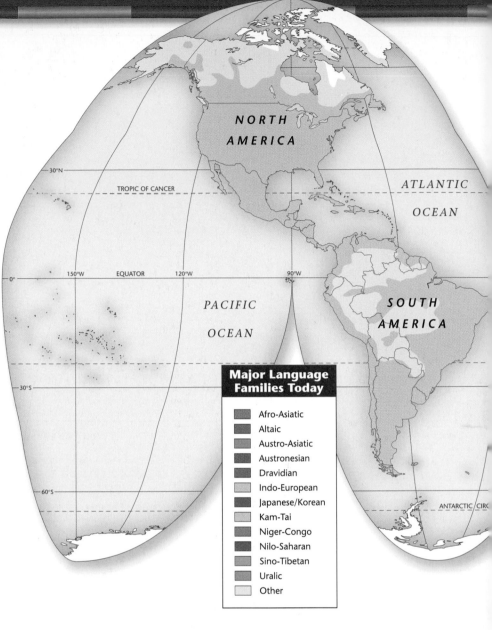

NORTH AMERICA

ATLANTIC OCEAN

TROPIC OF CANCER

PACIFIC OCEAN

SOUTH AMERICA

EQUATOR

ANTARCTIC CIRC

Major Language Families Today

- Afro-Asiatic
- Altaic
- Austro-Asiatic
- Austronesian
- Dravidian
- Indo-European
- Japanese/Korean
- Kam-Tai
- Niger-Congo
- Nilo-Saharan
- Sino-Tibetan
- Uralic
- Other

▼ *The Golden Arches icon would help you identify this restaurant in Moscow even if you didn't know how to read the Cyrillic alphabet of the Russian language.*

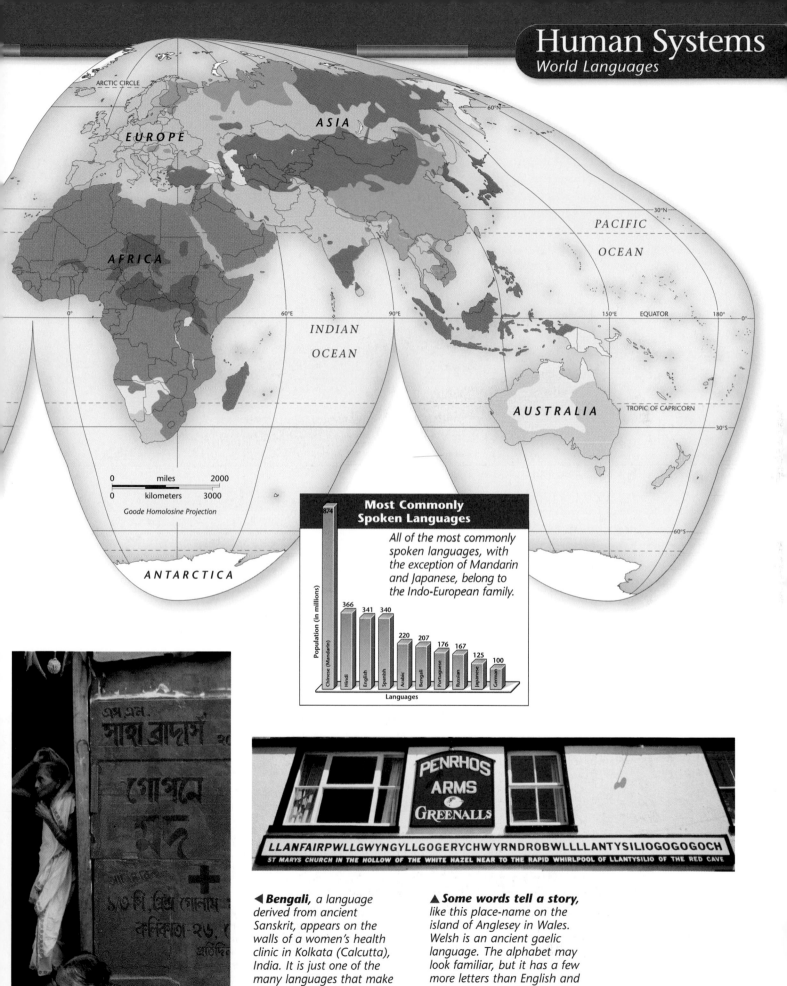

ARCTIC CIRCLE

EUROPE

ASIA

AFRICA

PACIFIC OCEAN

INDIAN OCEAN

AUSTRALIA

ANTARCTICA

TROPIC OF CAPRICORN

60°N

30°N

EQUATOR

30°S

60°S

0°   60°E   90°E   150°E   180°   0°

0 — miles — 2000
0 — kilometers — 3000
Goode Homolosine Projection

Most Commonly Spoken Languages

All of the most commonly spoken languages, with the exception of Mandarin and Japanese, belong to the Indo-European family.

Population (in millions)

Language	Population
Chinese (Mandarin)	874
Hindi	366
English	341
Spanish	340
Arabic	220
Bengali	207
Portuguese	176
Russian	167
Japanese	125
German	100

Languages

PENRHOS ARMS GREENALLS

LLANFAIRPWLLGWYNGYLLGOGERYCHWYRNDROBWLLLLANTYSILIOGOGOGOCH
ST MARYS CHURCH IN THE HOLLOW OF THE WHITE HAZEL NEAR TO THE RAPID WHIRLPOOL OF LLANTYSILIO OF THE RED CAVE

◄ **Bengali,** a language derived from ancient Sanskrit, appears on the walls of a women's health clinic in Kolkata (Calcutta), India. It is just one of the many languages that make up the the Indo-European language family.

▲ **Some words tell a story,** like this place-name on the island of Anglesey in Wales. Welsh is an ancient gaelic language. The alphabet may look familiar, but it has a few more letters than English and different pronunciations.

WORLD RELIGIONS

Religious beliefs, a central element of culture throughout the world, vary widely from place to place. Religious beliefs and practices help people deal with the unknown. But people in different places have developed a variety of belief systems.

Universalizing religions, such as Christianity, Islam, and Buddhism, actively seek converts. They have spread throughout the world from their origins in Asia. Other religions, including Judaism, Hinduism, and Shinto, tend to be associated with particular groups of people and are concentrated in certain places. These religions are called ethnic religions. Some groups, especially indigenous, or native, people living in the tropical forests of Africa and South America, believe that spirits inhabit all things in the natural world. Such belief systems are known as animistic religions.

Religion can play an important role in defining cultural identity. Places of worship are often a distinctive part of the cultural landscape. A cathedral, mosque, or temple can reveal much about the people who live in a particular place. Web Link

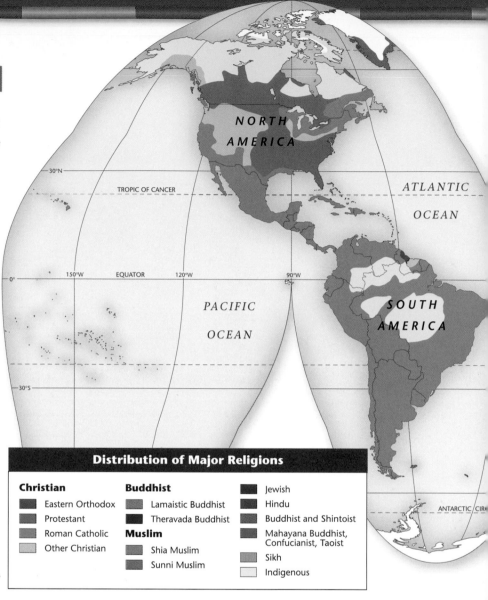

Distribution of Major Religions

Christian
- Eastern Orthodox
- Protestant
- Roman Catholic
- Other Christian

Buddhist
- Lamaistic Buddhist
- Theravada Buddhist

Muslim
- Shia Muslim
- Sunni Muslim

- Jewish
- Hindu
- Buddhist and Shintoist
- Mahayana Buddhist, Confucianist, Taoist
- Sikh
- Indigenous

▲ **Most of Hinduism's** 900 million followers live in India and other countries of South Asia. The goddess Durga (above) is regarded as Mother of the Universe and protector of the righteous.

▼ **Jerusalem is holy** to Muslims, Christians, and Jews, a fact that has led to tension and conflict. Below, a Russian orthodox church is silhouetted against the Wailing Wall, while sunlight reflects off the Dome of the Rock mosque.

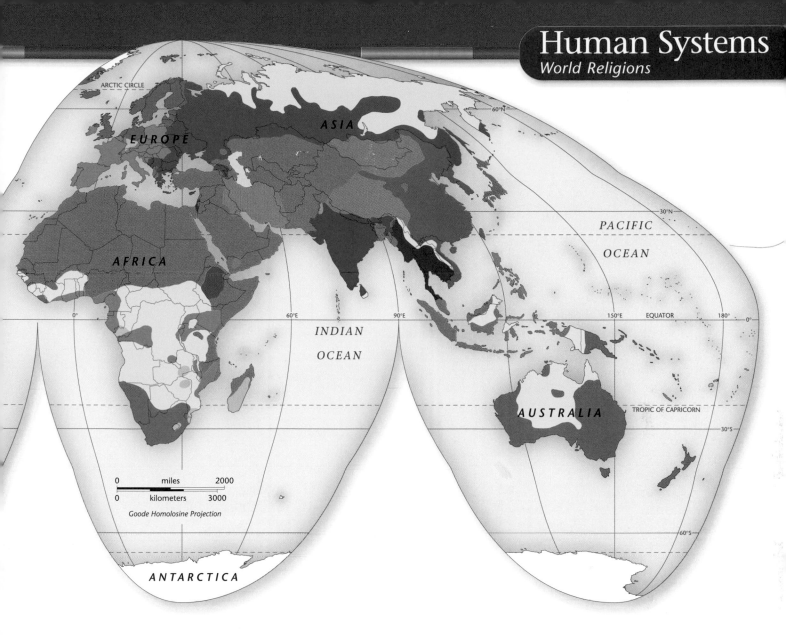

ARCTIC CIRCLE

EUROPE

ASIA

60°N

AFRICA

PACIFIC

OCEAN

30°N

0°

60°E

90°E

INDIAN

OCEAN

150°E

EQUATOR

180°

0°

AUSTRALIA

TROPIC OF CAPRICORN

30°S

| 0 | miles | 2000 |
| 0 | kilometers | 3000 |

Goode Homolosine Projection

60°S

ANTARCTICA

▲ **Muslim worshippers** surround the sacred Kaaba stone, which lies shrouded in black cloth at the center of the Grand Mosque in Mecca. Each year two million Muslims make a *hajj*, or pilgrimage, here to Islam's holiest shrine.

▼ **Statues of Buddha** and temples, such as these built in the 13th century at Wat Chang Hom in northern Thailand, create a unique cultural landscape in southeastern and eastern Asia where most of Buddhism's 350 million followers live.

PREDOMINANT WORLD ECONOMIES

Economic activities are the many different ways that people create products and generate income to meet their needs and wants. Long ago most people lived by hunting and gathering. Today, most engage in a variety of other activities that are commonly grouped into the following categories. Primary activities: agriculture, fishing, forestry; secondary activities: manufacturing and processing industries; tertiary activities: services, such as finance, medicine, education; and quaternary activities: information exchange and e-commerce—buying and selling over the Internet. The more developed economies of the world have shifted from secondary activities toward tertiary and quaternary activities. Less developed economies continue to rely on primary activities. **Web Link**

Predominant Economies

- • Selected population center
- Agriculture
- Agriculture and forestry
- Fishing
- Forestry (lumber and pulpwood)
- Hunting, fishing and forestry
- Subsistence agriculture
- Little or no economic activity
- Manufacturing
- Nomadic herding
- Stock raising on ranges

▲ **Subsistence Agriculture.** *Many people in developing countries, such as these farmers in Peru, use traditional methods to grow crops for their daily food requirements rather than for commercial sale.*

◀ **Logging.** *Workers ready logs to float down the Columbia River in Washington State. Processing plants will turn the logs into paper products or cut them into lumber for the construction industry.*

▶ **Fishing.** *Tuna is one of the chief commercial fishes as well as a favorite among big game fishermen. Japan is the world's leading harvester of tuna. Albacore, shown here, is one of the top commercial varieties.*

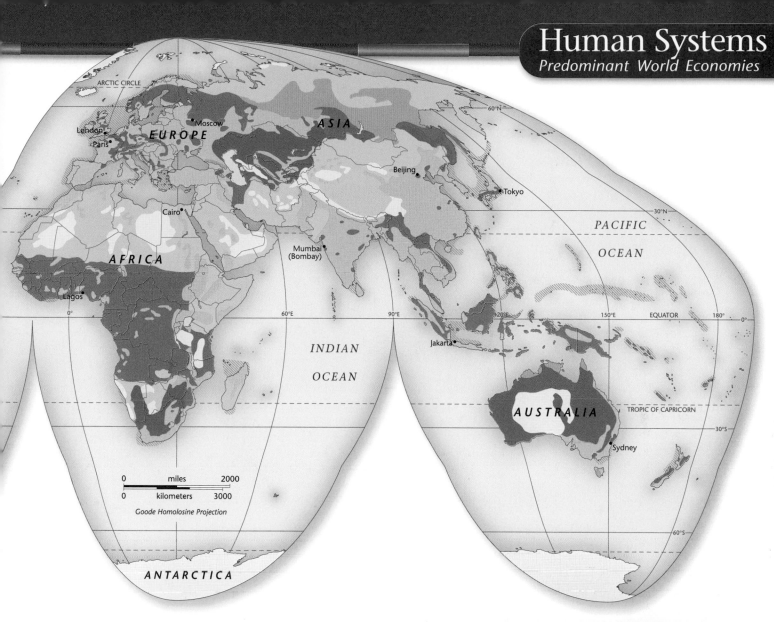

ARCTIC CIRCLE

EUROPE

London
Paris

Moscow

ASIA

Beijing

Tokyo

60°N

Cairo

30°N

AFRICA

Mumbai
(Bombay)

PACIFIC

OCEAN

Lagos

0°

60°E

90°E

150°E

EQUATOR

180°

0°

INDIAN

OCEAN

Jakarta

AUSTRALIA

TROPIC OF CAPRICORN

30°S

Sydney

| 0 | miles | 2000 |
| 0 | kilometers | 3000 |

Goode Homolosine Projection

60°S

ANTARCTICA

▶ **Education and Communications.** *These services combine to allow students to interact with scientists working in the field. Here students explore the underwater ecology of California's Monterey Bay as part of renowned ocean explorer Robert Ballard's JASON Project.*

▲ **Manufacturing.** *This mill in Slovakia processes raw materials—coal and iron ore—to make steel, which in turn is used by other industries to produce cars, machinery, and other kinds of manufactured goods.*

▶ **The Internet.** *This has opened a whole new way of exchanging information. E-mail connects people in places near and far, while e-commerce allows them to buy and sell products without ever leaving home.*

WORLD FOOD

At the beginning of the 21st century, the world's population numbered 6.3 billion people—more than six billion hungry mouths to feed! Productive cropland, though, like other natural resources, is unevenly distributed. In addition, access to modern farming methods and technology varies from country to country. Some countries produce large surpluses while others struggle to feed their people. Grains such as rice, corn, and wheat provide 80 percent of the world's food energy supply. Web Link

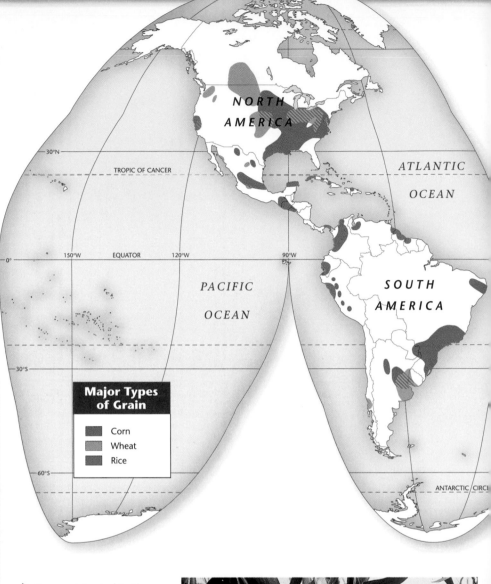

NORTH AMERICA

30°N

TROPIC OF CANCER

ATLANTIC OCEAN

150°W   EQUATOR   120°W   90°W

0°

PACIFIC OCEAN

SOUTH AMERICA

30°S

Major Types of Grain

- Corn
- Wheat
- Rice

60°S

ANTARCTIC CIRCLE

▶ **Corn** originated in the Americas but was carried by Europeans to Europe, Asia, and Africa. Corn is an important food grain for both people and livestock.

▲ **Rice** is an important staple food crop, especially in eastern and southern Asia. Although China produces about one-third of the world's rice, it is also a major importer of rice to feed its population of more than a billion people.

◀ **Wheat** is the world's leading export grain. It is a main ingredient in bread and pasta and is grown on every inhabited continent. Each year trade in this grain exceeds 100 million tons.

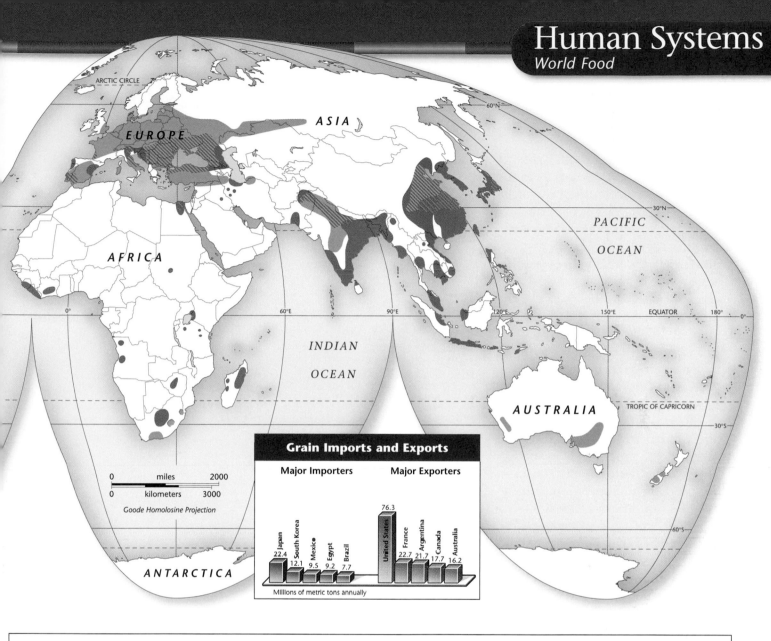

Grain Imports and Exports

Major Importers

Japan	South Korea	Mexico	Egypt	Brazil
22.4	12.1	9.5	9.2	7.7

Major Exporters

United States	France	Argentina	Canada	Australia
76.3	22.7	21.7	17.7	16.2

Millions of metric tons annually

Goode Homolosine Projection

▶ **The demand for food** becomes greater as world population increases. Fertilizer use rose almost 275 percent between 1965 and 1995, as farmers tried to improve crop yields to meet rising demand.

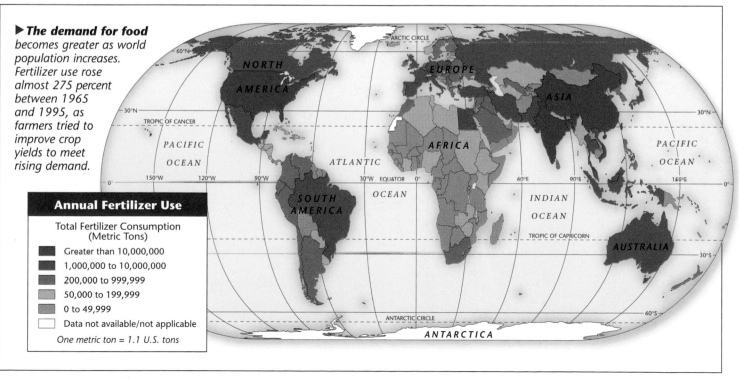

Annual Fertilizer Use

Total Fertilizer Consumption (Metric Tons)

- Greater than 10,000,000
- 1,000,000 to 10,000,000
- 200,000 to 999,999
- 50,000 to 199,999
- 0 to 49,999
- Data not available/not applicable

One metric ton = 1.1 U.S. tons

WORLD WATER

Water is essential for life and is one of Earth's most valuable natural resources. It is even more important than food. More than 70 percent of Earth's surface is covered with water, but most of it—about 97 percent—is salty. Without treatment it is not usable for drinking or growing crops. The remaining 3 percent is fresh, but most of this is either trapped in glaciers or ice caps or lies too deep underground to be tapped economically.

Water is a renewable resource. We can use it over and over because the hydrologic, or water, cycle purifies water as it moves through the processes of evaporation, condensation, precipitation, runoff, and infiltration. But careless use can diminish the supply of usable fresh water. Water may become polluted as a result of runoff from industries, cultivated fields, and urban areas. In addition, water, like other natural resources, is unevenly distributed on Earth. Some countries have an abundance of water while others face serious shortages, especially in parts of Asia and Africa. (Web Link)

Note: Color blocks in photos below are keyed to the graph.

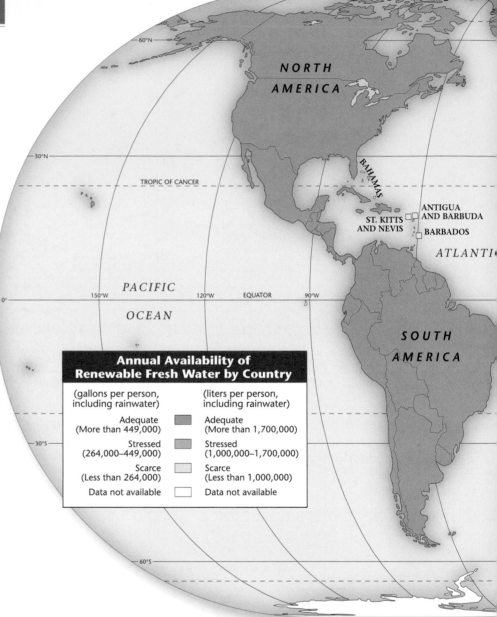

Annual Availability of Renewable Fresh Water by Country

(gallons per person, including rainwater)

Adequate (More than 449,000)	Adequate (More than 1,700,000)
Stressed (264,000–449,000)	Stressed (1,000,000–1,700,000)
Scarce (Less than 264,000)	Scarce (Less than 1,000,000)
Data not available	Data not available

(liters per person, including rainwater)

▲ **Domestic Water Use.** *In much of the less developed world, people haul water daily for household use, as in this village in Central America.*

▲ **Agricultural Water Use.** *Irrigation has made agriculture possible in dry areas such as the San Pedro Valley in Arizona, shown here.*

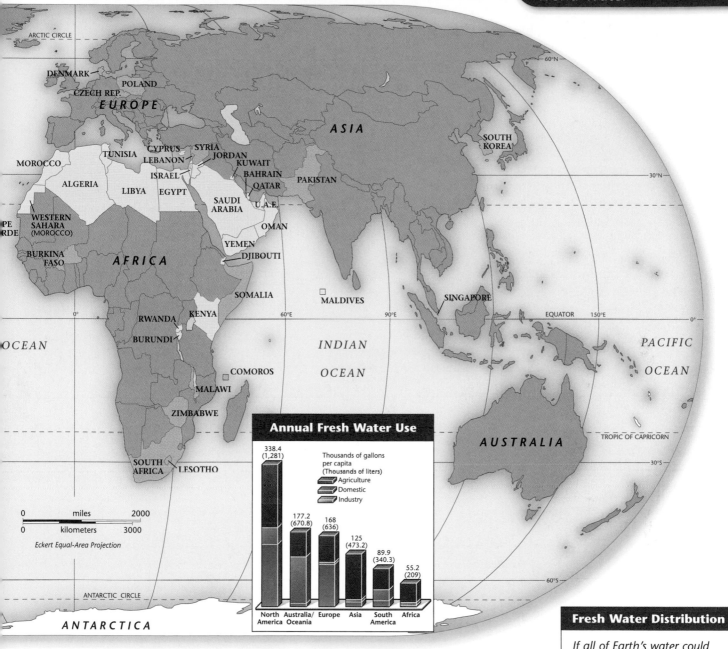

Annual Fresh Water Use

Thousands of gallons per capita
(Thousands of liters)

- Agriculture
- Domestic
- Industry

North America	338.4 (1,281)
Australia/Oceania	177.2 (670.8)
Europe	168 (636)
Asia	125 (473.2)
South America	89.9 (340.3)
Africa	55.2 (209)

0 — miles — 2000
0 — kilometers — 3000
Eckert Equal-Area Projection

▲ **Industrial Water Use.** Hydroelectric projects, such as this dam in Tucuruí, Brazil, harness running water to generate electricity that powers industry.

▲ **Water Stress.** By using groundwater faster than it is renewed, agriculture in dry areas puts stress on limited water supplies.

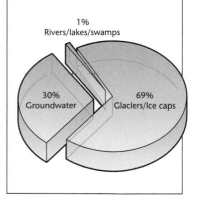

Fresh Water Distribution

If all of Earth's water could fit into a gallon (4.5 liter) jug, only slightly more than a tablespoon of it would be available fresh water. This graph shows the sources of Earth's fresh water.

1%
Rivers/lakes/swamps

30%
Groundwater

69%
Glaciers/Ice caps

WORLD ENERGY & MINERAL RESOURCES

Beginning in the 19th century, as the Industrial Revolution spread across Europe and around the world, the demand for energy and mineral resources skyrocketed. Fossil fuels—first coal, then oil—provided the energy that kept the wheels of industry turning. Minerals such as iron ore (essential for the production of steel) and copper (used for electrical wiring) became increasingly important.

Energy and minerals, like all nonrenewable resources, are in limited supply and are unevenly distributed. Countries with major deposits play an important role in the global economy. For example, the Organization of Petroleum Exporting Countries (OPEC) influences the world supply of oil and, therefore, fuel prices.

(Web Link)

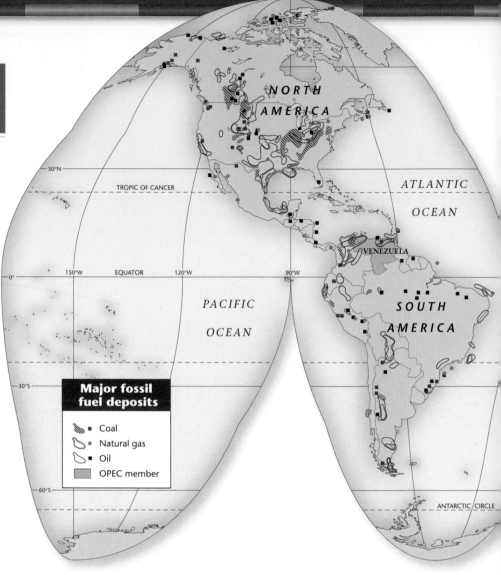

Major fossil fuel deposits

- ◨ ■ Coal
- ◔ ● Natural gas
- ◠ ■ Oil
- ▨ OPEC member

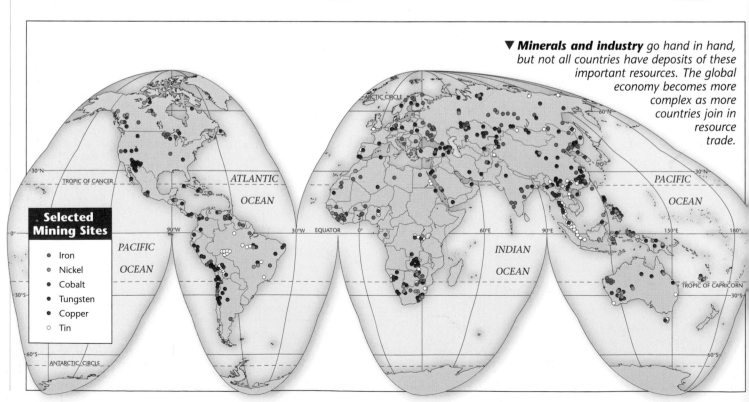

▼ *Minerals and industry* go hand in hand, but not all countries have deposits of these important resources. The global economy becomes more complex as more countries join in resource trade.

Selected Mining Sites

- ● Iron
- ● Nickel
- ● Cobalt
- ● Tungsten
- ● Copper
- ○ Tin

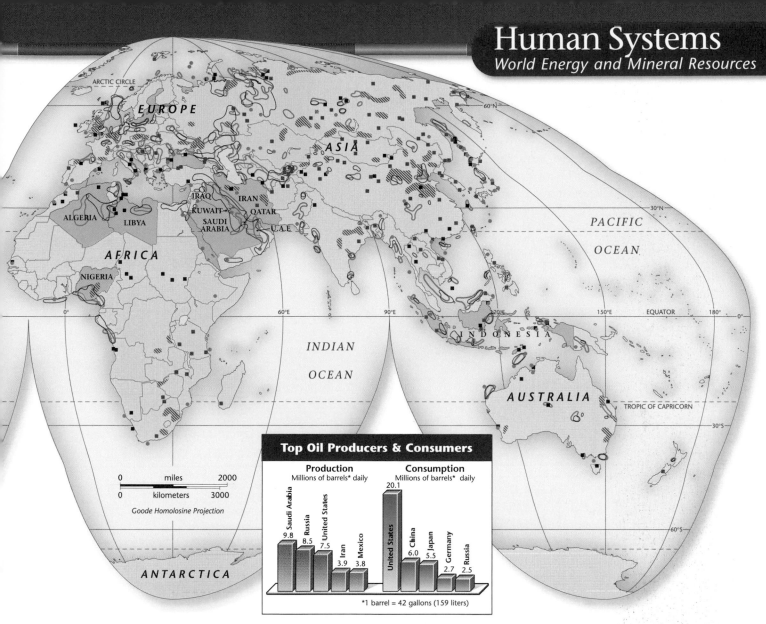

ARCTIC CIRCLE

EUROPE

ASIA

60°N

ALGERIA   LIBYA   IRAQ   IRAN   QATAR
           KUWAIT   SAUDI
           ARABIA   U.A.E.

30°N

PACIFIC

AFRICA   OCEAN

NIGERIA

0°   60°E   90°E   120°E   150°E   EQUATOR   180°   0°

INDONESIA

INDIAN

OCEAN

AUSTRALIA

TROPIC OF CAPRICORN

0   miles   2000
0   kilometers   3000

30°S

Goode Homolosine Projection

60°S

ANTARCTICA

Top Oil Producers & Consumers

Production
Millions of barrels* daily

Saudi Arabia 9.8
Russia 8.5
United States 7.5
Iran 3.9
Mexico 3.8

Consumption
Millions of barrels* daily

United States 20.1
China 6.0
Japan 5.5
Germany 2.7
Russia 2.5

*1 barrel = 42 gallons (159 liters)

▶ **Reactors** near Sacramento, California, produce nuclear energy, and solar panels (foreground) capture energy from the sun. These two sources of energy are important alternatives to nonrenewable fossil fuels.

▲ **A wind energy farm** near Tehachapi, California, uses windmills to capture the energy of winds blowing off the Pacific Ocean.

▼ **Dependence on oil** for motor vehicles, industries, and domestic power and heating makes the United States the world's leading consumer of this energy resource.

◀ **A geothermal power plant,** fueled by heat from deep within Earth, produces energy to heat homes in Iceland. Runoff creates a warm pool for bathers.

WORLD CONFLICTS

The world map reveals a complex mosaic of people and cultures. Sometimes these differences can be a source of conflict. For example, when two groups claim the same territory, conflict may result. Or, when major cultural differences such as religion overlap, previously peaceful people may turn to violence. Political differences, opposing value systems, or competition for resources can also create tensions that hold the potential for conflict.

Some conflicts are relatively short-lived, while others last years. For example, when the communist governments of Eastern Europe collapsed, the country of Yugoslavia broke into several new countries. Conflict in Slovenia, which is culturally homogeneous, did not last very long. But Bosnia and Herzegovina faced years of civil war, as groups with different languages, religions, and traditions struggled for control. In the Middle East, territorial disputes between Muslim Palestinians and Jewish Israelis have been a source of turmoil for more than 50 years. And in eastern Asia, ethnic minorities in Myanmar, Indonesia, and the Philippines frequently protest domination by the majority group.

In September 2001, conflict came to the previously safe shores of the United States. In a protest against the global power of the United States, members of a terrorist network known as al Qaeda launched attacks against American symbols of political and economic power. This group and other terrorist cells have also directed attacks in other parts of the world. These actions have resulted in a so-called war on terror, led by the United States. Web Link

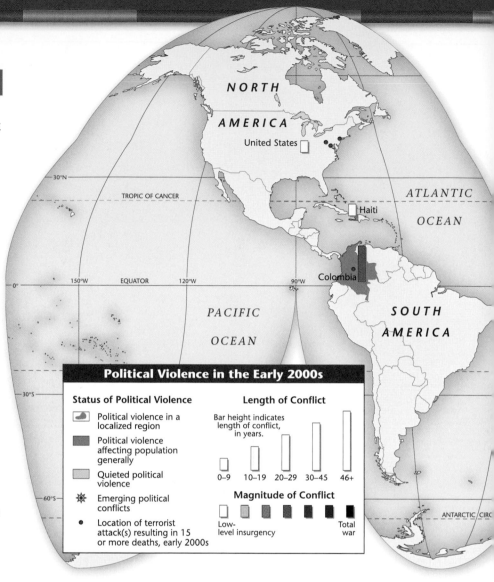

Political Violence in the Early 2000s

Status of Political Violence

- Political violence in a localized region
- Political violence affecting population generally
- Quieted political violence
- Emerging political conflicts
- Location of terrorist attack(s) resulting in 15 or more deaths, early 2000s

Length of Conflict

Bar height indicates length of conflict, in years.

0–9   10–19   20–29   30–45   46+

Magnitude of Conflict

Low-level insurgency .... Total war

▲ **On September 11, 2001,** terrorists used commercial airliners as weapons to attack symbols of U.S. wealth and power in New York City (above) and Washington, D.C.

▼ **Israel is building a wall** (below) between itself and the Palestinian West Bank partly as a defense against terrorist attacks. Both Israelis and Palestinians claim the region as a homeland, resulting in ongoing territorial disputes.

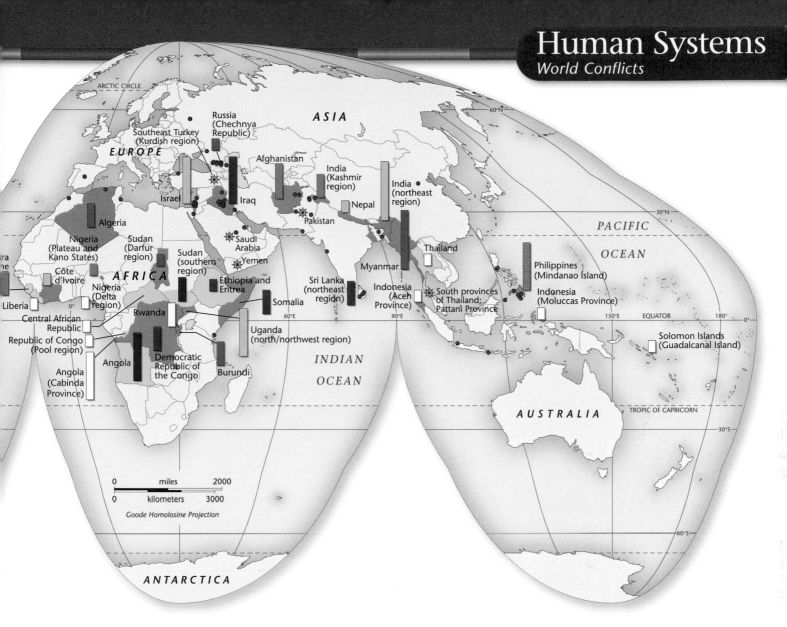

Map labels:

ARCTIC CIRCLE

ASIA

EUROPE

Russia (Chechnya Republic)

Southeast Turkey (Kurdish region)

Afghanistan

India (Kashmir region)

India (northeast region)

Israel

Iraq

Nepal

Algeria

Pakistan

PACIFIC OCEAN

Nigeria (Plateau and Kano States)

Sudan (Darfur region)

Saudi Arabia

Thailand

Côte d'Ivoire

AFRICA

Sudan (southern region)

Yemen

Myanmar

Philippines (Mindanao Island)

Nigeria (Delta region)

Ethiopia and Eritrea

Sri Lanka (northeast region)

Indonesia (Aceh Province)

Indonesia (Moluccas Province)

Liberia

Somalia

South provinces of Thailand; Pattani Province

Central African Republic

Rwanda

Uganda (north/northwest region)

INDIAN OCEAN

Republic of Congo (Pool region)

Solomon Islands (Guadalcanal Island)

Angola

Democratic Republic of the Congo

Burundi

Angola (Cabinda Province)

AUSTRALIA

TROPIC OF CAPRICORN

0 miles 2000

0 kilometers 3000

Goode Homolosine Projection

ANTARCTICA

▲ **The Territory of Jammu and Kashmir** has been a focus of tension and conflict between predominantly Hindu India and Muslim Pakistan ever since the partition of British India in 1947. Here, crowds protest a 2004 election in the city of Srinagar, India.

▼ **Open fighting in Chechnya,** a largely Muslim region in Russia, broke out in 1994 when it attempted to declare independence. The war, which led to claims of human rights abuses by the Russian Army and Chechnyan fighters, destroyed Groznya, the capital city, and left the economy in ruins.

WORLD REFUGEES

Every day, people relocate to new cities, new states, or even to new countries. Most move by choice, but some people, called refugees, move to escape war and persecution that make it impossible to remain where they are. Refugees have no choice but to flee to find safety. Such forced movement creates severe hardship especially for families who may have to leave behind all their possessions. They may find themselves in a strange new place where they do not speak the local language, where customs are unfamiliar, and where basic necessities, such as food, water, shelter, sanitation, and medical care, are in short supply.

A specialized agency of the United Nations, the Office of the High Commissioner for Refugees (UNHCR), is responsible for the safety and well-being of refugees worldwide and for ensuring the protection of and respect for their rights. UNHCR works to find solutions to refugee situations through voluntary return to home countries, integration in a host country, or resettlement to another country.

Web Link

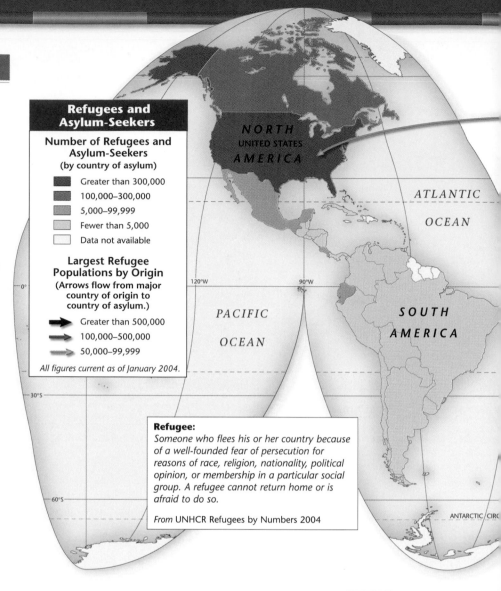

Refugees and Asylum-Seekers

Number of Refugees and Asylum-Seekers
(by country of asylum)

- Greater than 300,000
- 100,000–300,000
- 5,000–99,999
- Fewer than 5,000
- Data not available

Largest Refugee Populations by Origin
(Arrows flow from major country of origin to country of asylum.)

- Greater than 500,000
- 100,000–500,000
- 50,000–99,999

All figures current as of January 2004.

Refugee:
Someone who flees his or her country because of a well-founded fear of persecution for reasons of race, religion, nationality, political opinion, or membership in a particular social group. A refugee cannot return home or is afraid to do so.

From UNHCR Refugees by Numbers 2004

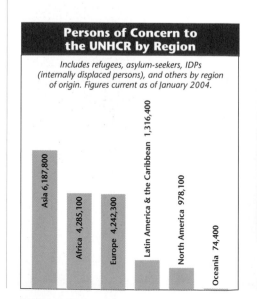

Persons of Concern to the UNHCR by Region

Includes refugees, asylum-seekers, IDPs (internally displaced persons), and others by region of origin. Figures current as of January 2004.

- Asia 6,187,800
- Africa 4,285,100
- Europe 4,242,300
- Latin America & the Caribbean 1,316,400
- North America 978,100
- Oceania 74,400

▲ **Many Kurds,** *a people who live mainly in Iraq and Turkey, fled to the remote mountains of northern Iraq to escape spreading hostilities. This region, referred to as Kurdistan, is the traditional homeland of these stateless people.*

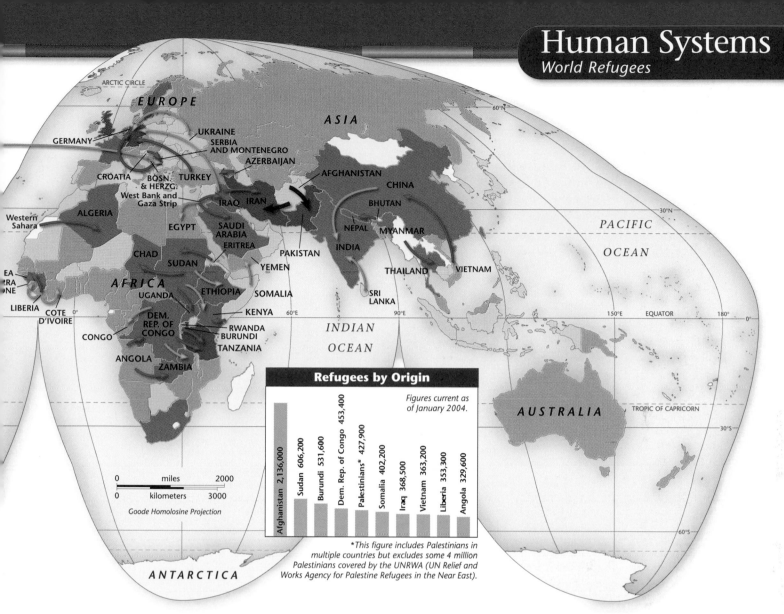

ARCTIC CIRCLE

EUROPE

ASIA

GERMANY

UKRAINE
SERBIA
AND MONTENEGRO
AZERBAIJAN

CROATIA
BOSN. TURKEY
& HERZG.
West Bank and
Gaza Strip

AFGHANISTAN

CHINA

ALGERIA

IRAQ IRAN

BHUTAN

PACIFIC

Western
Sahara

EGYPT

SAUDI
ARABIA
ERITREA

NEPAL
MYANMAR

OCEAN

CHAD

SUDAN

PAKISTAN

INDIA

EA
RA
NE

YEMEN

AFRICA

UGANDA

ETHIOPIA

SOMALIA

THAILAND

VIETNAM

LIBERIA

COTE
D'IVOIRE

KENYA

SRI
LANKA

CONGO

DEM.
REP. OF
CONGO

RWANDA
BURUNDI
TANZANIA

INDIAN

OCEAN

ANGOLA

ZAMBIA

AUSTRALIA

TROPIC OF CAPRICORN

0   miles   2000
0   kilometers   3000

Goode Homolosine Projection

Refugees by Origin

Figures current as of January 2004.

Origin	Refugees
Afghanistan	2,136,000
Sudan	606,200
Burundi	531,600
Dem. Rep. of Congo	453,400
Palestinians*	427,900
Somalia	402,200
Iraq	368,500
Vietnam	363,200
Liberia	353,300
Angola	329,600

*This figure includes Palestinians in multiple countries but excludes some 4 million Palestinians covered by the UNRWA (UN Relief and Works Agency for Palestine Refugees in the Near East).

ANTARCTICA

▲ **Afghan women** in traditional robes, called burkas, climb on colorful buses for the trip home from refugee camps in Pakistan.

▲ **Thousands of Sudanese** refugees have been forced to leave their homes. Some, called internally displaced persons, or IDPs (above), remain in camps within Sudan. Others are refugees who have crossed into Chad to escape rebel forces attacking their villages.

GLOBALIZATION

The close of the 20th century saw a technology revolution that changed the way people and countries of the world relate to each other. This revolution in technology is an important part of a process known as globalization.

Globalization refers to the complex network of interconnections that link people, companies, and places together without regard for national boundaries. Although it began as early as the 19th century, when countries became increasingly active in international trade, the process of globalization has gained momentum in recent years, affecting many different aspects of daily life.

Because of improvements in communications and transportation, many companies now employ workers in distant countries. Some workers make clothing; some perform accounting tasks; and others work in call centers answering inquiries about product services. Communications improvements also allow banking transactions to take place faster and over greater distances than ever before. Companies that have offices and conduct business in multiple countries around the world are called transnational companies.

One important aspect of today's global communications system is the Internet, a vast system of computer networks that enables people to access information and to communicate around the world in just seconds. Today there are more than 600 million Internet users worldwide, most in North America and Europe. Ideas and images travel over the Internet to distant places, introducing change and making places more and more alike. _Web Link_

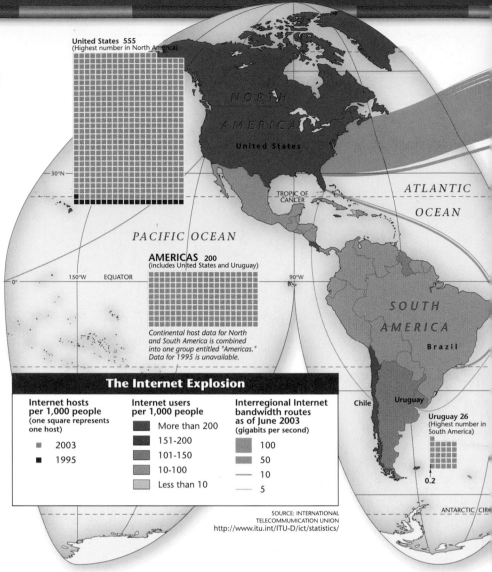

United States 555
(Highest number in North America)

AMERICAS 200
(includes United States and Uruguay)

Continental host data for North and South America is combined into one group entitled "Americas." Data for 1995 is unavailable.

Uruguay 26
(Highest number in South America)

The Internet Explosion

Internet hosts per 1,000 people (one square represents one host)	Internet users per 1,000 people	Interregional Internet bandwidth routes as of June 2003 (gigabits per second)
■ 2003	More than 200	100
■ 1995	151-200	50
	101-150	10
	10-100	5
	Less than 10	

SOURCE: INTERNATIONAL
TELECOMMUNICATION UNION
http://www.itu.int/ITU-D/ict/statistics/

▼ **Maquiladoras,** assembly plants concentrated mainly near the U.S.-Mexico border, rely on low-cost labor to produce finished goods for consumers in the U.S. and around the world. These women in Ciudad Juarez work on audio speakers for export.

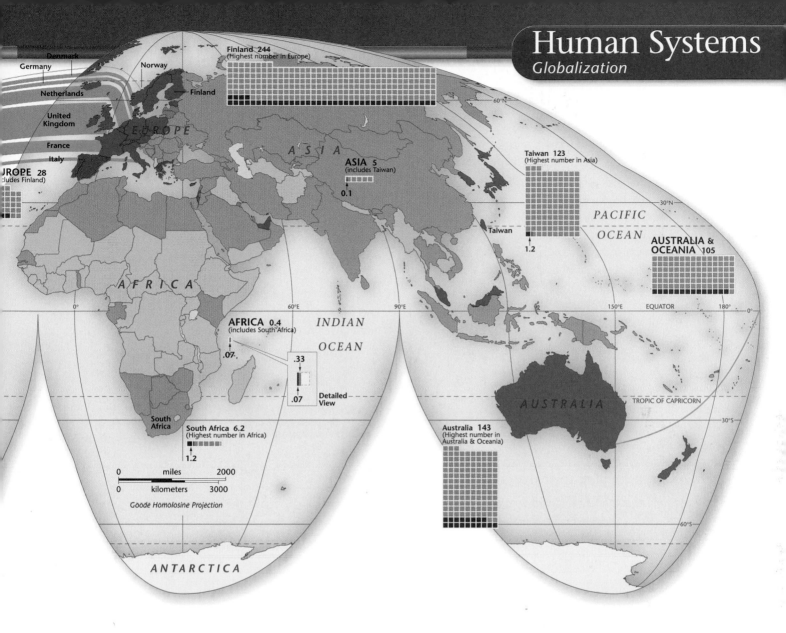

Denmark
Germany
Norway
Netherlands
Finland
United Kingdom
France
Italy

EUROPE

Finland 244
(Highest number in Europe)

EUROPE 28
(includes Finland)

A S I A

ASIA 5
(includes Taiwan)
0.1

Taiwan 123
(Highest number in Asia)

Taiwan
1.2

PACIFIC OCEAN

AUSTRALIA & OCEANIA 105

AFRICA

INDIAN OCEAN

AFRICA 0.4
(includes South Africa)

.07

.33

Detailed View

.07

AUSTRALIA

TROPIC OF CAPRICORN

South Africa

South Africa 6.2
(Highest number in Africa)

1.2

0 miles 2000
0 kilometers 3000

Goode Homolosine Projection

Australia 143
(Highest number in Australia & Oceania)

ANTARCTICA

▲ *Blending popular and traditional culture,* these young Chinese women share a cell phone while enjoying a cup of tea. Almost 300 million cell phones are used in China, linking people and places for both leisure and work.

Global Cell Phone Usage

The availability of cell phones is one example of the technology divide between more and less developed regions of the world. Being "connected" is essential to participation in the global system that links people and places.

Cell Phones per 100 People

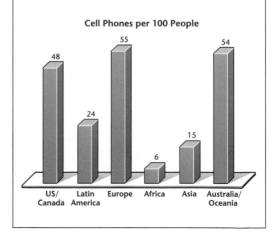

US/Canada	Latin America	Europe	Africa	Asia	Australia/Oceania
48	24	55	6	15	54

CULTURAL DIFFUSION

In the past, when groups of people lived in relative isolation, cultures were quite distinct and varied widely from place to place. Customs, styles, and preferences were handed down from one generation to the next without much change. Such cultures are known as folk cultures.

Today, thanks to high-speed communication, trade, and travel, cultures all around the world encounter and adopt new ideas. This pattern of diffusion introduces new customs, clothing and music trends, food habits, and lifestyles into cultures everywhere at almost the same time. Some people are concerned that this fast-changing trend in popular culture may result in a loss of cultural distinctiveness that makes places unique. For example, fast food chains once found only in the United States can now be seen in major cities around the world. And denim jeans, once a distinctively American clothing style, are worn by young people everywhere in place of more traditional clothing.

An important key to the spread of popular culture is the increasing contact between people and places around the world. Cellular telephones have become popular, not just in the United States and Europe, but also in developing countries where traditional telephone lines are not widely available. Satellite television and cybercafes have helped open the world to styles and trends popular in western countries. And tourists, traveling to places that were once remote and isolated, carry with them new ideas and fashions that are catalysts for bringing about cultural change.

Web Link

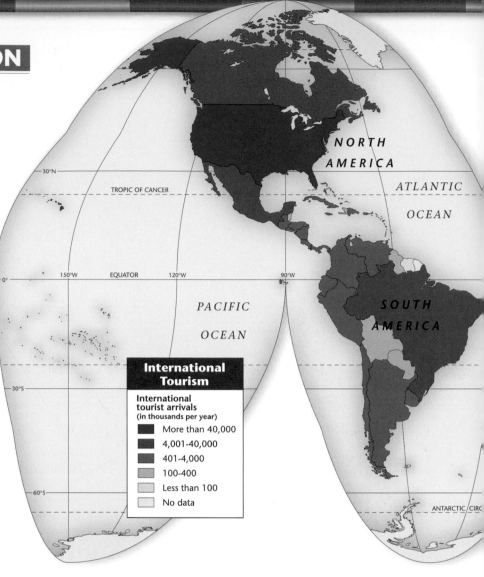

International Tourism

International tourist arrivals (in thousands per year)

- More than 40,000
- 4,001–40,000
- 401–4,000
- 100–400
- Less than 100
- No data

▼ **The influence of immigrant cultures** on the American landscape is evident in ethnic communities such as Chinatown in the heart of New York City.

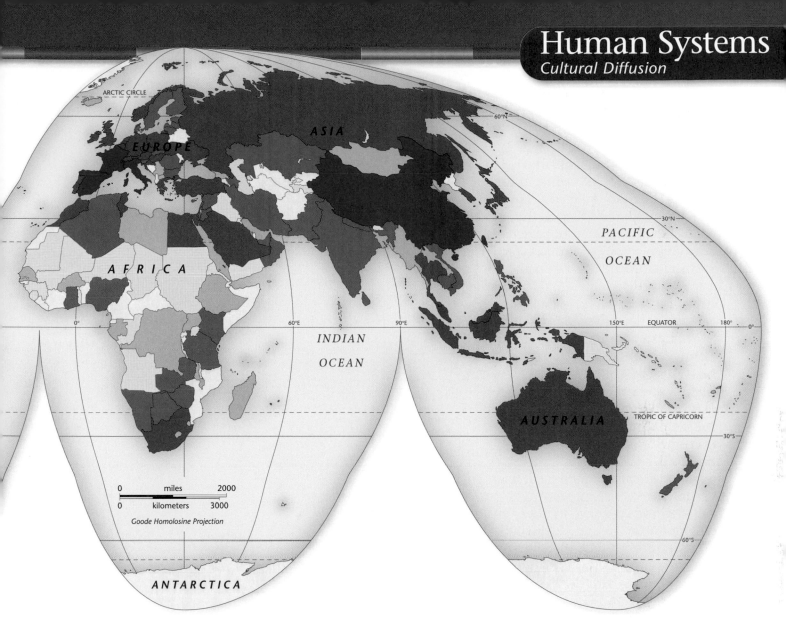

ARCTIC CIRCLE

EUROPE

ASIA

60°N

AFRICA

30°N

PACIFIC OCEAN

0°

60°E

90°E

150°E

EQUATOR

180°

0°

INDIAN OCEAN

AUSTRALIA

TROPIC OF CAPRICORN

30°S

| 0 | miles | 2000 |
| 0 | kilometers | 3000 |

Goode Homolosine Projection

60°S

ANTARCTICA

▼ **Women in dark robes** stroll through a mall in Manama, Bahrain. Stores and movie theaters introduce Western fashions and ideas that are in sharp contrast to those of traditional Arab culture.

▲ **Taking a break** from a traditional ceremony, a Maasai warrior in Kenya enjoys a soft drink that was once uniquely American.

TIME ZONES

The *Fiji Times*, a newspaper published in Suva, capital of the Fiji Islands, carries the message "The First Newspaper Published in the World Today" on the front page of each edition. How can this newspaper from a small island country make such a claim? Fiji lies west of the date line, an invisible boundary designated to mark the beginning of each new day. The date line is just part of the system we have adopted to keep track of the passage of days.

For most of human history, people determined time by observing the position of the sun in the sky. Slight differences in time did not matter until, in the mid-19th century, the spread of railroads and telegraph lines changed forever the importance of time. High-speed transportation and communications required schedules, and schedules required that everyone agree on the time.

In 1884, an international conference, convened in Washington, D.C., established an international system of 24 time zones based on the fact that Earth turns from west to east 15 degrees of longitude every hour. Each time zone has a central meridian and is 15 degrees wide, 7 1/2 degrees to either side of the named central meridian. Web Link

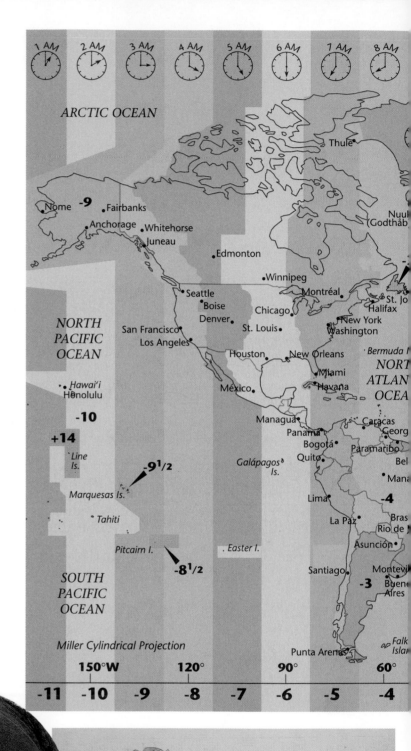

▶ **The prime meridian's** path is lit up by light bulbs strung across Greenwich Park just north of the Royal Observatory, in England. The photographer used a special lens called a fish-eye to make the park resemble a globe. Of course, on the real Earth, meridians and parallels (lines of longitude and latitude) are imaginary and cannot be seen.

▲ **A system of standard time** put trains on schedules, which helped reduce the chance of collisions and the loss of lives and property caused by them.

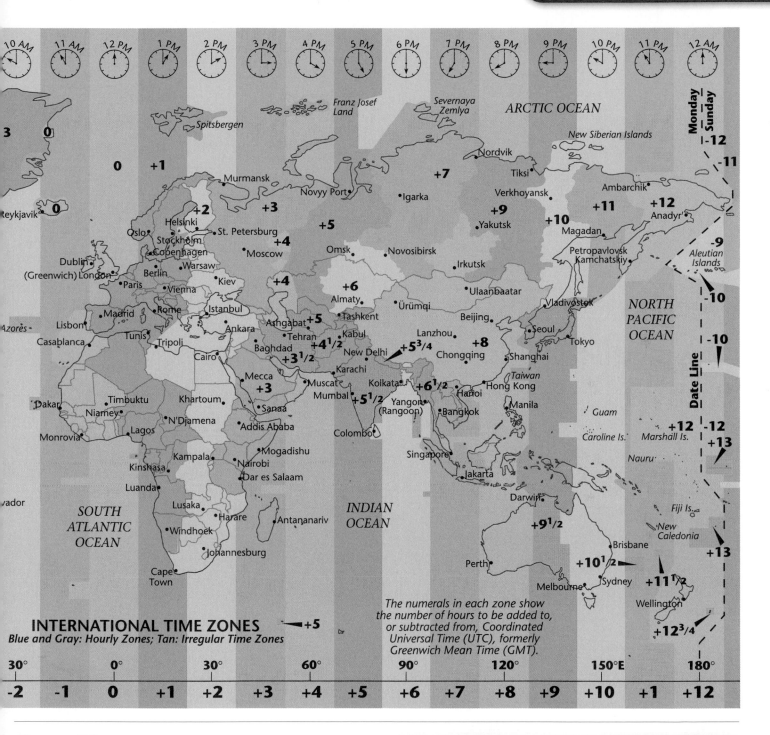

10 AM 11 AM 12 PM 1 PM 2 PM 3 PM 4 PM 5 PM 6 PM 7 PM 8 PM 9 PM 10 PM 11 PM 12 AM

ARCTIC OCEAN

Franz Josef Land
Severnaya Zemlya
Spitsbergen
New Siberian Islands

Monday | Sunday
-12
-11

-3 0 0 +1
Murmansk +7 Tiksi Ambarchik +12
Nordvik Verkhoyansk +11 Anadyr'
Reykjavik 0 +2 +3 Novyy Port Igarka +9 +10 Magadan -9
Helsinki St. Petersburg +5 Yakutsk Petropavlovsk Aleutian Islands
Oslo Stockholm +4 Omsk Novosibirsk Kamchatskiy -10
Dublin Copenhagen Moscow Irkutsk Vladivostok NORTH
(Greenwich) London Berlin Warsaw +4 +6 Ulaanbaatar PACIFIC
Paris Vienna Kiev Almaty Ürümqi Beijing Seoul OCEAN -10
Azores Madrid Rome Istanbul Tashkent Lanzhou +8 Tokyo Date Line
Lisbon Ashgabat +5 Chongqing Shanghai
Casablanca Tunis Ankara Kabul +5¾ Taiwan
Tripoli Baghdad +4½ New Delhi Hong Kong
Cairo +3½ Karachi Kolkata +6½ Hanoi Manila Guam +12 -12
Mecca Muscat Mumbai +5½ Yangon Bangkok Caroline Is. Marshall Is. +13
Dakar +3 (Rangoon) Nauru
Timbuktu Khartoum Sanaa Colombo Singapore
Niamey N'Djamena Addis Ababa Jakarta
Monrovia Lagos Kampala Nairobi Fiji Is.
Kinshasa Dar es Salaam Darwin +13
Luanda INDIAN +9½ New Caledonia
Lusaka Harare OCEAN Brisbane
vador SOUTH Antananariv +10½ +13
ATLANTIC Windhoek Perth Sydney +11¾
OCEAN Johannesburg Melbourne Wellington
Cape Town +12¾

INTERNATIONAL TIME ZONES
Blue and Gray: Hourly Zones; Tan: Irregular Time Zones →+5

The numerals in each zone show the number of hours to be added to, or subtracted from, Coordinated Universal Time (UTC), formerly Greenwich Mean Time (GMT).

30°	0°	30°	60°	90°	120°	150°E	180°
-2	-1	0	+1	+2	+3	+4	+5	+6	+7	+8	+9	+10	+1	+12

Date Line

The date line (180°) is directly opposite the prime meridian (0°). As Earth rotates, each new day officially begins as the 180° line passes 12 midnight. If you travel west across the date line, you advance one day; If you travel east across the date line, you fall back one day.

Notice on the map how the line zigs to the east as it passes through the South Pacific so that the islands of Fiji will not be split between two different days. Also notice that India is 5½ hours ahead of Coordinated Universal Time (formerly Greenwich Mean Time), and China has only one time zone, even though the country spans more than 60 degrees of longitude. These differences are the result of decisions made at the country level.

North America

Viewed from high above, North America stretches from the frozen expanses of the Arctic Ocean and Greenland to the lush green of Panama's tropical forests. Hudson Bay and the Great Lakes, fingerprints of long-departed glaciers, dominate the continent's east, while the brown landscapes of the west and southwest tell of dry lands where water is scarce.

Facts & Figures

- **Land area:** 9,449,500 sq mi (24,474,000 sq km)

- **Population:** 510,051,000

- **Highest point:** Mount McKinley (Denali), Alaska: 20,320 ft (6,194 m)

- **Lowest point:** Death Valley, California: 282 ft (86 m) below sea level

- **Longest river:** Mississippi-Missouri, United States: 3,710 mi (5,971 km)

- **Largest lake:** Lake Superior, U.S.-Canada: 31,701 sq mi (82,100 sq km)

- **Number of independent countries:** 23

- **Largest country:** Canada: 3,855,101 sq mi (9,984,670 sq km)

- **Smallest country:** St. Kitts and Nevis: 104 sq mi (269 sq km)

- **Most populous country:** United States: Pop. 293,633,000

- **Least populous country:** St. Kitts and Nevis: Pop. 47,000

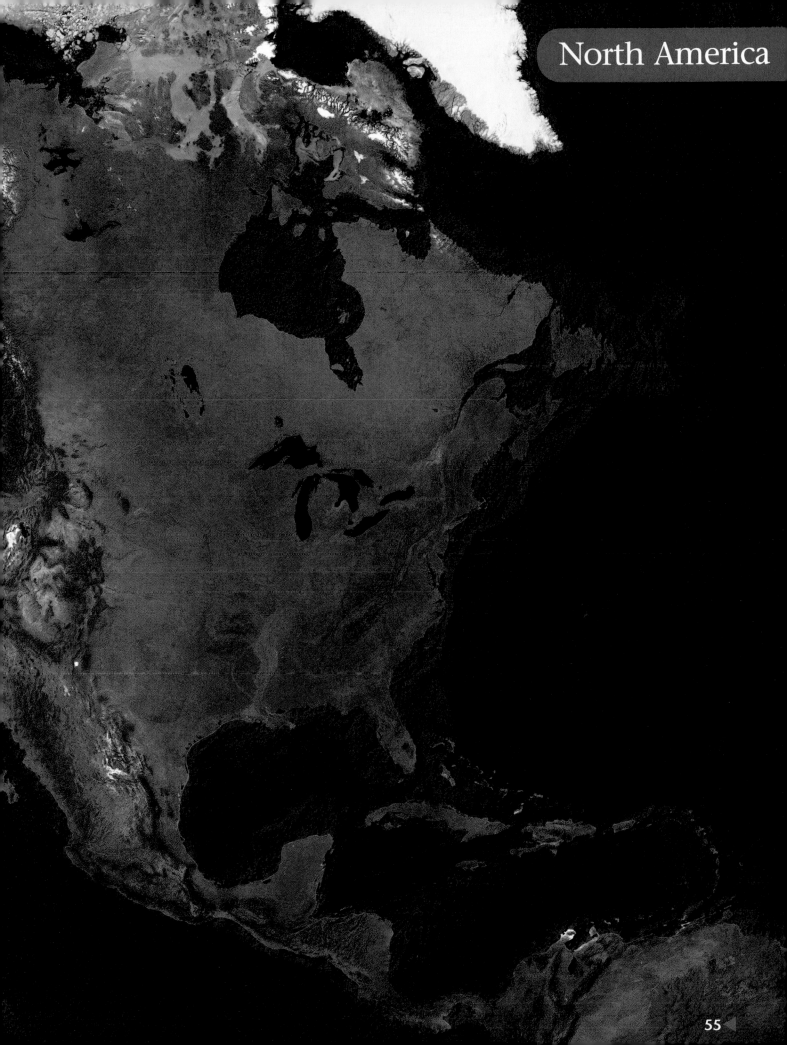

North America

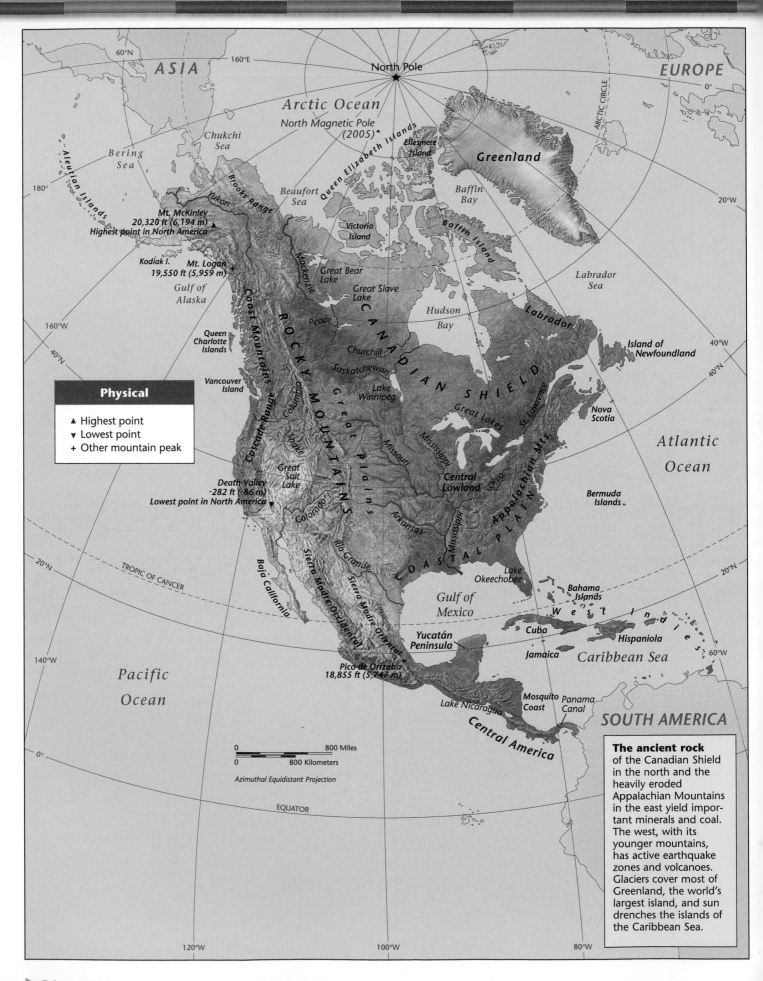

Physical

▲ Highest point
▼ Lowest point
+ Other mountain peak

ASIA

EUROPE

North Pole

Arctic Ocean

North Magnetic Pole
(2005) *

*Chukchi
Sea*

*Bering
Sea*

Aleutian Islands

60°N

160°E

0°

20°W

ARCTIC CIRCLE

*Ellesmere
Island*

Queen Elizabeth Islands

Greenland

*Beaufort
Sea*

*Baffin
Bay*

*Victoria
Island*

Baffin Island

Brooks Range

Mt. McKinley
20,320 ft (6,194 m) ▲
Highest point in North America

Yukon

180°

*Labrador
Sea*

Mackenzie

*Great Bear
Lake*

Baffin Bay

Kodiak I.
Mt. Logan
19,550 ft (5,959 m) +

*Gulf of
Alaska*

*Great Slave
Lake*

C A N A D I A N   S H I E L D

*Hudson
Bay*

Labrador

160°W

*Island of
Newfoundland*

40°W

40°N

Peace

Coast Mountains

*Queen
Charlotte
Islands*

R O C K Y   M O U N T A I N S

Churchill

Saskatchewan

*Lake
Winnipeg*

Great Lakes

St. Lawrence

*Nova
Scotia*

40°N

*Vancouver
Island*

Columbia

Snake

G r e a t   P l a i n s

Missouri

*Atlantic
Ocean*

Cascade Range

*Great
Salt
Lake*

*Central
Lowland*

Ohio

Appalachian Mts.

Death Valley
-282 ft (-86 m)
Lowest point in North America ▼

Colorado

Arkansas

Mississippi

*Bermuda
Islands*

Mississippi

C O A S T A L   P L A I N

Rio Grande

Baja California

Sierra Madre Occidental

Sierra Madre Oriental

20°N

TROPIC OF CANCER

*Lake
Okeechobee*

*Bahama
Islands*

W e s t   I n d i e s

20°N

140°W

*Gulf of
Mexico*

Cuba

Hispaniola

60°W

*Yucatán
Peninsula*

Jamaica

Caribbean Sea

Pico de Orizaba
18,855 ft (5,747 m)

*Pacific
Ocean*

*Mosquito
Coast*

*Panama
Canal*

Lake Nicaragua

SOUTH AMERICA

C e n t r a l   A m e r i c a

120°W

100°W

80°W

0°

EQUATOR

0		800 Miles
0		800 Kilometers

Azimuthal Equidistant Projection

The ancient rock of the Canadian Shield in the north and the heavily eroded Appalachian Mountains in the east yield important minerals and coal. The west, with its younger mountains, has active earthquake zones and volcanoes. Glaciers cover most of Greenland, the world's largest island, and sun drenches the islands of the Caribbean Sea.

North America

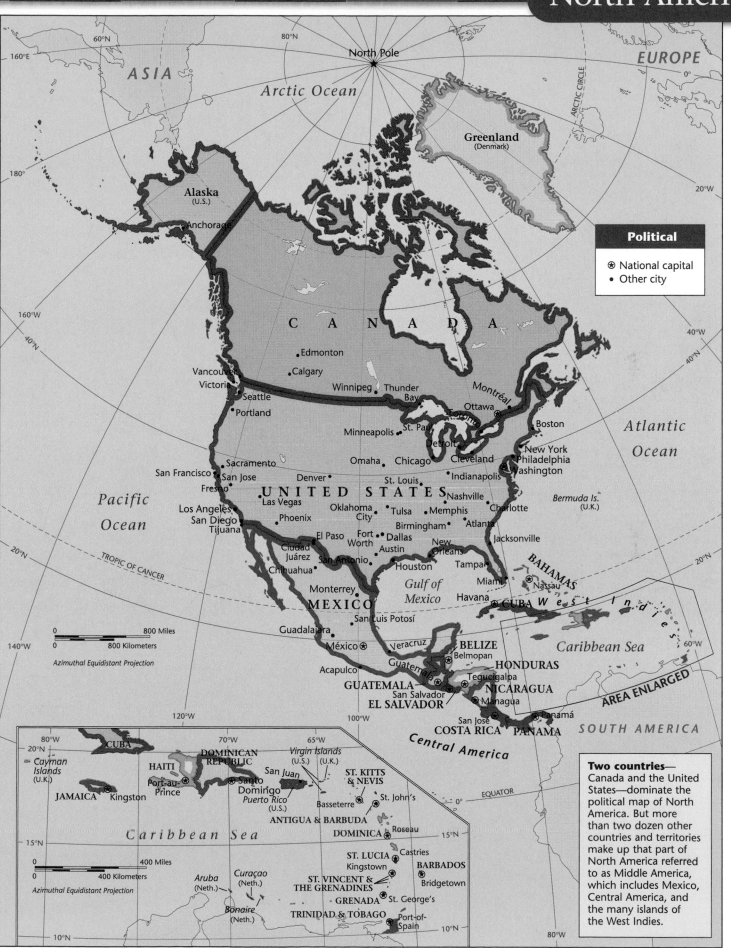

80°N

North Pole

ASIA

Arctic Ocean

EUROPE

Greenland
(Denmark)

ARCTIC CIRCLE

160°E

60°N

20°W

180°

20°W

Alaska
(U.S.)

•Anchorage

Political
⊗ National capital
• Other city

160°W

40°N

40°W

40°W

40°N

C A N A D A

•Edmonton

•Calgary

Vancouver
Victoria

Winnipeg •Thunder
Bay

Montréal

Seattle
•Portland

Ottawa ⊗

Toronto

Boston

*Atlantic
Ocean*

Minneapolis

St. Paul

Detroit

Omaha• Chicago•

Cleveland•

New York

*Pacific
Ocean*

Sacramento•

San Francisco•
San Jose•
Fresno•

Denver•

St. Louis•

U N I T E D   S T A T E S

Nashville•

Las Vegas•

Los Angeles•
San Diego•
Tijuana

Phoenix•

Oklahoma
City•

Tulsa• Memphis•

Birmingham•

Philadelphia•
Washington⊗

Indianapolis•

Charlotte•

Bermuda Is.
(U.K.)

Atlanta•

El Paso•

Fort
Worth•

Dallas•
Austin•

New
Orleans•

Jacksonville•

20°N

TROPIC OF CANCER

Ciudad
Juárez•

San Antonio•

Houston•

Tampa•

BAHAMAS
⊗Nassau

20°N

Chihuahua•

*Gulf of
Mexico*

Miami•

Monterrey•

Havana

W e s t   I n d i e s

MEXICO

⊗CUBA

140°W

0	800 Miles
0	800 Kilometers

Azimuthal Equidistant Projection

San Luis Potosí•

Guadalajara•

Veracruz•

México⊗

BELIZE
•Belmopan

Caribbean Sea

60°W

Acapulco•

Guatemala•

HONDURAS

•Tegucigalpa

NICARAGUA

AREA ENLARGED

GUATEMALA⊗
San Salvador⊗
EL SALVADOR

⊗Managua

120°W

100°W

San José⊗

COSTA RICA

•Panamá

PANAMA

Central America

SOUTH AMERICA

80°W

20°N

CUBA

*Cayman
Islands*
(U.K.)

**DOMINICAN
REPUBLIC**

70°W

Virgin Islands
(U.S.) (U.K.)

65°W

HAITI

San Juan

**ST. KITTS
& NEVIS**

Port-au-
Prince⊗

⊗Santo
Domingo

Puerto Rico
(U.S.)

JAMAICA ⊗Kingston

Basseterre⊗

⊗St. John's

0°

EQUATOR

ANTIGUA & BARBUDA

15°N

C a r i b b e a n   S e a

DOMINICA⊗ •Roseau

15°N

ST. LUCIA ⊗Castries

Kingstown⊗

BARBADOS

0	400 Miles
0	400 Kilometers

Azimuthal Equidistant Projection

Aruba
(Neth.)

Curaçao
(Neth.)

**ST. VINCENT &
THE GRENADINES**

⊗Bridgetown

GRENADA ⊗St. George's

Bonaire
(Neth.)

TRINIDAD & TOBAGO

⊗Port-of-
Spain

10°N

10°N

80°W

Two countries—
Canada and the United
States—dominate the
political map of North
America. But more
than two dozen other
countries and territories
make up that part of
North America referred
to as Middle America,
which includes Mexico,
Central America, and
the many islands of
the West Indies.

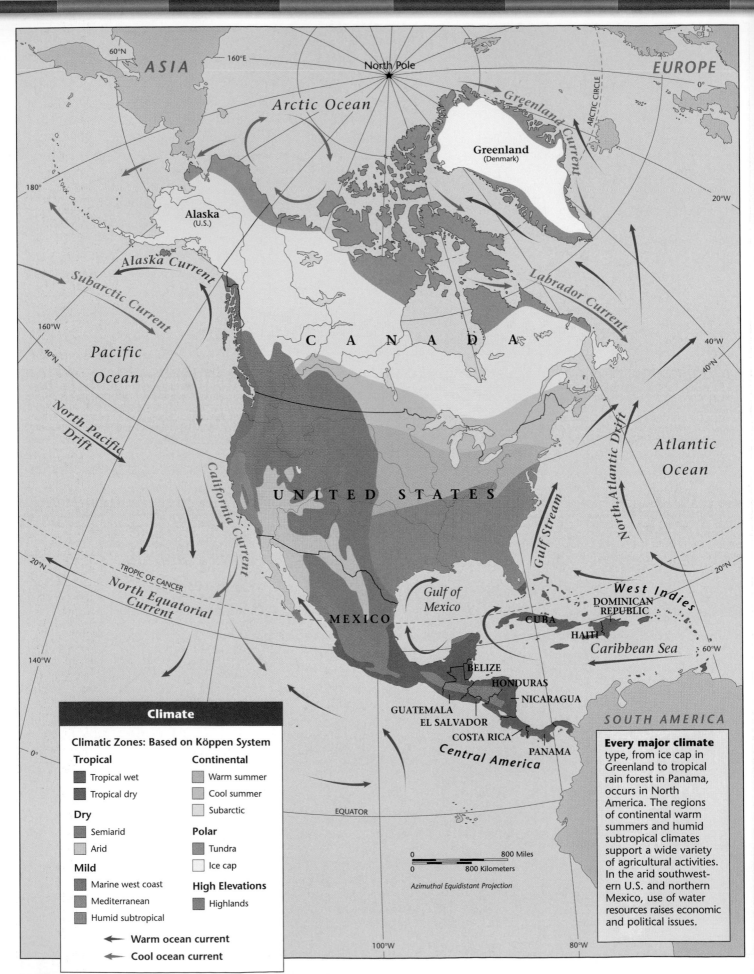

ASIA

60°N

160°E

North Pole

Arctic Ocean

EUROPE

0°

20°W

ARCTIC CIRCLE

Greenland Current

Greenland
(Denmark)

180°

Alaska
(U.S.)

Alaska Current

Subarctic Current

160°W

40°N

Pacific
Ocean

*North Pacific
Drift*

C A N A D A

Labrador Current

40°W

40°N

North Atlantic Drift

Atlantic
Ocean

California Current

U N I T E D   S T A T E S

20°N

TROPIC OF CANCER

*North Equatorial
Current*

MEXICO

Gulf of
Mexico

Gulf Stream

West Indies

DOMINICAN
REPUBLIC

CUBA

20°N

60°W

140°W

HAITI

Caribbean Sea

BELIZE

HONDURAS

NICARAGUA

GUATEMALA
EL SALVADOR

COSTA RICA

PANAMA

SOUTH AMERICA

0°

Central America

EQUATOR

800 Miles

800 Kilometers

Azimuthal Equidistant Projection

100°W

80°W

Climate

Climatic Zones: Based on Köppen System

Tropical
- Tropical wet
- Tropical dry

Dry
- Semiarid
- Arid

Mild
- Marine west coast
- Mediterranean
- Humid subtropical

Continental
- Warm summer
- Cool summer
- Subarctic

Polar
- Tundra
- Ice cap

High Elevations
- Highlands

← Warm ocean current

← Cool ocean current

Every major climate type, from ice cap in Greenland to tropical rain forest in Panama, occurs in North America. The regions of continental warm summers and humid subtropical climates support a wide variety of agricultural activities. In the arid southwestern U.S. and northern Mexico, use of water resources raises economic and political issues.

North America

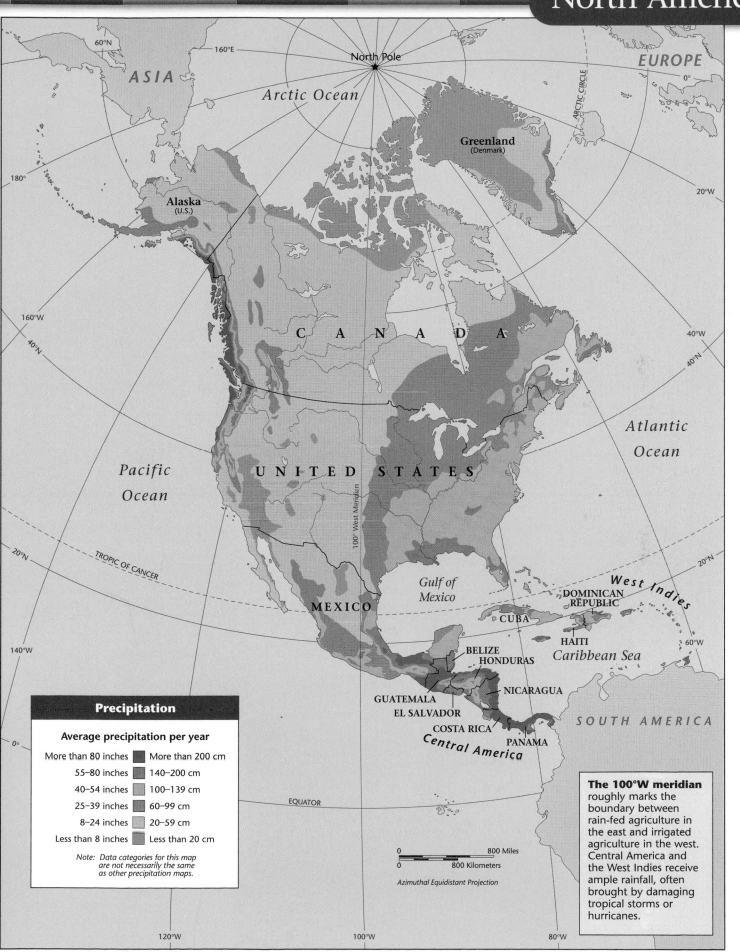

ASIA

Arctic Ocean

North Pole

EUROPE

ARCTIC CIRCLE

Greenland
(Denmark)

Alaska
(U.S.)

C A N A D A

Atlantic
Ocean

Pacific
Ocean

U N I T E D   S T A T E S

100° West Meridian

TROPIC OF CANCER

Gulf of
Mexico

West Indies

DOMINICAN
REPUBLIC

CUBA

MEXICO

HAITI
Caribbean Sea

BELIZE
HONDURAS

GUATEMALA   NICARAGUA
EL SALVADOR

COSTA RICA   PANAMA

Central America

SOUTH AMERICA

EQUATOR

Precipitation

Average precipitation per year

More than 80 inches		More than 200 cm
55–80 inches		140–200 cm
40–54 inches		100–139 cm
25–39 inches		60–99 cm
8–24 inches		20–59 cm
Less than 8 inches		Less than 20 cm

*Note: Data categories for this map
are not necessarily the same
as other precipitation maps.*

0   800 Miles

0   800 Kilometers

Azimuthal Equidistant Projection

The 100°W meridian
roughly marks the
boundary between
rain-fed agriculture in
the east and irrigated
agriculture in the west.
Central America and
the West Indies receive
ample rainfall, often
brought by damaging
tropical storms or
hurricanes.

59

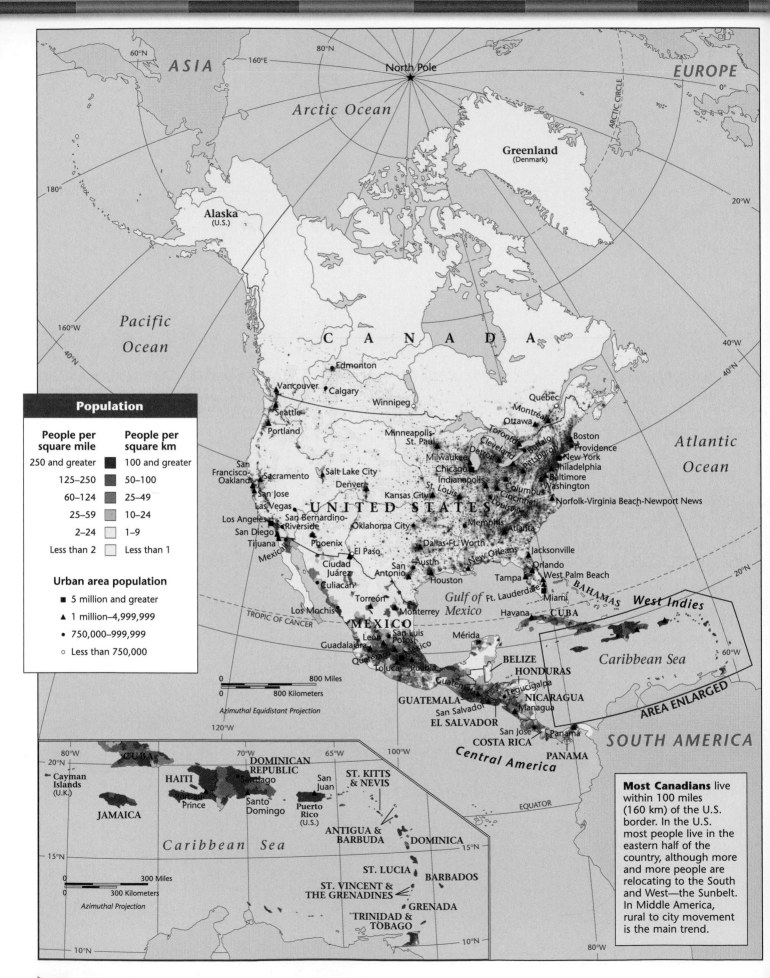

Population

People per square mile
- 250 and greater
- 125–250
- 60–124
- 25–59
- 2–24
- Less than 2

People per square km
- 100 and greater
- 50–100
- 25–49
- 10–24
- 1–9
- Less than 1

Urban area population
- ■ 5 million and greater
- ▲ 1 million–4,999,999
- ● 750,000–999,999
- ○ Less than 750,000

Most Canadians live within 100 miles (160 km) of the U.S. border. In the U.S. most people live in the eastern half of the country, although more and more people are relocating to the South and West—the Sunbelt. In Middle America, rural to city movement is the main trend.

ASIA

EUROPE

Arctic Ocean

North Pole

Greenland (Denmark)

Alaska (U.S.)

Pacific Ocean

C A N A D A

Atlantic Ocean

Edmonton

Calgary

Winnipeg

Québec

Vancouver

Montréal

Seattle

Ottawa

Toronto

Boston

Portland

Minneapolis

Providence

St. Paul

Buffalo

New York

Cleveland

Pittsburgh

Philadelphia

Salt Lake City

Milwaukee

Detroit

Baltimore

San Francisco-Oakland

Sacramento

Chicago

Washington

Denver

Indianapolis

Columbus

San Jose

Kansas City

St. Louis

Cincinnati

Louisville

Norfolk-Virginia Beach-Newport News

U N I T E D   S T A T E S

Las Vegas

Los Angeles

San Bernardino-Riverside

Oklahoma City

Memphis

Atlanta

San Diego

Tijuana

Phoenix

Dallas-Ft. Worth

Mexicali

El Paso

Austin

New Orleans

Jacksonville

Ciudad Juárez

San Antonio

Houston

Orlando

West Palm Beach

Culiacán

Tampa

Ft. Lauderdale

Torreón

Gulf of Mexico

Miami

BAHAMAS

West Indies

Los Mochis

Monterrey

Havana

CUBA

TROPIC OF CANCER

M E X I C O

Mérida

Caribbean Sea

León

San Luis Potosí

Guadalajara

Querétaro

México

BELIZE

Toluca

Puebla

HONDURAS

GUATEMALA

Guatemala

Tegucigalpa

NICARAGUA

San Salvador

Managua

EL SALVADOR

San Jose

Panamá

AREA ENLARGED

COSTA RICA

PANAMA

SOUTH AMERICA

Central America

EQUATOR

0   800 Miles
0   800 Kilometers

Azimuthal Equidistant Projection

CUBA

Cayman Islands (U.K.)

DOMINICAN REPUBLIC

Santiago

San Juan

ST. KITTS & NEVIS

HAITI

Port-au-Prince

Santo Domingo

Puerto Rico (U.S.)

JAMAICA

ANTIGUA & BARBUDA

DOMINICA

Caribbean   Sea

ST. LUCIA

BARBADOS

ST. VINCENT & THE GRENADINES

GRENADA

TRINIDAD & TOBAGO

0   300 Miles
0   300 Kilometers

Azimuthal Projection

North America

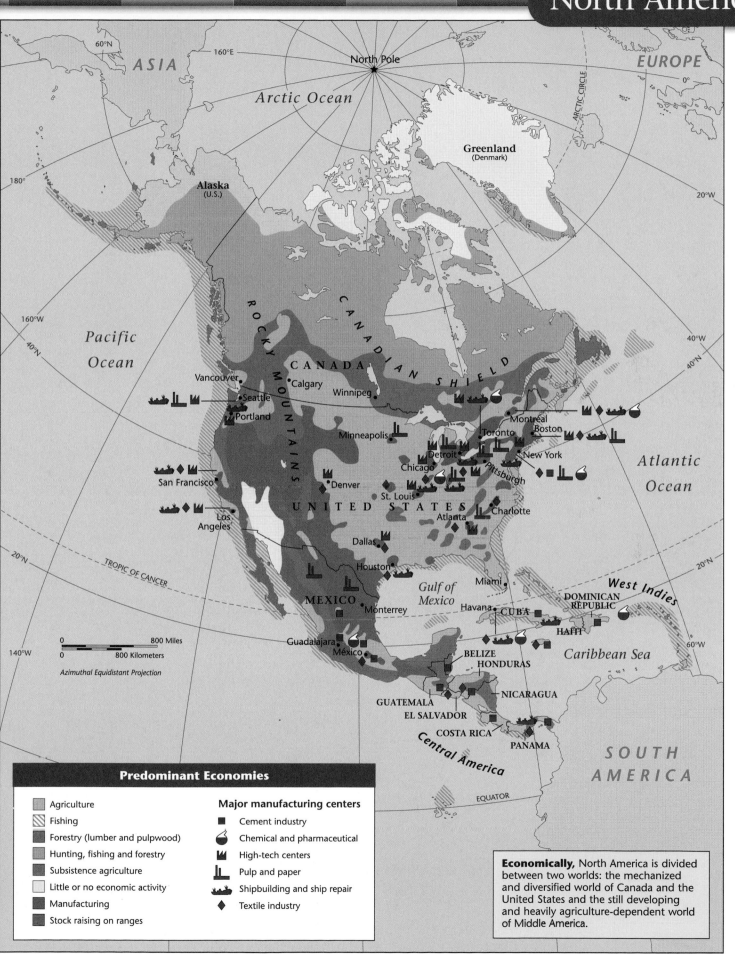

ASIA

160°E

North Pole

EUROPE

0°

Arctic Ocean

160°W

180°

Alaska
(U.S.)

Greenland
(Denmark)

ARCTIC CIRCLE

20°W

40°W

Pacific
Ocean

40°N

ROCKY MOUNTAINS

CANADIAN SHIELD

CANADA

Vancouver

Calgary

Winnipeg

Seattle

Portland

Minneapolis

Montréal

Toronto

Boston

Atlantic
Ocean

40°N

San Francisco

Denver

Detroit

Chicago

Pittsburgh

New York

40°W

Los
Angeles

UNITED STATES

St. Louis

Atlanta

Charlotte

Dallas

Houston

Miami

Gulf of
Mexico

20°N

West Indies

20°N

TROPIC OF CANCER

MEXICO

Monterrey

Havana

CUBA

DOMINICAN
REPUBLIC

Guadalajara

México

BELIZE
HONDURAS

HAITI

Caribbean Sea

60°W

0   800 Miles

0   800 Kilometers

Azimuthal Equidistant Projection

140°W

GUATEMALA

EL SALVADOR

NICARAGUA

COSTA RICA

PANAMA

Central America

SOUTH
AMERICA

EQUATOR

Predominant Economies

- Agriculture
- Fishing
- Forestry (lumber and pulpwood)
- Hunting, fishing and forestry
- Subsistence agriculture
- Little or no economic activity
- Manufacturing
- Stock raising on ranges

Major manufacturing centers

- Cement industry
- Chemical and pharmaceutical
- High-tech centers
- Pulp and paper
- Shipbuilding and ship repair
- Textile industry

Economically, North America is divided
between two worlds: the mechanized
and diversified world of Canada and the
United States and the still developing
and heavily agriculture-dependent world
of Middle America.

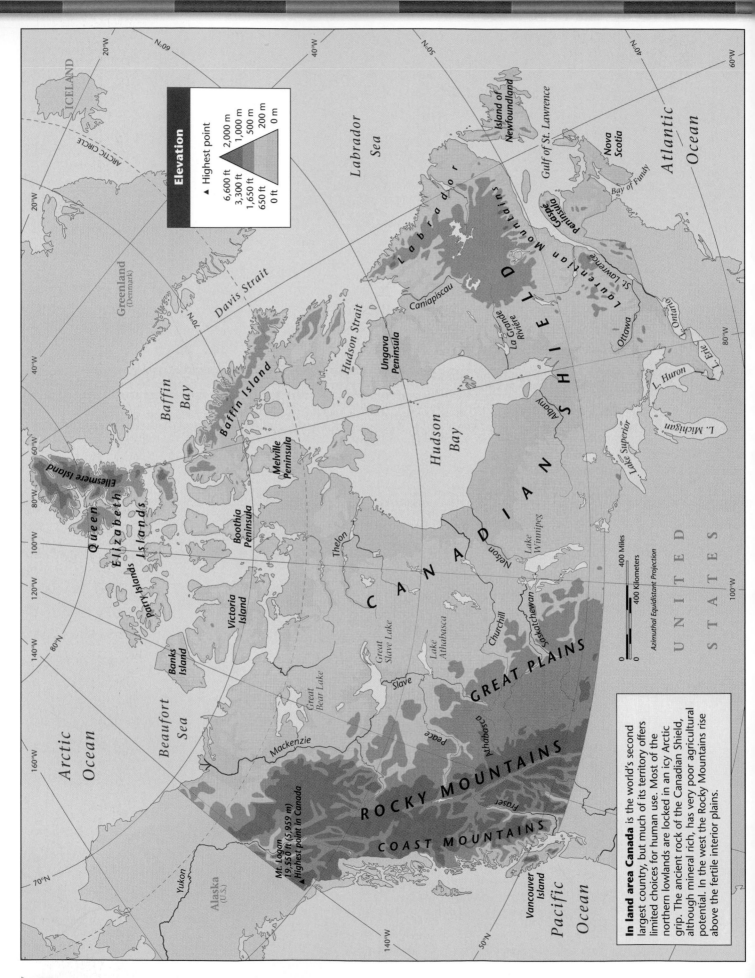

Elevation

▲ Highest point

6,600 ft	2,000 m
3,300 ft	1,000 m
1,650 ft	500 m
650 ft	200 m
0 ft	0 m

ICELAND

Greenland (Denmark)

ARCTIC CIRCLE

Labrador Sea

Davis Strait

Baffin Bay

Baffin Island

Hudson Strait

Ungava Peninsula

Island of Newfoundland

Gulf of St. Lawrence

Nova Scotia

Bay of Fundy

Atlantic Ocean

C A N A D I A N   S H I E L D

Labrador

Laurentian Mountains

Gaspé Peninsula

St. Lawrence

Caniapiscau

La Grande Rivière

Ottawa

L. Ontario

L. Erie

L. Huron

L. Michigan

Lake Superior

Queen Elizabeth Islands

Ellesmere Island

Parry Islands

Melville Peninsula

Boothia Peninsula

Victoria Island

Banks Island

Beaufort Sea

Arctic Ocean

Yukon

Alaska (U.S.)

Mackenzie

Great Bear Lake

Great Slave Lake

Slave

Thelon

Hudson Bay

Albany

Nelson

Lake Winnipeg

Lake Athabasca

Athabasca

Churchill

Saskatchewan

G R E A T   P L A I N S

Peace

Mt. Logan 19,550 ft (5,959 m) ▲ Highest point in Canada

R O C K Y   M O U N T A I N S

Fraser

C O A S T   M O U N T A I N S

Vancouver Island

Pacific Ocean

U N I T E D   S T A T E S

400 Miles

400 Kilometers

Azimuthal Equidistant Projection

In land area Canada is the world's second largest country, but much of its territory offers limited choices for human use. Most of the northern lowlands are locked in an icy Arctic grip. The ancient rock of the Canadian Shield, although mineral rich, has very poor agricultural potential. In the west the Rocky Mountains rise above the fertile interior plains.

Political
- ⊛ National capital
- ⊙ Provincial or territorial capital
- • Other city

400 Miles
400 Kilometers
0
0

Azimuthal Equidistant Projection

ICELAND

Greenland (Denmark)

ARCTIC CIRCLE

Atlantic Ocean

Ellesmere Island

Baffin Island

Banks Island

Victoria Island

Resolute

Iqaluit

Igloolik

Cape Dorset

Ivujivik

Cambridge Bay

Kugluktuk

Tuktoyaktuk

Inuvik

NORTHWEST TERRITORIES

Yellowknife

Hay River

Fort Smith

NUNAVUT

Hudson Bay

Churchill

Fort Severn

Fort Albany

Kuujjuaq

Schefferville

Happy Valley-Goose Bay

L'Anse aux Meadows

St. John's

NEWFOUNDLAND AND LABRADOR

Sept-Îles

Chisasibi

QUEBEC

Chicoutimi

Québec

Montréal

PRINCE EDWARD ISLAND

Charlottetown

NEW BRUNSWICK

Fredericton

NOVA SCOTIA

Halifax

Kingston

Ottawa ⊛

Niagara Falls

Toronto

Hamilton

London

Windsor

ONTARIO

Timmins

Sudbury

Sault Ste. Marie

Thunder Bay

Winnipeg ⊙

MANITOBA

The Pas

SASKATCHEWAN

Uranium City

Prince Albert

Saskatoon

Regina ⊙

Moose Jaw

Medicine Hat

ALBERTA

Edmonton ⊙

Calgary

Lethbridge

BRITISH COLUMBIA

Dawson Creek

Prince George

Prince Rupert

Vancouver

Victoria ⊙

YUKON TERRITORY

Whitehorse ⊙

Haines Junction

Alaska (U.S.)

UNITED STATES

Arctic Ocean

Pacific Ocean

Ten provinces and three territories (including Nunavut) make up Canada. The provinces of Ontario and Quebec form Canada's core, with more than half the country's population and almost three-quarters of its industrial capacity.

70°N

ARCTIC CIRCLE

80°N

50°N

60°N

20°W

40°W

60°W

80°W

100°W

120°W

140°W

160°W

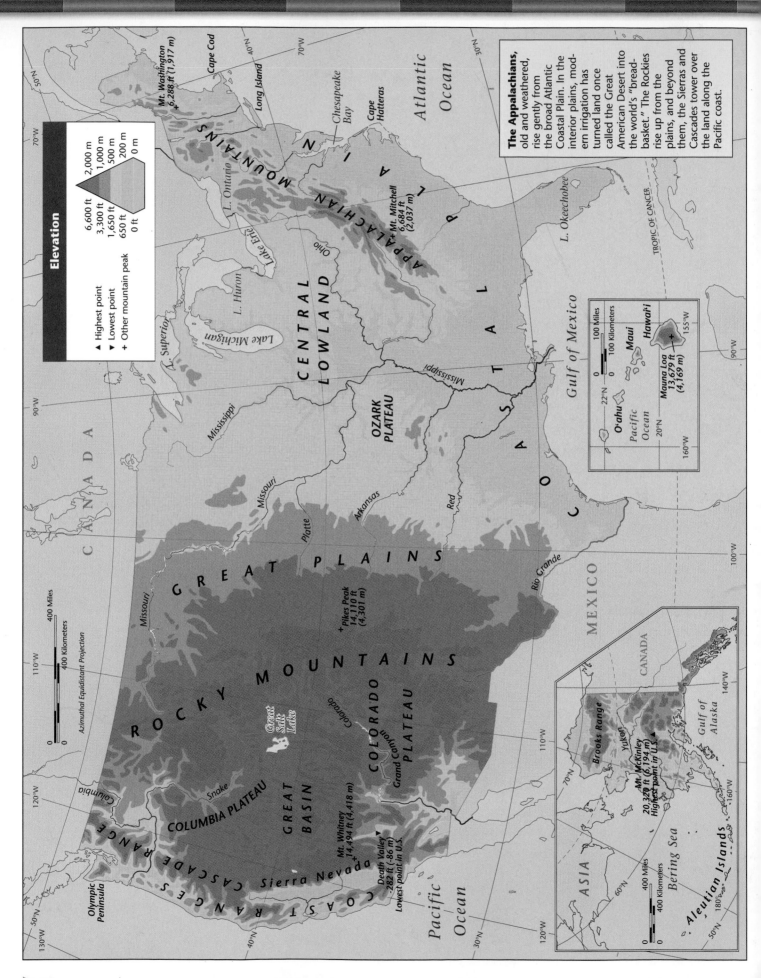

The **Appalachians**, old and weathered, rise gently from the broad Atlantic Coastal Plain. In the interior plains, modern irrigation has turned land once called the Great American Desert into the world's "breadbasket." The Rockies rise up from the plains, and beyond them, the Sierras and Cascades tower over the land along the Pacific coast.

Elevation

6,600 ft	2,000 m
3,300 ft	1,000 m
1,650 ft	500 m
650 ft	200 m
0 ft	0 m

▲ Highest point
▼ Lowest point
+ Other mountain peak

Mt. Washington
6,288 ft (1,917 m)

Cape Cod

Long Island

Chesapeake Bay

Cape Hatteras

Atlantic Ocean

APPALACHIAN MOUNTAINS

+ Mt. Mitchell
6,684 ft
(2,037 m)

CENTRAL LOWLAND

L. Ontario

Lake Erie

Ohio

L. Huron

Lake Michigan

L. Superior

CANADA

Mississippi

OZARK PLATEAU

Mississippi

Missouri

Arkansas

Red

L. Okeechobee

Gulf of Mexico

COASTAL PLAIN

TROPIC OF CANCER

Platte

GREAT PLAINS

+ Pikes Peak
14,110 ft
(4,301 m)

Rio Grande

MEXICO

Missouri

ROCKY MOUNTAINS

Great Salt Lake

Colorado

COLORADO PLATEAU

Grand Canyon

GREAT BASIN

Snake

COLUMBIA PLATEAU

Columbia

Mt. Whitney
14,494 ft (4,418 m)

Death Valley
282 ft (−86 m)
Lowest point in U.S.

Sierra Nevada

COAST RANGES

CASCADE RANGE

Olympic Peninsula

Pacific Ocean

400 Miles
400 Kilometers
Azimuthal Equidistant Projection

100 Miles
100 Kilometers

O'ahu

Maui

Pacific Ocean

Hawai'i

Mauna Loa
13,679 ft
(4,169 m)

22°N

20°N

160°W

155°W

ASIA

CANADA

Brooks Range

Yukon

Mt. McKinley
20,320 ft (6,194 m)
Highest point in U.S.

Gulf of Alaska

Bering Sea

Aleutian Islands

400 Miles
400 Kilometers

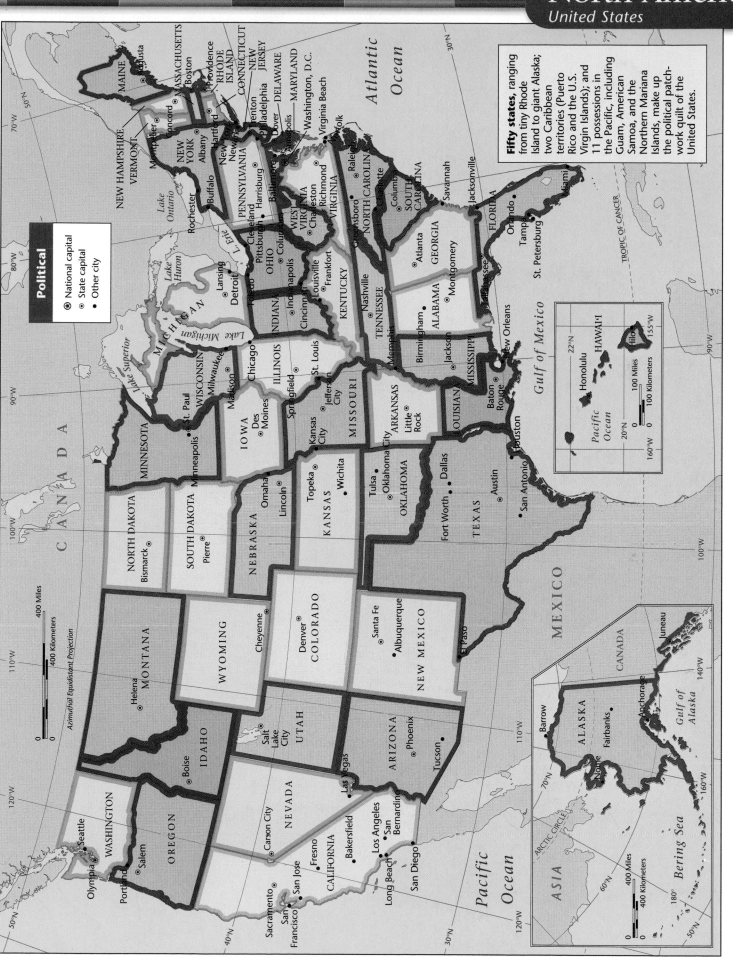

North America
United States

Political
⊛ National capital
◉ State capital
• Other city

Fifty states, ranging from tiny Rhode Island to giant Alaska; two Caribbean territories (Puerto Rico and the U.S. Virgin Islands); and 11 possessions in the Pacific, including Guam, American Samoa, and the Northern Mariana Islands, make up the political patch-work quilt of the United States.

Atlantic Ocean

MAINE
Augusta
NEW HAMPSHIRE
VERMONT
Montpelier
Concord
MASSACHUSETTS
Boston
Providence
RHODE ISLAND
CONNECTICUT
NEW JERSEY
NEW YORK
Albany
Hartford
New York
Newark
Trenton
Philadelphia
DELAWARE
MARYLAND
Dover
Washington, D.C.
Annapolis
Harrisburg
Baltimore
Buffalo
Rochester
PENNSYLVANIA
Pittsburgh
WEST VIRGINIA
Charleston
Richmond
VIRGINIA
Virginia Beach
Norfolk
Raleigh
NORTH CAROLINA
Greensboro
Charlotte
Columbia
SOUTH CAROLINA
Savannah
Jacksonville

Lake Ontario
L. Erie
Lake Huron
Cleveland
Columbus
OHIO
Toledo
Detroit
Lansing
MICHIGAN
Lake Michigan
Indianapolis
INDIANA
Cincinnati
Louisville
Frankfort
KENTUCKY
Nashville
TENNESSEE
Memphis
Atlanta
GEORGIA
Montgomery
ALABAMA
Birmingham
Tallahassee
FLORIDA
Orlando
Tampa
St. Petersburg
Miami
TROPIC OF CANCER

Lake Superior
WISCONSIN
Milwaukee
Madison
Chicago
ILLINOIS
Springfield
St. Louis
MISSOURI
Jefferson City
ARKANSAS
Little Rock
Jackson
MISSISSIPPI
LOUISIANA
Baton Rouge
New Orleans
Gulf of Mexico

CANADA
St. Paul
Minneapolis
MINNESOTA
IOWA
Des Moines
Kansas City
Topeka
KANSAS
Wichita
Omaha
Lincoln
NEBRASKA
OKLAHOMA
Oklahoma City
Tulsa
Dallas
Fort Worth
Austin
TEXAS
Houston
San Antonio

NORTH DAKOTA
Bismarck
SOUTH DAKOTA
Pierre

MONTANA
Helena
WYOMING
Cheyenne
Denver
COLORADO
Santa Fe
Albuquerque
NEW MEXICO
El Paso
MEXICO

HAWAI'I
Honolulu
Hilo
Pacific Ocean
22°N
20°N
160°W
155°W
100 Miles
100 Kilometers

IDAHO
Boise
Salt Lake City
UTAH
NEVADA
Carson City
Las Vegas
ARIZONA
Phoenix
Tucson

WASHINGTON
Seattle
Olympia
Portland
Salem
OREGON
Sacramento
San Francisco
San Jose
Fresno
Bakersfield
CALIFORNIA
Los Angeles
San Bernardino
Long Beach
San Diego
Pacific Ocean

ALASKA
Barrow
Fairbanks
Anchorage
Nome
Juneau
CANADA
Gulf of Alaska
ASIA
Bering Sea
ARCTIC CIRCLE
70°N
60°N
180°
160°W
140°W
50°N
400 Miles
400 Kilometers

400 Miles
400 Kilometers
Azimuthal Equidistant Projection

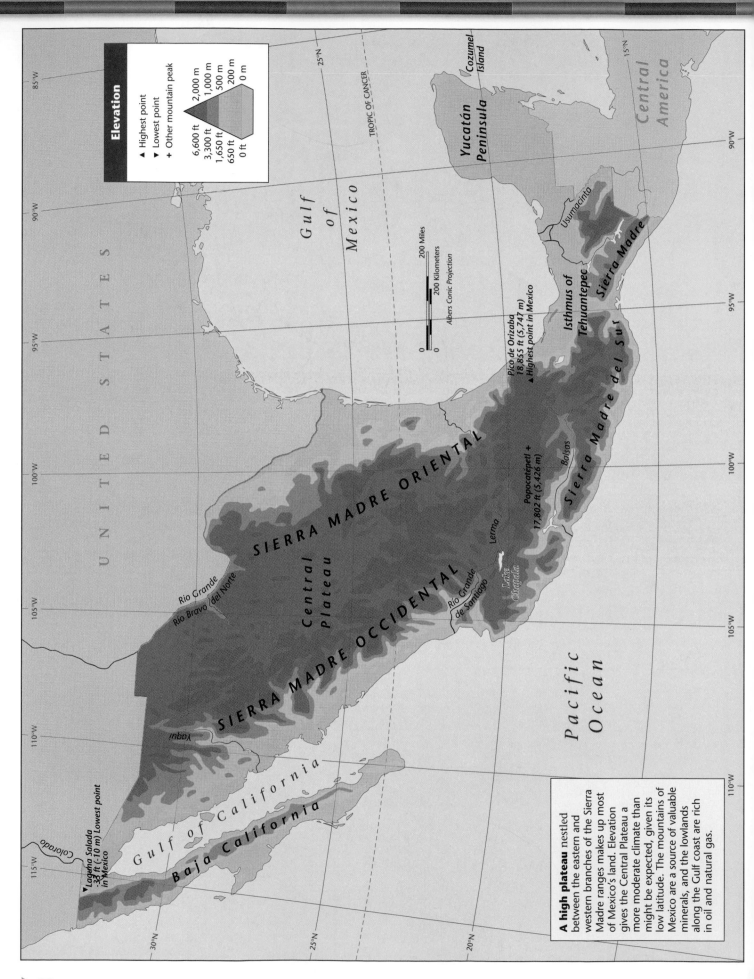

Elevation

▲ Highest point
▼ Lowest point
+ Other mountain peak

6,600 ft	2,000 m
3,300 ft	1,000 m
1,650 ft	500 m
650 ft	200 m
0 ft	0 m

UNITED STATES

Gulf of Mexico

TROPIC OF CANCER

Cozumel Island

Yucatán Peninsula

Usumacinta

Central America

Sierra Madre

Isthmus of Tehuantepec

Pico de Orizaba
18,855 ft (5,747 m)
▲ Highest point in Mexico

200 Miles
200 Kilometers
Albers Conic Projection

SIERRA MADRE ORIENTAL

Central Plateau

SIERRA MADRE OCCIDENTAL

Rio Grande
Rio Bravo del Norte

Rio Grande de Santiago

Lerma

Lake Chapala

Balsas

Popocatépetl +
17,802 ft (5,426 m)

Sierra Madre del Sur

Yaqui

Colorado

▲Laguna Salada
-33 ft (-10 m) Lowest point
in Mexico

Gulf of California

Baja California

Pacific Ocean

A **high plateau** nestled between the eastern and western branches of the Sierra Madre ranges makes up most of Mexico's land. Elevation gives the Central Plateau a more moderate climate than might be expected, given its low latitude. The mountains of Mexico are a source of valuable minerals, and the lowlands along the Gulf coast are rich in oil and natural gas.

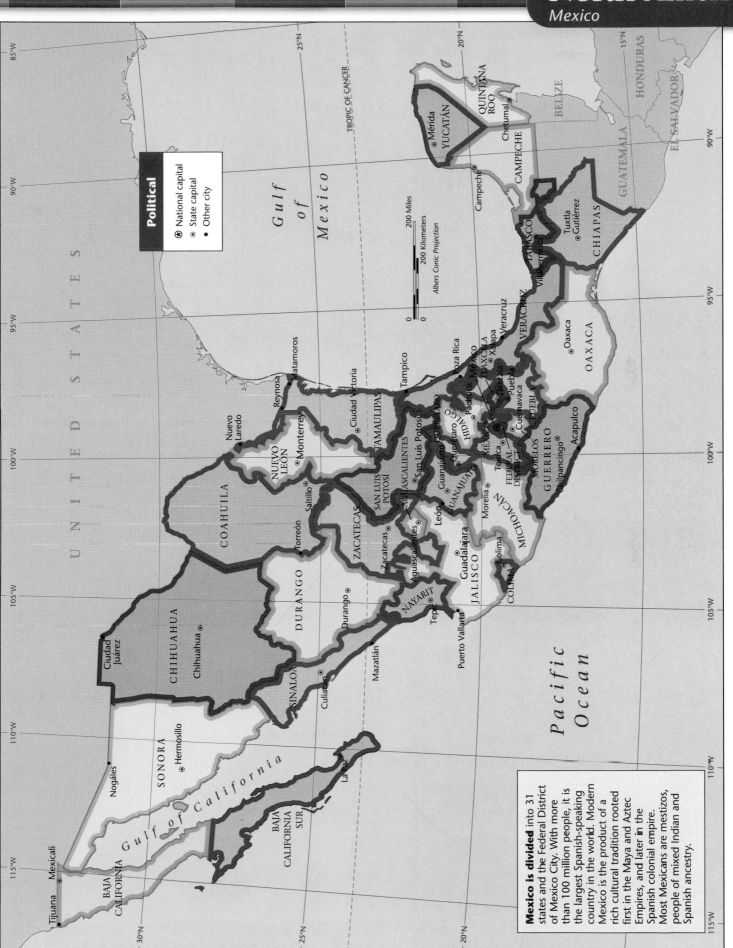

Political
- ⊛ National capital
- ⊙ State capital
- • Other city

200 Miles

200 Kilometers

Albers Conic Projection

Gulf of Mexico

Pacific Ocean

Gulf of California

UNITED STATES

HONDURAS

EL SALVADOR

GUATEMALA

BELIZE

QUINTANA ROO

YUCATÁN

CAMPECHE

CHIAPAS

TABASCO

VERACRUZ

OAXACA

GUERRERO

MORELOS

PUEBLA

TLAXCALA

MÉXICO

FEDERAL DISTRICT

HIDALGO

QUERÉTARO

MICHOACÁN

GUANAJUATO

JALISCO

COLIMA

NAYARIT

AGUASCALIENTES

ZACATECAS

SAN LUIS POTOSÍ

TAMAULIPAS

NUEVO LEÓN

COAHUILA

DURANGO

SINALOA

CHIHUAHUA

SONORA

BAJA CALIFORNIA

BAJA CALIFORNIA SUR

Mérida • Chetumal • Campeche • Tuxtla Gutiérrez • Villahermosa • Veracruz • Xalapa • Oaxaca • Poza Rica • Pachuca • Querétaro • Toluca • Cuernavaca • Chilpancingo • Acapulco • Morelia • Colima • Guadalajara • León • Guanajuato • San Luis Potosí • Aguascalientes • Zacatecas • Tepic • Puerto Vallarta • Mazatlán • Culiacán • Durango • Torreón • Saltillo • Monterrey • Nuevo Laredo • Ciudad Victoria • Tampico • Matamoros • Reynosa • Chihuahua • Ciudad Juárez • Hermosillo • Nogáles • La Paz • Mexicali • Tijuana • Mexico • Puebla

TROPIC OF CANCER

Mexico is divided into 31 states and the Federal District of Mexico City. With more than 100 million people, it is the largest Spanish-speaking country in the world. Modern Mexico is the product of a rich cultural tradition rooted first in the Maya and Aztec Empires, and later in the Spanish colonial empire. Most Mexicans are mestizos, people of mixed Indian and Spanish ancestry.

Natural Hazards: Selected Statistics

Hurricanes
This list names North America's eight strongest recorded hurricanes as of 2004. In other parts of the world hurricanes are called cyclones and typhoons.

1980 Allen: 165 mph/265 kmph*

1969 Camille: 165 mph/265 kmph

1950 Dog: 160 mph/257 kmph

1988 Gilbert: 160 mph/257 kmph

1977 Anita: 150 mph/241 kmph

1961 Carla: 150 mph/241 kmph

1979 David: 150 mph/241 kmph

1955 Janet: 150 mph//241 kmph

*maximum wind speed recorded

Tornadoes
The following states had the highest average annual number of tornadoes from 1950 to 1998.

Texas: 125

Oklahoma: 52

Florida: 49

Kansas: 48

Nebraska: 38

Iowa: 31

Illinois: 28

Missouri: 25

Louisiana: 24

Mississippi: 24

Earthquakes
This list shows the number of earthquakes in North America in the 20th century that had a magnitude of 8.0 to 9.9 on the Richter scale.

Mexico: 8

Alaska (U.S.): 7

Guatemala: 2

British Columbia (Canada): 1

California (U.S.): 1

Dominican Republic: 1
(see map page 57)

Panama: 1

FOCUS ON

Natural Hazards

The forces of nature inspire awe. They can also bring damage and destruction, especially when people locate homes and businesses in places that are at risk of experiencing violent storms, earthquakes, volcanoes, floods, wildfires, or other natural hazards.

Tornadoes, violent, swirling storms with winds that can exceed 200 miles (300 km) per hour, strike the U.S. more than 800 times each year. Hurricanes, massive low-pressure storms that form over warm ocean waters, bring destructive winds and rain primarily to the Gulf of Mexico and the southeastern mainland. Melting spring snows and heavy rains trigger flooding; periods of drought make other regions vulnerable to wildfires. These and other hazards of nature are not limited to this continent. Natural hazards pose serious threats to lives and property wherever people live.

▲ **Volcanoes.** From deep inside Earth, molten rock, called magma, rises and breaks through the surface, sometimes quietly, but more often violently, shooting billowing ash clouds as shown here at Mount St. Helens, in Washington State.

▼ **Wildfires.** Putting lives and property at great risk, wildfires destroy millions of acres of forest each year. At the same time, fires help renew ecosystems by removing debris and encouraging seedling growth.

▶ **Floods.** Towns and farmland that occupy fertile plains along rivers are always in danger from floods. In 1993 the great Mississippi River floods devastated millions of people in the midwestern United States.

Web Link for information on natural hazards: www.usgs.gov/hazards/#hazinfo

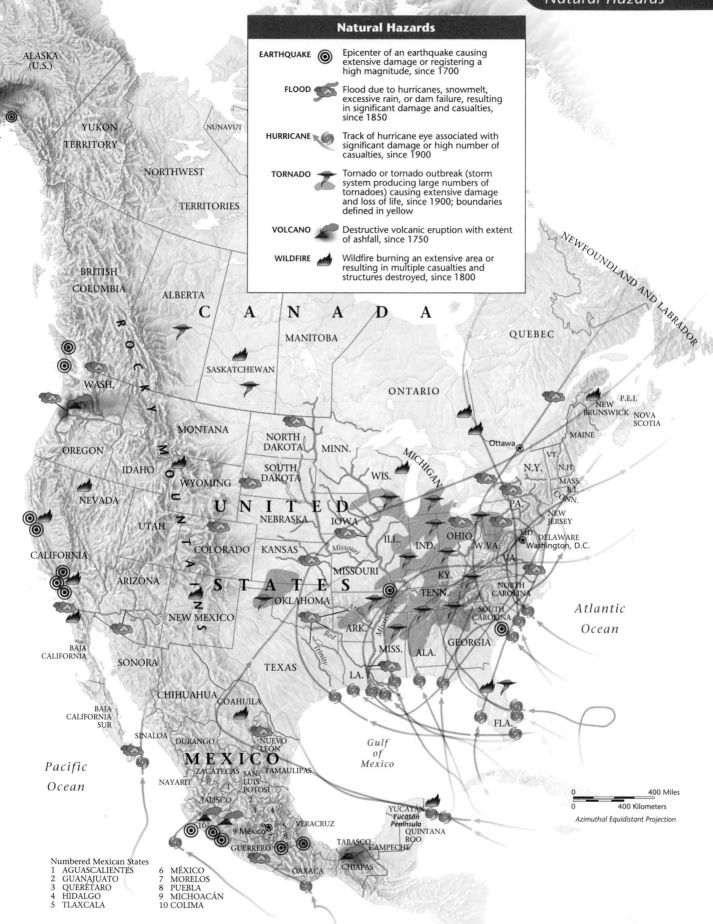

Natural Hazards

EARTHQUAKE — Epicenter of an earthquake causing extensive damage or registering a high magnitude, since 1700

FLOOD — Flood due to hurricanes, snowmelt, excessive rain, or dam failure, resulting in significant damage and casualties, since 1850

HURRICANE — Track of hurricane eye associated with significant damage or high number of casualties, since 1900

TORNADO — Tornado or tornado outbreak (storm system producing large numbers of tornadoes) causing extensive damage and loss of life, since 1900; boundaries defined in yellow

VOLCANO — Destructive volcanic eruption with extent of ashfall, since 1750

WILDFIRE — Wildfire burning an extensive area or resulting in multiple casualties and structures destroyed, since 1800

ALASKA (U.S.)

YUKON TERRITORY

NORTHWEST TERRITORIES

NUNAVUT

BRITISH COLUMBIA

ALBERTA

C A N A D A

MANITOBA

SASKATCHEWAN

ONTARIO

QUEBEC

NEWFOUNDLAND AND LABRADOR

WASH.

OREGON

IDAHO

MONTANA

NORTH DAKOTA

SOUTH DAKOTA

MINN.

WIS.

MICHIGAN

Ottawa

P.E.I.

NEW BRUNSWICK

NOVA SCOTIA

MAINE

VT.

N.H.

N.Y.

MASS.
R.I.
CONN.

NEW JERSEY

PA.

NEVADA

CALIFORNIA

UTAH

WYOMING

NEBRASKA

IOWA

ILL.

IND.

OHIO

W.VA.

VA.

MD.
Washington, D.C.

DELAWARE

ROCKY MOUNTAINS

U N I T E D

COLORADO

KANSAS

MISSOURI

Missouri

S T A T E S

ARIZONA

NEW MEXICO

OKLAHOMA

Arkansas

TENN.

KY.

NORTH CAROLINA

SOUTH CAROLINA

Atlantic Ocean

ARK.

Red

Trinity

Mississippi

MISS.

ALA.

GEORGIA

BAJA CALIFORNIA

TEXAS

LA.

Pacific Ocean

BAJA CALIFORNIA SUR

SONORA

CHIHUAHUA

COAHUILA

FLA.

SINALOA

DURANGO

NUEVO LEÓN

Gulf of Mexico

NAYARIT

ZACATECAS

SAN LUIS POTOSÍ

TAMAULIPAS

M E X I C O

JALISCO

2

3

4

1

10

9

México

7

5

8

6

VERACRUZ

YUCATÁN
Yucatán Peninsula

QUINTANA ROO

GUERRERO

TABASCO

CAMPECHE

OAXACA

CHIAPAS

0   400 Miles
0   400 Kilometers

Azimuthal Equidistant Projection

Numbered Mexican States
1 AGUASCALIENTES
2 GUANAJUATO
3 QUERÉTARO
4 HIDALGO
5 TLAXCALA
6 MÉXICO
7 MORELOS
8 PUEBLA
9 MICHOACÁN
10 COLIMA

South America

From the towering, snow-capped Andes in the west to the steamy rain forest of the Amazon Basin in the north, and from the fertile grasslands of the Pampas to the arid Atacama Desert along the Pacific coast, South America is a continent of extremes. North to south the continent extends from the tropical waters of the Caribbean Sea to the windblown islands of Tierra del Fuego. Its longest river, the Amazon, carries more water than any other river in the world.

Facts & Figures

▸ **Number of independent countries:** 12

▸ **Largest country:** Brazil: 3,300,169 sq mi (8,547,403 sq km)

▸ **Population:** 364,992,000

▸ **Highest point:** Aconcagua, Argentina: 22,834 ft (6,960 m)

▸ **Lowest point:** Valdés Peninsula, Argentina: 131 ft (40 m) below sea level

▸ **Smallest country:** Suriname: 63,037 sq mi (163,265 sq km)

▸ **Longest river:** Amazon: 4,000 mi (6,437 km)

▸ **Most populous country:** Brazil: Pop. 179,091,000

▸ **Largest lake:** Lake Titicaca, Bolivia-Peru: 3,200 sq mi (8,290 sq km)

▸ **Least populous country:** Suriname: Pop. 449,000

▸ **Land area:** 6,880,500 sq mi (17,819,000 sq km)

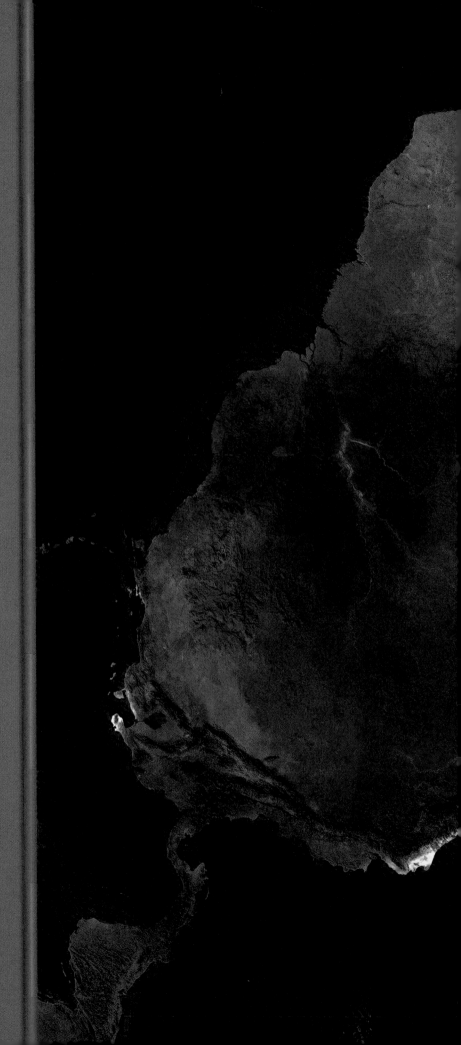

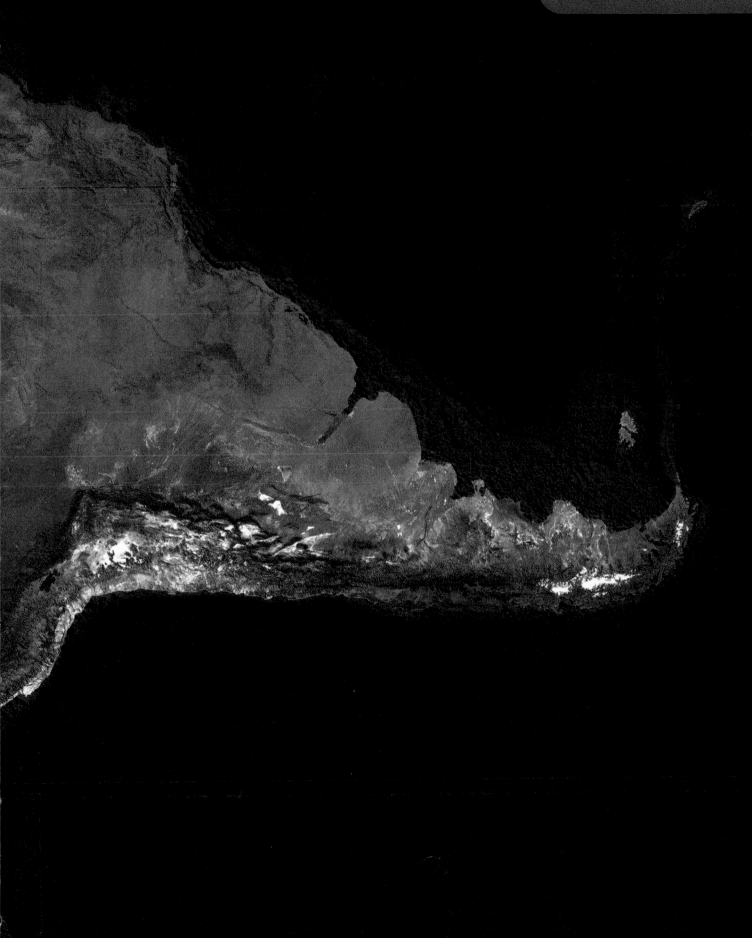

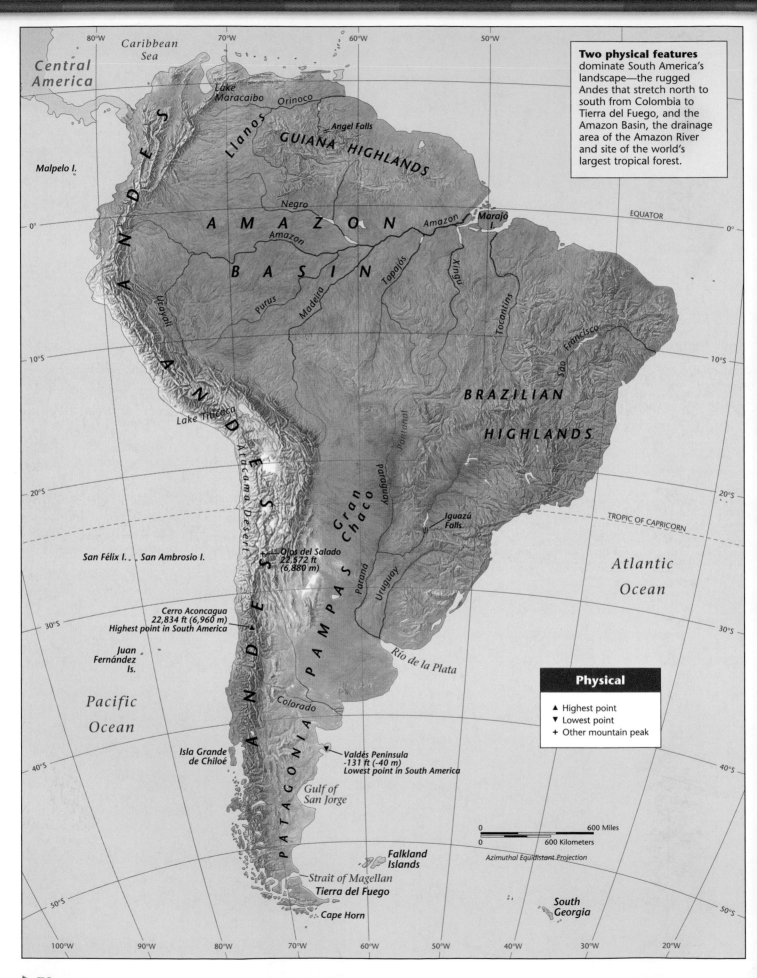

Two physical features dominate South America's landscape—the rugged Andes that stretch north to south from Colombia to Tierra del Fuego, and the Amazon Basin, the drainage area of the Amazon River and site of the world's largest tropical forest.

Caribbean Sea

Central America

Malpelo I.

Lake Maracaibo

Orinoco

Llanos

GUIANA HIGHLANDS

Angel Falls

A N D E S

EQUATOR

AMAZON

Negro

Amazon

Marajó I.

BASIN

Ucayali

Purus

Madeira

Topajós

Xingu

Tocantins

São Francisco

Lake Titicaca

BRAZILIAN

HIGHLANDS

Atacama Desert

San Félix I.   San Ambrosio I.

Ojos del Salado
22,572 ft
(6,880 m)

Pantanal

Paraguay

Gran Chaco

TROPIC OF CAPRICORN

Iguazú Falls

Cerro Aconcagua
22,834 ft (6,960 m)
Highest point in South America

A N D E S

PAMPAS

Paraná

Uruguay

Atlantic Ocean

Juan Fernández Is.

Pacific Ocean

Colorado

Río de la Plata

Physical

▲ Highest point
▼ Lowest point
+ Other mountain peak

Isla Grande de Chiloé

PATAGONIA

Valdés Peninsula
-131 ft (-40 m)
Lowest point in South America

Gulf of San Jorge

0   600 Miles
0   600 Kilometers

Azimuthal Equidistant Projection

Falkland Islands

South Georgia

Strait of Magellan
Tierra del Fuego

Cape Horn

South America

Twelve countries and one French territory (French Guiana) make up South America. The continent was under mainly Spanish and Portuguese control from the 16th to the 19th century. Colonial influence is still evident in the use of Spanish and Portuguese languages and in the widespread presence of the Roman Catholic church.

Caribbean Sea

Barranquilla
Maracaibo
Caracas
Barquisimeto
Valencia
VENEZUELA
Medellín
Bogotá
Cali
COLOMBIA
Georgetown
Paramaribo
GUYANA
SURINAME
Cayenne
French Guiana (France)

EQUATOR
Quito
ECUADOR
Guayaquil
Manaus
Belém
EQUATOR

PERU
Fortaleza
Natal
Recife

Lima
BOLIVIA
La Paz
B R A Z I L
Salvador (Bahia)

Santa Cruz
Sucre
Goiânia
Brasília
Belo Horizonte

PARAGUAY
Nova Iguaçu
São Paulo
Rio de Janeiro
Santos
Curitiba
TROPIC OF CAPRICORN

Asunción

San Miguel de Tucumán
CHILE
Porto Alegre

Atlantic Ocean

Córdoba
Santa Fe
Rosario
URUGUAY
Buenos Aires
La Plata
Montevideo

Valparaíso
Santiago

Pacific Ocean

ARGENTINA
Mar del Plata

Political
⊛ National capital
• Other city

0   600 Miles
0   600 Kilometers
Azimuthal Equidistant Projection

Stanley
Falkland Islands (U.K.)

South Georgia (U.K.)

Caribbean
Sea

Central
America

North Equatorial Current

Tropical climates dominate
most of South America.
Elevation moderates the
tropical heat, which has
influenced settlement and
land-use patterns on the
continent. Mild climates in
the south support agriculture
in Chile, Argentina,
and Uruguay.

VENEZUELA

GUYANA

French
Guiana
(France)

COLOMBIA

SURINAME

South Equatorial Current

ECUADOR

EQUATOR

PERU

B R A Z I L

Brazil Current

BOLIVIA

Peru Current

PARAGUAY

TROPIC OF CAPRICORN

Atlantic
Ocean

URUGUAY

Pacific
Ocean

CHILE

ARGENTINA

Falkland Current

Climate

Climatic Zones:
Based on Köppen System

Tropical   **Mild**

Tropical wet   Marine west coast

Tropical dry   Mediterranean

Dry   Humid subtropical

Semiarid   **High Elevations**

Arid   Highlands

                      Uplands

0   600 Miles
0   600 Kilometers

Azimuthal Equidistant Projection

← Warm ocean current
← Cool ocean current

Cape Horn Current

South America

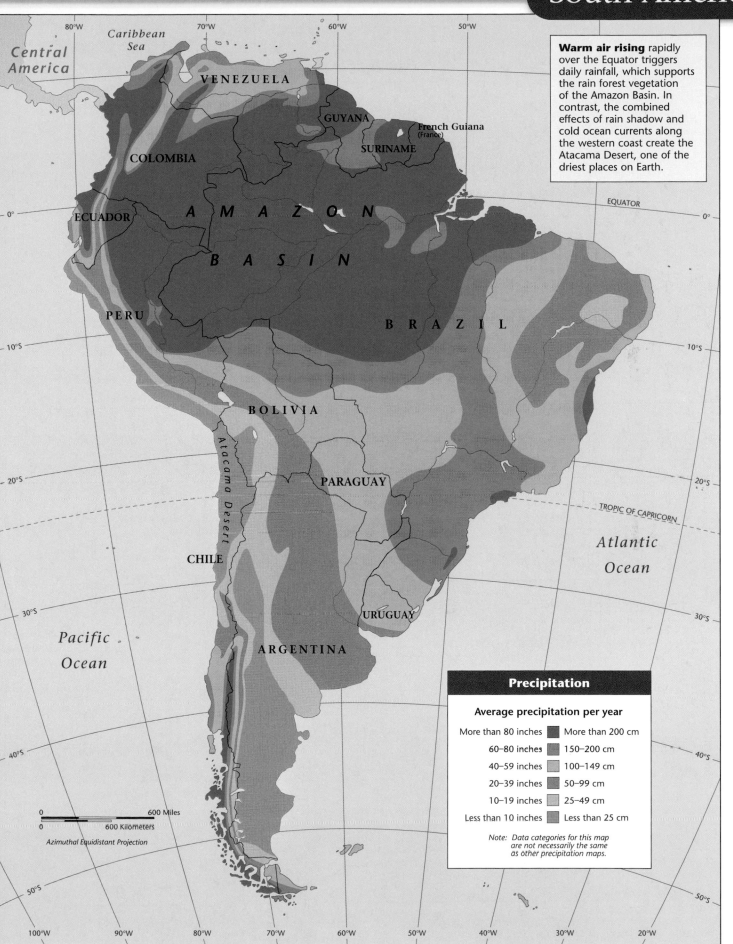

Caribbean Sea

Central America

VENEZUELA

GUYANA

French Guiana (France)

SURINAME

COLOMBIA

ECUADOR

A M A Z O N

B A S I N

EQUATOR

PERU

B R A Z I L

Atacama Desert

BOLIVIA

PARAGUAY

TROPIC OF CAPRICORN

Atlantic Ocean

CHILE

URUGUAY

Pacific Ocean

ARGENTINA

Warm air rising rapidly over the Equator triggers daily rainfall, which supports the rain forest vegetation of the Amazon Basin. In contrast, the combined effects of rain shadow and cold ocean currents along the western coast create the Atacama Desert, one of the driest places on Earth.

0   600 Miles
0   600 Kilometers

Azimuthal Equidistant Projection

Precipitation

Average precipitation per year

More than 80 inches	More than 200 cm
60–80 inches	150–200 cm
40–59 inches	100–149 cm
20–39 inches	50–99 cm
10–19 inches	25–49 cm
Less than 10 inches	Less than 25 cm

Note: Data categories for this map are not necessarily the same as other precipitation maps.

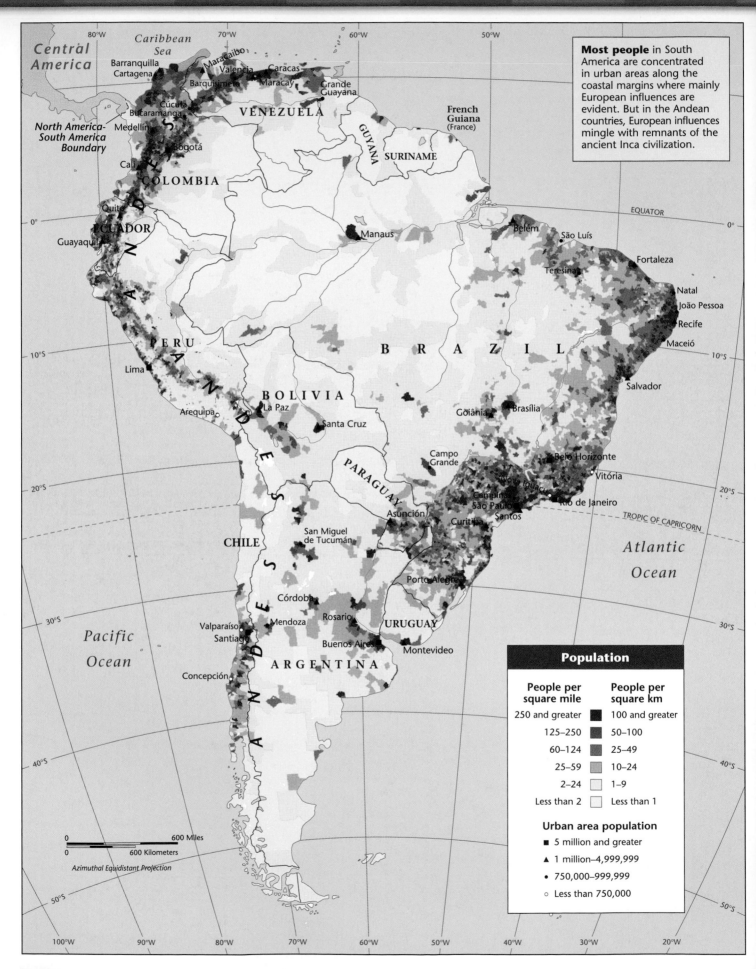

Central America

Caribbean Sea

Barranquilla
Cartagena

North America-
South America
Boundary

Maracaibo
Valencia
Barquisimeto
Cúcuta
Bucaramanga
Medellín
Cali
Bogotá
Quito
ECUADOR
Guayaquil

VENEZUELA

Caracas
Maracay

Grande
Guayana

GUYANA

SURINAME

French
Guiana
(France)

COLOMBIA

A
N
D
E
S

PERU

Lima

Arequipa

BOLIVIA

La Paz

Santa Cruz

EQUATOR

Manaus

Belém

São Luís

Teresina

Fortaleza

Natal
João Pessoa
Recife
Maceió

B R A Z I L

Salvador

Goiânia

Brasília

Campo
Grande

Belo Horizonte
Vitória

PARAGUAY

Asunción

Nova Iguaçu
Campinas
São Paulo
Santos

Rio de Janeiro

Curitiba

TROPIC OF CAPRICORN

CHILE

San Miguel
de Tucumán

*Atlantic
Ocean*

Córdoba

Porto Alegre

Mendoza

Rosario

URUGUAY

Valparaíso
Santiago

Buenos Aires

Montevideo

*Pacific
Ocean*

Concepción

A R G E N T I N A

A
N
D
E
S

0   600 Miles
0   600 Kilometers

Azimuthal Equidistant Projection

Most people in South
America are concentrated
in urban areas along the
coastal margins where mainly
European influences are
evident. But in the Andean
countries, European influences
mingle with remnants of the
ancient Inca civilization.

Population

**People per
square mile**

250 and greater

125–250

60–124

25–59

2–24

Less than 2

**People per
square km**

100 and greater

50–100

25–49

10–24

1–9

Less than 1

Urban area population

■ 5 million and greater

▲ 1 million–4,999,999

● 750,000–999,999

○ Less than 750,000

South America

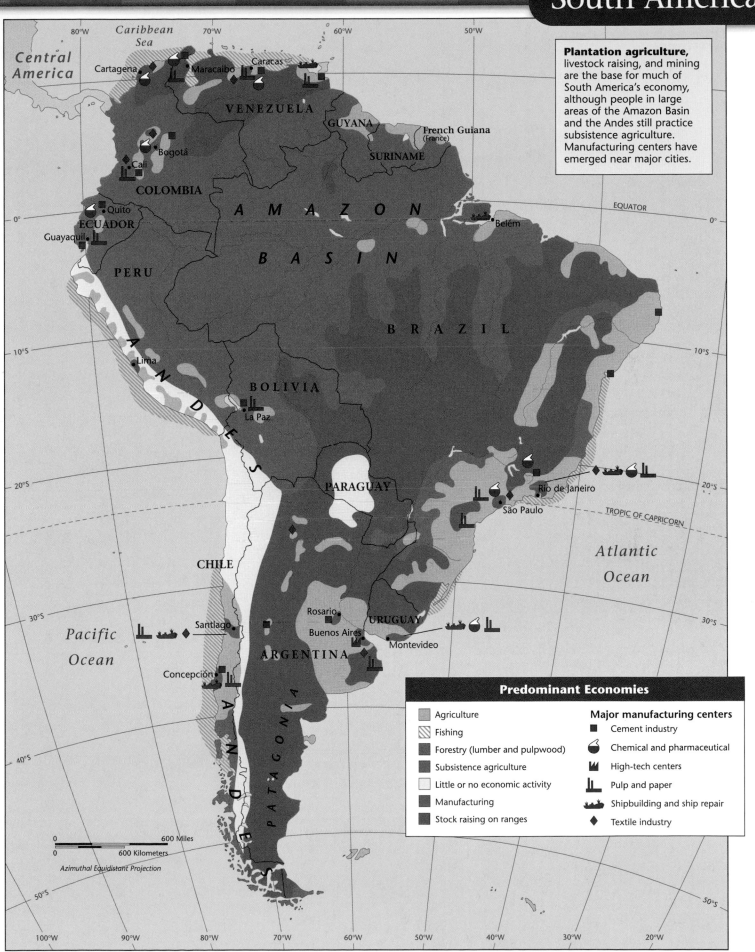

Plantation agriculture, livestock raising, and mining are the base for much of South America's economy, although people in large areas of the Amazon Basin and the Andes still practice subsistence agriculture. Manufacturing centers have emerged near major cities.

Caribbean Sea

Central America

Cartagena

Maracaibo

Caracas

VENEZUELA

GUYANA

SURINAME

French Guiana (France)

Bogotá

Cali

COLOMBIA

Quito

ECUADOR

Guayaquil

AMAZON BASIN

EQUATOR

Belém

PERU

BRAZIL

Lima

BOLIVIA

La Paz

PARAGUAY

Rio de Janeiro

São Paulo

TROPIC OF CAPRICORN

Atlantic Ocean

CHILE

Pacific Ocean

Rosario

Santiago

Buenos Aires

URUGUAY

Montevideo

ARGENTINA

Concepción

PATAGONIA

ANDES

ANDES

0   600 Miles
0   600 Kilometers
Azimuthal Equidistant Projection

Predominant Economies

Agriculture	
Fishing	
Forestry (lumber and pulpwood)	
Subsistence agriculture	
Little or no economic activity	
Manufacturing	
Stock raising on ranges	

Major manufacturing centers

Cement industry	
Chemical and pharmaceutical	
High-tech centers	
Pulp and paper	
Shipbuilding and ship repair	
Textile industry	

Amazon Rain Forest

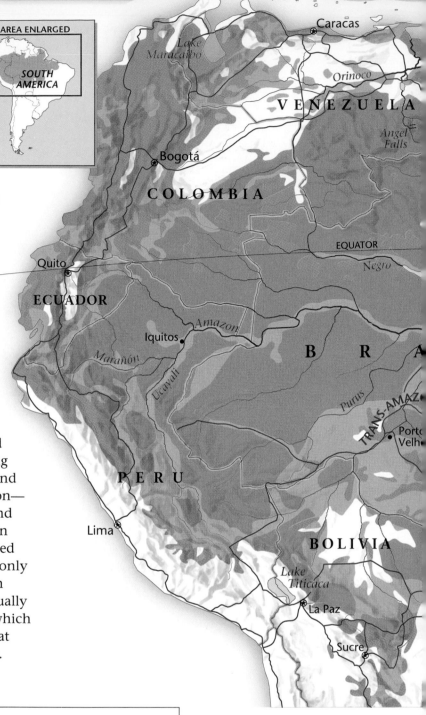

AREA ENLARGED

SOUTH
AMERICA

The Amazon rain forest, which covers approximately 2.7 million square miles (7 million sq km), is the world's largest tropical forest. Located mainly in Brazil, the Amazon rain forest accounts for more than 20 percent of all the world's tropical forests. Known in Brazil as the selva, the rain forest is a vast storehouse of biological diversity, filled with plants and animals both familiar and exotic. According to estimates, at least half of all species are found in tropical forests, but many of these species have not yet been identified.

Tropical forests contain many valuable resources, including cacao (chocolate), nuts, spices, rare hardwoods, and plant extracts used to make medicines. Some drugs used in treating cancer and heart disease come from plants found only in tropical forests. But human intervention—logging, mining, and clearing land for crops and grazing—has put tropical forests at great risk. In Brazil, roads cut into the rain forest have opened the way for settlers, who clear away the forest only to discover soil too poor in nutrients to sustain agriculture for more than a few years. Land usually is cleared by a method called slash-and-burn, which contributes to global warming by releasing great amounts of carbon dioxide into the atmosphere.

Tropical Forests

Tropical rain forests grow in parts of every continent except Europe and Antarctica. Together, the tropical forests of South America and Africa make up three-quarters of the world's total. Brazil alone has more than 300 million acres (120 million hectares)—more than any other country.

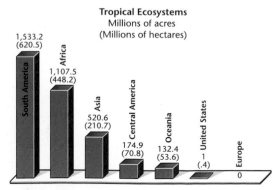

Tropical Ecosystems
Millions of acres
(Millions of hectares)

- South America 1,533.2 (620.5)
- Africa 1,107.5 (448.2)
- Asia 520.6 (210.7)
- Central America 174.9 (70.8)
- Oceania 132.4 (53.6)
- United States 1 (.4)
- Europe 0

▶ **Price of progress.** *Clearing trees to make way for expanding economic activities leads to widespread environmental destruction. Slash-and-burn agriculture exposes fragile soils to heat and torrential rains, and the runoff from mining operations pollutes streams and rivers. In an effort to reverse this trend, some countries and international organizations have set up national parks, reserves, and other protected areas.*

Web Link for information on rain forests: http://www.srl.caltech.edu/personnel/krubal/rainforest/Edit560s6/www/facts.ht

▶ **Dense canopy of the rain forest** *stands in sharp contrast to the silt-laden waters of one of the Amazon's many tributaries. Although seemingly endless, the forest in Brazil is decreasing in size at the rate of almost 15,000 acres (6,070 ha) per day.*

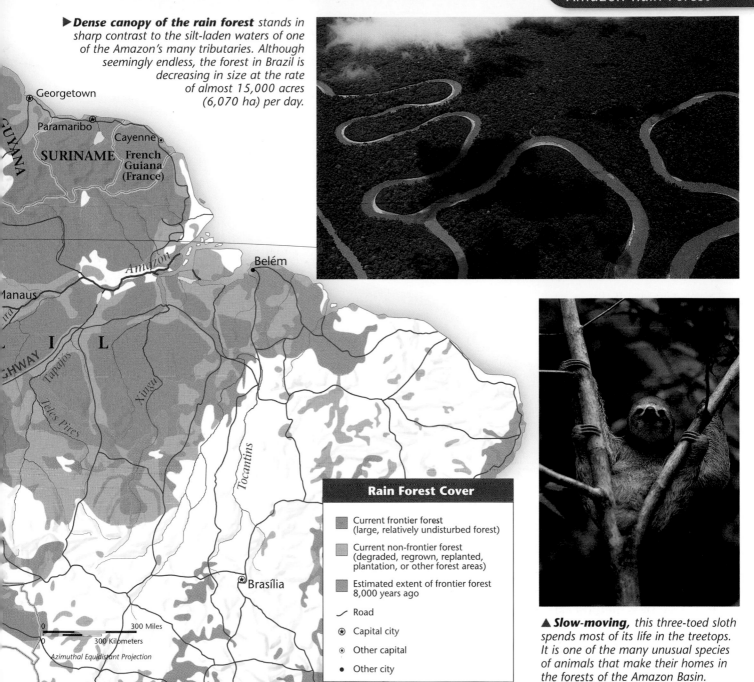

Georgetown

Paramaribo

Cayenne

SURINAME French Guiana (France)

GUYANA

Amazon

Belém

Manaus

B R A S I L

HIGHWAY

Tapajós

Xingu

Teles Pires

Tocantins

⊛ Brasília

0   300 Miles
0   300 Kilometers

Azimuthal Equidistant Projection

Rain Forest Cover

- Current frontier forest (large, relatively undisturbed forest)
- Current non-frontier forest (degraded, regrown, replanted, plantation, or other forest areas)
- Estimated extent of frontier forest 8,000 years ago
- ⟋ Road
- ⊛ Capital city
- ⊙ Other capital
- • Other city

▲ **Slow-moving,** *this three-toed sloth spends most of its life in the treetops. It is one of the many unusual species of animals that make their homes in the forests of the Amazon Basin.*

▲ **Slash-and-burn** *is a method used in the tropics for clearing land for farms. But the soil is poor in nutrients, and good yields are short-lived.*

▲ **Mining operations,** *such as this tin mine, remove forests to gain access to mineral deposits.*

79 ◀

Europe

Smaller than every other continent except Australia, Europe is a mosaic of islands and peninsulas. In fact, Europe itself is one big peninsula, jutting westward from the huge land-mass of Asia and nearly touching Africa to the south. Europe's ragged coastline measures more than one and a half times the length of the Equator—38,279 miles (61,603 km) to be exact—giving 31 of its 44 countries direct access to the sea.

Facts & Figures

▶ **Land area:** 3,837,400 sq mi
(9,938,000 sq km)

▶ **Population:** 728,392,000

▶ **Highest point:** Mount El'brus, Russia:
18,510 ft (5,642 m)

▶ **Lowest point:** Caspian Sea:
92 ft (28 m) below sea level

▶ **Longest river:** Volga, Russia:
2,290 mi (3,685 km)

▶ **Largest lake entirely in Europe:**
Ladoga, Russia: 6,853 sq mi (17,703 sq km)

▶ **Number of independent countries:**
44 (including Russia)

▶ **Largest country entirely in Europe:**
Ukraine 233,090 sq mi (603,700 sq km)

▶ **Smallest country:** Vatican City:
0.2 sq mi (0.4 sq km)

▶ **Most populous country entirely in
Europe:** Germany: Pop. 82,621,000

▶ **Least populous country:**
Vatican City: Pop. 1,000

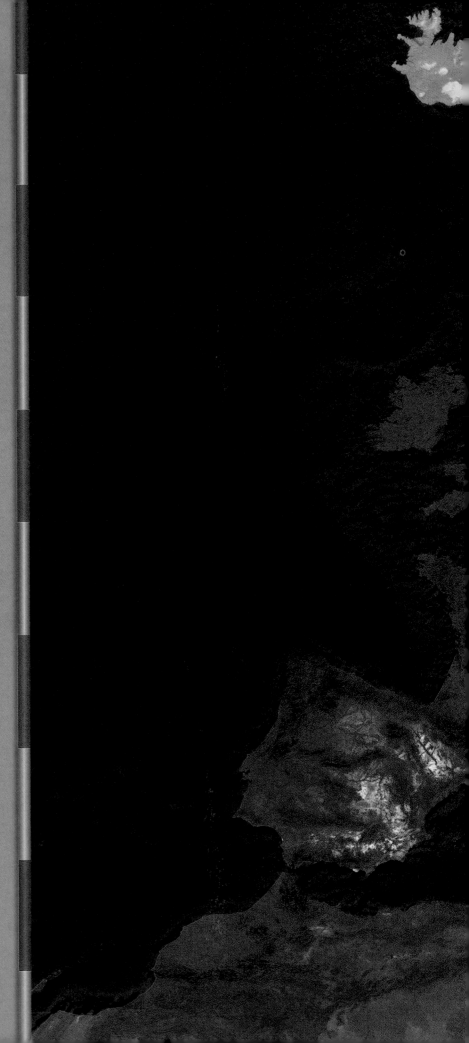

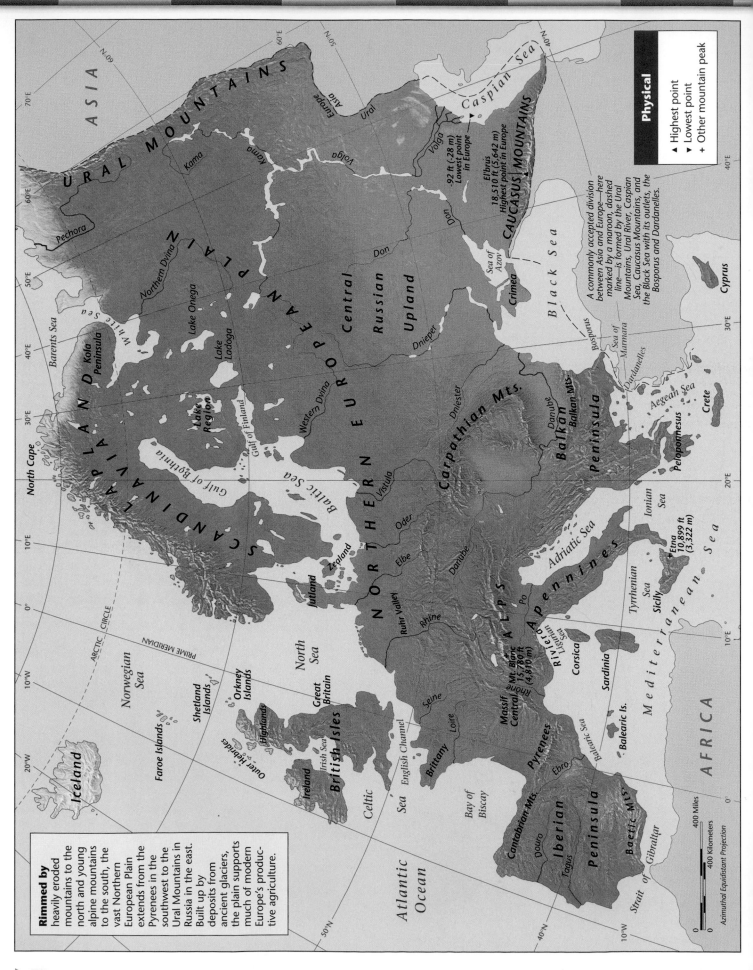

Azimuthal Equidistant Projection

Physical

▲ Highest point
▼ Lowest point
+ Other mountain peak

Rimmed by heavily eroded mountains to the north and young alpine mountains to the south, the vast Northern European Plain extends from the Pyrenees in the southwest to the Ural Mountains in Russia in the east. Built up by deposits from ancient glaciers, the plain supports much of modern Europe's productive agriculture.

A commonly accepted division between Asia and Europe—here marked by a maroon, dashed line—is formed by the Ural Mountains, Ural River, Caspian Sea, Caucasus Mountains, and the Black Sea with its outlets, the Bosporus and Dardanelles.

ASIA

URAL MOUNTAINS

Pechora
Kama
Kama
Volga
Volga
Ural
Europe
Asia

Caspian Sea

-92 ft (-28 m) Lowest point in Europe

Elbrus 18,510 ft (5,642 m) Highest point in Europe

CAUCASUS MOUNTAINS

Don
Don
Sea of Azov
Crimea

Black Sea

Bosporus
Sea of Marmara
Dardanelles

Cyprus

NORTHERN EUROPEAN PLAIN

Central Russian Upland

Northern Dvina
Lake Onega
Lake Ladoga
Western Dvina
Dnieper
Dniester

Barents Sea
Kola Peninsula
White Sea

Lake Region

Gulf of Finland
Gulf of Bothnia

Baltic Sea

Carpathian Mts.

Danube
Balkan Mts.
Balkan Peninsula

Aegean Sea
Crete
Peloponnesus

North Cape

SCANDINAVIAN UPLAND

Vistula
Oder
Elbe
Danube

Zealand
Jutland

Adriatic Sea

Apennines

ALPS

Po
Rhine
Ruhr Valley

Tyrrhenian Sea
Sicily
+Etna 10,899 ft (3,322 m)

Ionian Sea

Mediterranean Sea

Norwegian Sea

Faroe Islands

Shetland Islands
Orkney Islands

North Sea

Highlands
Outer Hebrides

Great Britain

British Isles

Ireland
Irish Sea
Celtic Sea
English Channel

Brittany

Seine
Loire

Bay of Biscay

Massif Central

Mt. Blanc 15,780 ft (4,810 m)

Rhône
Riviera
Ligurian Sea

Corsica
Sardinia
Balearic Sea
Balearic Is.

Pyrenees

Cantabrian Mts.
Douro
Tagus
Ebro
Baetic Mts.

Iberian Peninsula

Strait of Gibraltar

AFRICA

Iceland

Atlantic Ocean

ARCTIC CIRCLE
PRIME MERIDIAN

400 Miles
400 Kilometers

82

Political
- ⊛ National capital
- • Other city
- ▢ Small country

Europe has 44 independent countries that range in size from giant Russia to tiny Vatican City. Because Russia's capital is located in and most of its people live west of the Urals, the country is usually considered part of Europe. Iceland, United Kingdom, Ireland, Malta, and Cyprus are all island countries.

A commonly accepted division between Asia and Europe—here marked by a maroon, dashed line—is formed by the Ural Mountains, Ural River, Caspian Sea, Caucasus Mountains, and the Black Sea with its outlets, the Bosporus and Dardanelles.

ASIA

RUSSIA

KAZAKHSTAN

Caspian Sea

AZERBAIJAN · Baku

GEORGIA

Ufa · Perm' · Orenburg · Astrakhan' · Grozny

Kirov · Nizhniy Novgorod · Samara · Penza · Saratov · Volgograd · Rostov

Kazan' · Ryazan' · Dnipropetrovs'k

Yaroslavl' · Tver' · Moscow ⊛ · Smolensk · Bryansk · Kursk · Kharkiv · Donets'k · Poltava

St. Petersburg

Murmansk

Barents Sea

Arkhangel'sk

FINLAND

Helsinki ⊛

ESTONIA · Tallinn ⊛

Riga · LATVIA

LITHUANIA · Vilnius · Kaunas

Kaliningrad (Russia)

BELARUS · Minsk · Homyel' · Vitsyebsk

UKRAINE · Kiev ⊛ · L'viv · Vinnytsya · Odesa · Simferopol' · Sevastopol'

MOLDOVA · Chişinău

Black Sea · Varna

ROMANIA · Bucharest

BULGARIA · Sofia

TURKEY · Istanbul · Thessaloníki

GREECE · Athens ⊛ · Crete

CYPRUS · Nicosia ⊛

Norwegian Sea

Faroe Islands (Denmark)

Shetland Islands

Orkney Islands

ICELAND · Reykjavik ⊛

SWEDEN

NORWAY · Oslo ⊛

Stockholm ⊛ · Göteborg

Baltic Sea

DENMARK · Copenhagen ⊛

Gdańsk

POLAND · Warsaw ⊛ · Łódź · Wrocław · Kraków · Bydgoszcz

CZECH REP. · Prague ⊛

SLOVAKIA · Bratislava

HUNGARY · Budapest ⊛

AUSTRIA · Vienna ⊛ · Munich

SLOV. · Ljubljana · Zagreb

CROATIA · SERB. & MONT. · Belgrade · Sarajevo

BOSN. & HERZG.

MACED. · Skopje

ALBANIA · Tirana · Podgorica

SCOTLAND · Glasgow · Edinburgh

N. IRELAND · Belfast

IRELAND · Dublin

UNITED KINGDOM · Manchester · Birmingham · Liverpool

WALES · Cardiff

ENGLAND · London ⊛

North Sea

NETH. · Amsterdam ⊛ · The Hague

BELGIUM · Brussels ⊛

LUX.

GERMANY · Berlin ⊛ · Hamburg · Frankfurt · Kiel

FRANCE · Paris ⊛ · Lyon · Nantes · Bordeaux · Toulouse · Nice · Marseille

SWITZ. · Bern ⊛ · Zürich

LIECH.

MONACO

ANDORRA

ITALY · Rome ⊛ · Milan · Turin · Venice · Genoa · Naples

SAN MARINO

VATICAN CITY

Corsica (France)

Sardinia (Italy)

Sicily · Palermo · Catania · Messina

MALTA · Valletta ⊛

Mediterranean Sea

Bay of Biscay

Atlantic Ocean

PORTUGAL · Lisbon ⊛ · Oporto

SPAIN · Madrid ⊛ · Barcelona · Valencia · Bilbao · Valladolid · Zaragoza · Seville · Murcia · Málaga

Gibraltar (U.K.)

Balearic Is. (Spain)

AFRICA

PRIME MERIDIAN

ARCTIC CIRCLE

400 Miles

400 Kilometers

Azimuthal Equidistant Projection

83 ◀

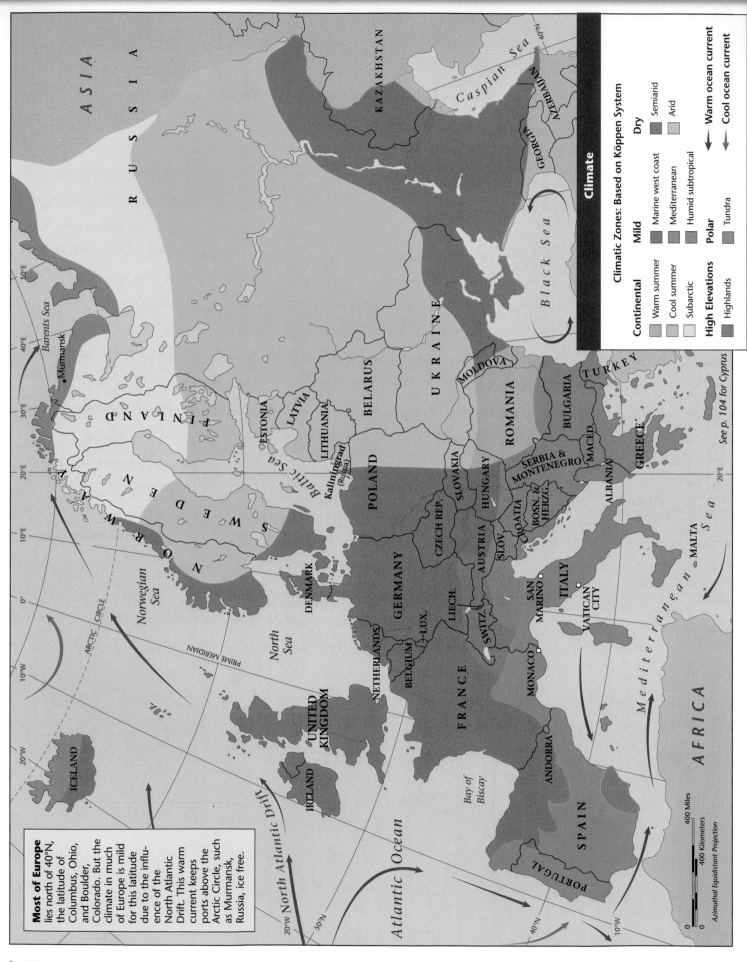

Climate

Climatic Zones: Based on Köppen System

Continental
- Warm summer
- Cool summer
- Subarctic

Mild
- Marine west coast
- Mediterranean
- Humid subtropical

Dry
- Semiarid
- Arid

Polar
- Tundra

High Elevations
- Highlands

→ Warm ocean current
→ Cool ocean current

Most of Europe lies north of 40°N, the latitude of Columbus, Ohio, and Boulder, Colorado. But the climate in much of Europe is mild for this latitude due to the influence of the North Atlantic Drift. This warm current keeps ports above the Arctic Circle, such as Murmansk, Russia, ice free.

See p. 104 for Cyprus

ASIA

RUSSIA

KAZAKHSTAN

Caspian Sea

AZERBAIJAN

GEORGIA

Black Sea

TURKEY

Barents Sea

•Murmansk

FINLAND

ESTONIA

LATVIA

LITHUANIA

BELARUS

UKRAINE

MOLDOVA

ROMANIA

BULGARIA

MACED.

SERBIA & MONTENEGRO

GREECE

ALBANIA

Baltic Sea

Kaliningrad (Russia)

POLAND

SLOVAKIA

HUNGARY

CZECH REP.

AUSTRIA

SLOV.

CROATIA

BOSN. & HERZG.

SWEDEN

NORWAY

Norwegian Sea

DENMARK

GERMANY

LIECH.

SWITZ.

ITALY

SAN MARINO

VATICAN CITY

MONACO

LUX.

NETHERLANDS

BELGIUM

FRANCE

ANDORRA

SPAIN

PORTUGAL

North Sea

UNITED KINGDOM

IRELAND

ICELAND

Atlantic Ocean

North Atlantic Drift

Bay of Biscay

Mediterranean Sea

MALTA

AFRICA

ARCTIC CIRCLE

PRIME MERIDIAN

20°W

10°W

0°

10°E

20°E

30°E

40°E

50°E

40°N

50°N

40°N

70°

400 Miles

400 Kilometers

0

0

Azimuthal Equidistant Projection

Europe

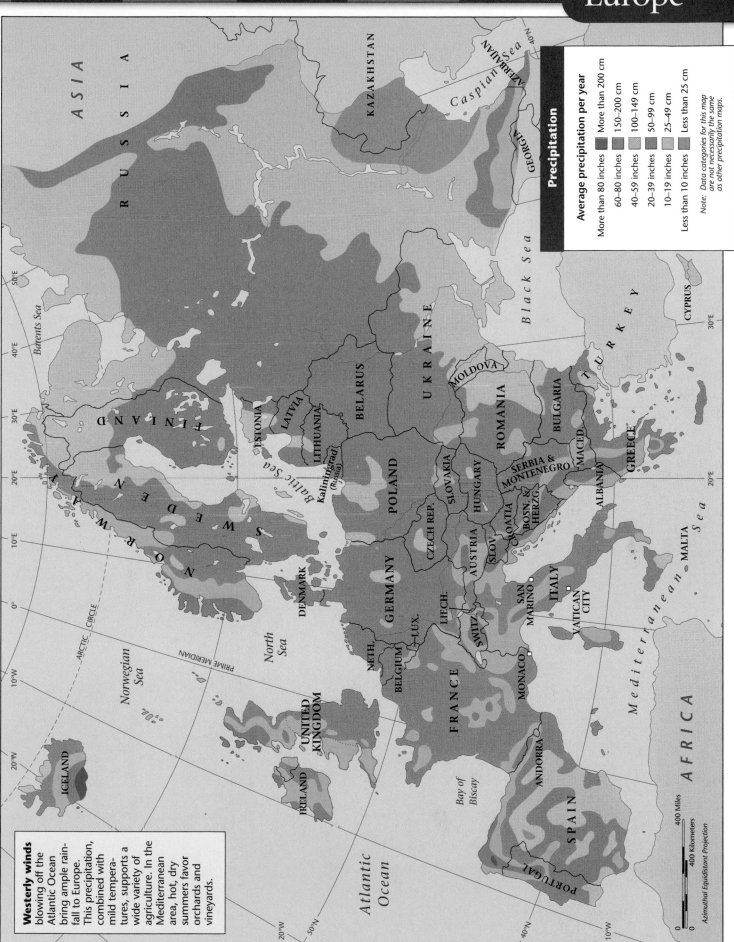

Precipitation

Average precipitation per year

More than 80 inches	More than 200 cm
60–80 inches	150–200 cm
40–59 inches	100–149 cm
20–39 inches	50–99 cm
10–19 inches	25–49 cm
Less than 10 inches	Less than 25 cm

Note: Data categories for this map are not necessarily the same as other precipitation maps.

Westerly winds blowing off the Atlantic Ocean bring ample rainfall to Europe. This precipitation, combined with mild temperatures, supports a wide variety of agriculture. In the Mediterranean area, hot, dry summers favor orchards and vineyards.

400 Miles

400 Kilometers

Azimuthal Equidistant Projection

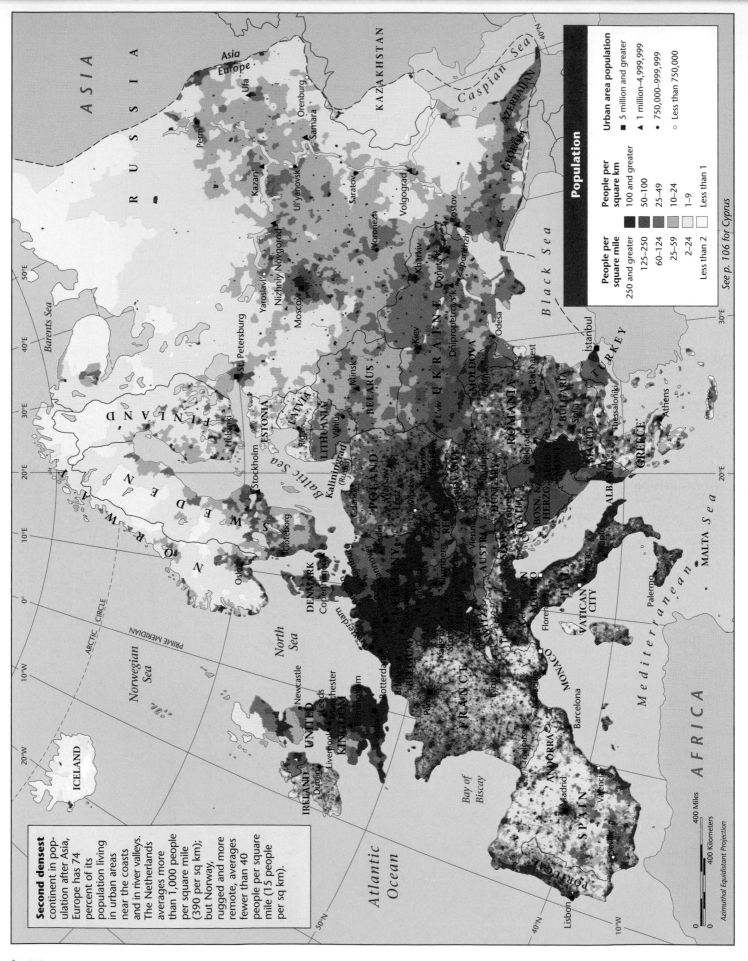

Second densest continent in population after Asia, Europe has 74 percent of its population living in urban areas near the coasts and in river valleys. The Netherlands averages more than 1,000 people per square mile (390 per sq km); but Norway, rugged and more remote, averages fewer than 40 people per square mile (15 people per sq km).

Population

Urban area population
- ■ 5 million and greater
- ▲ 1 million–4,999,999
- ● 750,000–999,999
- ○ Less than 750,000

People per square km
- 100 and greater
- 50–100
- 25–49
- 10–24
- 1–9
- Less than 1

People per square mile
- 250 and greater
- 125–250
- 60–124
- 25–59
- 2–24
- Less than 2

See p. 106 for Cyprus

Azimuthal Equidistant Projection

Europe

Major Manufacturing Centers

- Cement industry
- Chemical and pharmaceutical
- High-tech centers
- Pulp and paper
- Shipbuilding and ship repair
- Textile industry

The Industrial Revolution had its beginnings in Europe, and manufacturing is still an important part of the continent's economy. Main industrial centers in the United Kingdom and in Germany's Ruhr region are located near coal deposits, reflecting a time when coal was the main source of energy. Although agriculture is important, the region is not self-sufficient in food production.

Predominant Economies

- Agriculture
- Agriculture and forestry
- Fishing
- Forestry (lumber and pulpwood)
- Hunting, fishing and forestry
- Subsistence agriculture
- Little or no economic activity
- Manufacturing
- Nomadic herding
- Stock raising on ranges

See p. 107 for Cyprus

Azimuthal Equidistant Projection

400 Miles
400 Kilometers

ASIA

RUSSIA

KAZAKHSTAN

Caspian Sea

AZERBAIJAN

GEORGIA

Black Sea

TURKEY

Perm'

Yaroslavl'

Moscow

Volgograd

Kharkiv

UKRAINE

MOLDOVA

BELARUS

ROMANIA

BULGARIA

SERB. & MONT.

MACED.

ALBANIA

GREECE

Athens

FINLAND

ESTONIA

LATVIA

LITHUANIA

Kaliningrad (Russia)

POLAND

Warsaw

Lviv

SLOVAKIA

HUNGARY

CROATIA

BOSN. & HERZG.

SLOV.

SWEDEN

NORWAY

Baltic Sea

ARCTIC CIRCLE

PRIME MERIDIAN

DENMARK

Hamburg

Berlin

GERMANY

CZECH REP.

AUSTRIA

LIECH.

SWITZ.

ITALY

SAN MARINO

VATICAN CITY

MONACO

NETH.

BELGIUM

LUX.

FRANCE

Paris

North Sea

UNITED KINGDOM

London

IRELAND

ICELAND

Atlantic Ocean

ANDORRA

Barcelona

SPAIN

Madrid

PORTUGAL

MALTA

Mediterranean Sea

AFRICA

Time Line
Key Events in the Evolution of the European Union

1950 Union of Europe's coal and steel industries was proposed by Robert Schuman of France.

1951 European Coal and Steel Community (ECSC) was established, composed of Belgium, Italy, Netherlands, Luxembourg, France, and West Germany.

1957 European Economic Community (EEC) was set up to oversee economic integration of European nations.

1965 European Community (EC) was formed from EEC and other European organizations.

1973 Denmark, Republic of Ireland, and the United Kingdom became members of the EC.

1979 European Monetary System (EMS) was initiated.

1981 Greece became a member.

1986 Spain and Portugal became members.

1989 Plan for an Economic and Monetary Union (EMU) was endorsed.

1990 Former East Germany was admitted as part of a reunited Germany.

1993 Maastricht Treaty created the European Union (EU) after ratification by member countries.

1995 Austria, Finland, and Sweden became members of the EU.

1999 Euro was introduced as an accounting currency in 11 EMU member countries.

2002 Euro began circulating, replacing national currencies in all EMU member countries.

2004 Cyprus, Czech Republic, Estonia, Hungary, Latvia, Lithuania, Malta, Poland, Slovakia, and Slovenia became members of the EU, bringing the total membership to 25.

FOCUS ON

European Union

In the years following World War II, the countries of Europe looked for ways to restore political stability to the continent while rebuilding their war-ravaged economies. The first step toward the European Union was taken in 1950 when France proposed creating common institutions to govern coal and steel production in Europe jointly. In 1951 France, West Germany, Italy, Belgium, Netherlands, and Luxembourg created the European Coal and Steel Community with the goal of bringing former adversaries together. In 1965 that organization joined with others to form the European Community (EC).

The Maastricht Treaty took effect in 1993, establishing today's European Union (EU) and paving the way for a common foreign policy and a single European currency—the euro. The treaty also laid plans for the open flow of people, products, and services among member countries. In 1995 membership rose to 15 when Austria, Sweden, and Finland joined, and in May 2004 ten more countries were added: Estonia, Latvia, Lithuania, Poland, Czech Republic, Slovakia, Hungary, Cyprus, Slovenia, and Malta. Romania, Bulgaria, Croatia, and Turkey have applied for membership.

▲ **Main trade outlet** for Germany's heavily industrialized Ruhr Valley, the port of Rotterdam in the Netherlands accommodates massive supertankers and container ships.

Web Link for information on the European Union: www.europa.eu.int

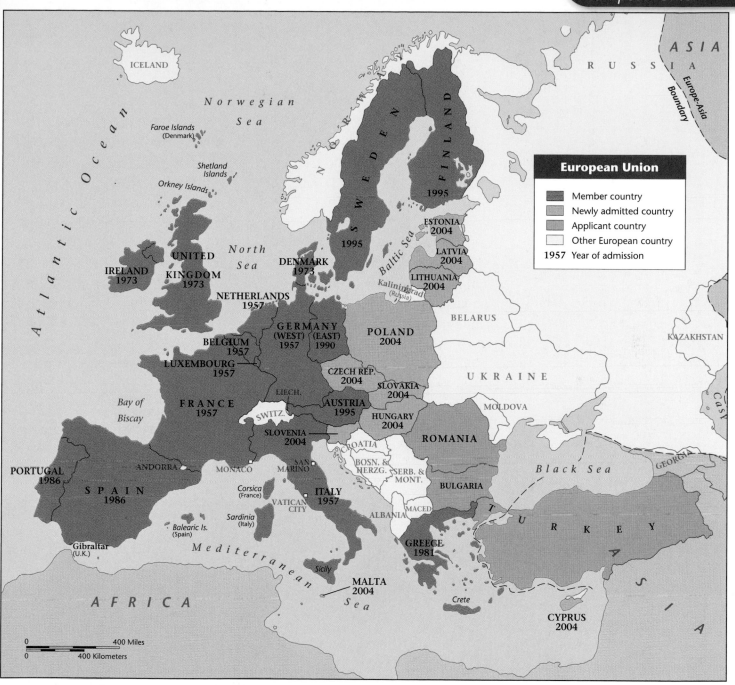

European Union

- Member country
- Newly admitted country
- Applicant country
- Other European country
- 1957 Year of admission

ICELAND

Norwegian Sea

Faroe Islands (Denmark)

Shetland Islands

Orkney Islands

SWEDEN 1995

FINLAND 1995

ESTONIA 2004

LATVIA 2004

LITHUANIA 2004

Kaliningrad (Russia)

Atlantic Ocean

IRELAND 1973

UNITED KINGDOM 1973

North Sea

DENMARK 1973

NETHERLANDS 1957

BELGIUM 1957

LUXEMBOURG 1957

GERMANY (WEST) 1957

GERMANY (EAST) 1990

POLAND 2004

BELARUS

KAZAKHSTAN

CZECH REP. 2004

SLOVAKIA 2004

UKRAINE

Bay of Biscay

FRANCE 1957

LIECH.

SWITZ.

AUSTRIA 1995

HUNGARY 2004

MOLDOVA

SLOVENIA 2004

CROATIA

ROMANIA

PORTUGAL 1986

ANDORRA

MONACO

SAN MARINO

BOSN. & HERZG.

SERB. & MONT.

Black Sea

GEORGIA

SPAIN 1986

Corsica (France)

VATICAN CITY

ITALY 1957

Sardinia (Italy)

ALBANIA

MACED.

BULGARIA

TURKEY

ASIA

RUSSIA

Europe-Asia Boundary

Balearic Is. (Spain)

Gibraltar (U.K.)

Mediterranean Sea

Sicily

MALTA 2004

GREECE 1981

Crete

CYPRUS 2004

AFRICA

Casp

0 — 400 Miles
0 — 400 Kilometers

European Union's Share of World Trade

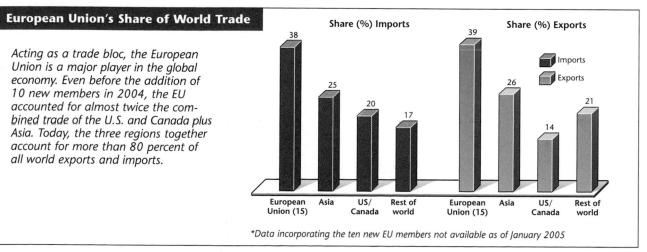

Acting as a trade bloc, the European Union is a major player in the global economy. Even before the addition of 10 new members in 2004, the EU accounted for almost twice the combined trade of the U.S. and Canada plus Asia. Today, the three regions together account for more than 80 percent of all world exports and imports.

Share (%) Imports

- European Union (15): 38
- Asia: 25
- US/Canada: 20
- Rest of world: 17

Share (%) Exports

- European Union (15): 39
- Asia: 26
- US/Canada: 14
- Rest of world: 21

- Imports
- Exports

Data incorporating the ten new EU members not available as of January 2005

Africa

From space, Africa appears divided into three regions: the northern third, dominated by the vast Sahara, largest hot desert in the world; a central green band of rain forests and tropical grasslands; and more dry lands to the south. Africa itself may be dividing literally: The Great Rift Valley, which runs from the Red Sea through the volcanic Afar Triangle to the lake district in the south (see map page 99), eventually may split apart the continent.

Facts & Figures

▶ **Land area:** 11,609,000 sq mi (30,065,000 sq km)

▶ **Population:** 884,966,000

▶ **Highest point:** Kilimanjaro, Tanzania; 19,340 ft (5,895 m)

▶ **Lowest point:** Lake Assal, Djibouti; 512 ft (156 m) below sea level

▶ **Longest river:** Nile; 4,241 mi (6,825 km)

▶ **Largest Lake:** Victoria; 26,836 sq mi (69,500 sq km)

▶ **Number of independent countries:** 53

▶ **Largest country:** Sudan; 967,500 sq mi (2,505,813 sq km)

▶ **Smallest country:** Seychelles; 176 sq mi (455 sq km)

▶ **Most populous country:** Nigeria; Pop. 137,253,000

▶ **Least populous country:** Seychelles; Pop. 80,000

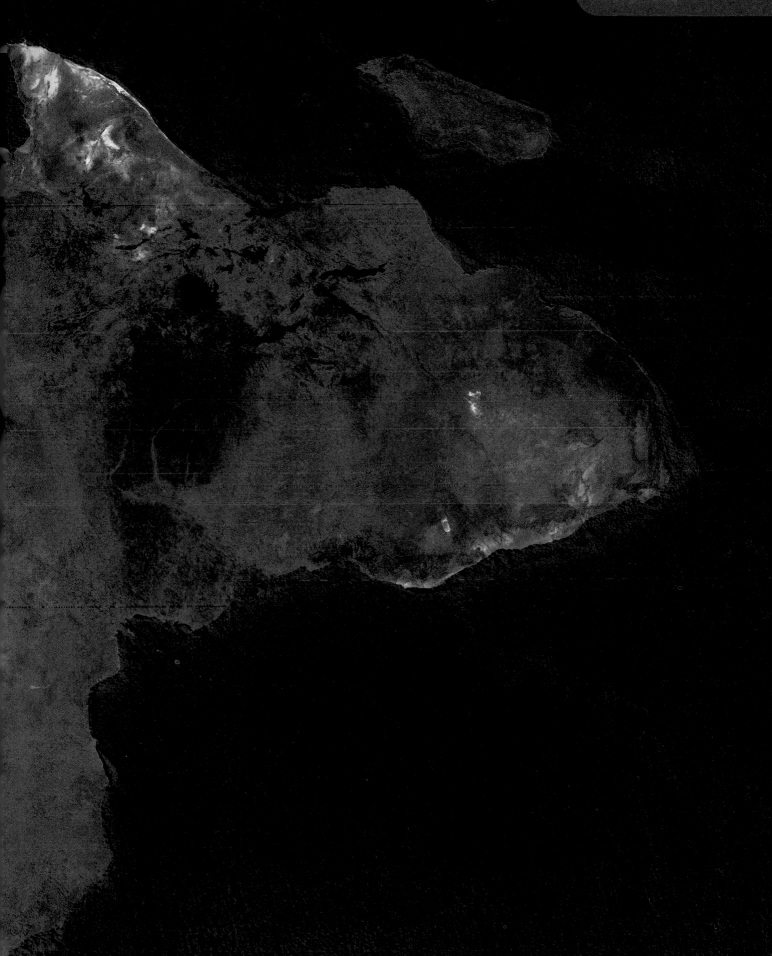

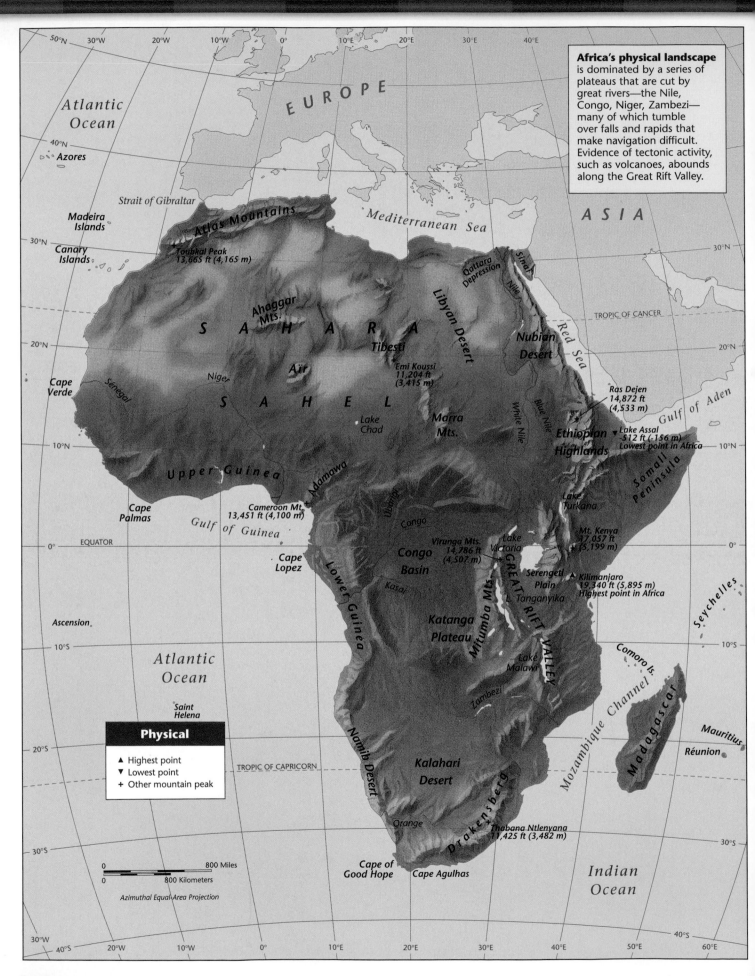

Atlantic
Ocean

EUROPE

Azores

40°N

Strait of Gibraltar

Madeira
Islands

Mediterranean Sea

ASIA

Canary
Islands

30°N

Atlas Mountains

Toubkal Peak
13,665 ft (4,165 m)

Qattara
Depression

Sinai

Nile

TROPIC OF CANCER

Africa's physical landscape
is dominated by a series of
plateaus that are cut by
great rivers—the Nile,
Congo, Niger, Zambezi—
many of which tumble
over falls and rapids that
make navigation difficult.
Evidence of tectonic activity,
such as volcanoes, abounds
along the Great Rift Valley.

S A H A R A

Ahaggar
Mts.

Libyan Desert

Nubian
Desert

Red Sea

20°N

Tibesti

Air

Emi Koussi
11,204 ft
(3,415 m)

S A H E L

Ras Dejen
14,872 ft
(4,533 m)

Gulf of Aden

Cape
Verde

Sénégal

Niger

White Nile

Blue Nile

Lake
Chad

Marra
Mts.

Ethiopian
Highlands

Lake Assal
-512 ft (-156 m)
Lowest point in Africa

10°N

Upper Guinea

Adamawa

Somali
Peninsula

Cape
Palmas

Cameroon Mt.
13,451 ft (4,100 m)

Gulf of Guinea

Ubangi

Congo

Lake
Turkana

EQUATOR

0°

Cape
Lopez

Congo
Basin

Virunga Mts.
14,786 ft
(4,507 m)

Lake
Victoria

Mt. Kenya
17,057 ft
(5,199 m)

Kasai

Ascension

Lower Guinea

Mitumba Mts.

Serengeti
Plain

L. Tanganyika

Kilimanjaro
19,340 ft (5,895 m)
Highest point in Africa

Seychelles

10°S

Atlantic
Ocean

Katanga
Plateau

GREAT RIFT VALLEY

Comoro Is.

Lake
Malawi

Saint
Helena

Mozambique Channel

Mauritius

20°S

Namib Desert

Zambezi

Madagascar

Réunion

Physical

TROPIC OF CAPRICORN

Kalahari
Desert

▲ Highest point
▼ Lowest point
+ Other mountain peak

Drakensberg

Indian
Ocean

Orange

Thabana Ntlenyana
11,425 ft (3,482 m)

30°S

0   800 Miles

0   800 Kilometers

Cape of
Good Hope

Cape Agulhas

Azimuthal Equal-Area Projection

Africa

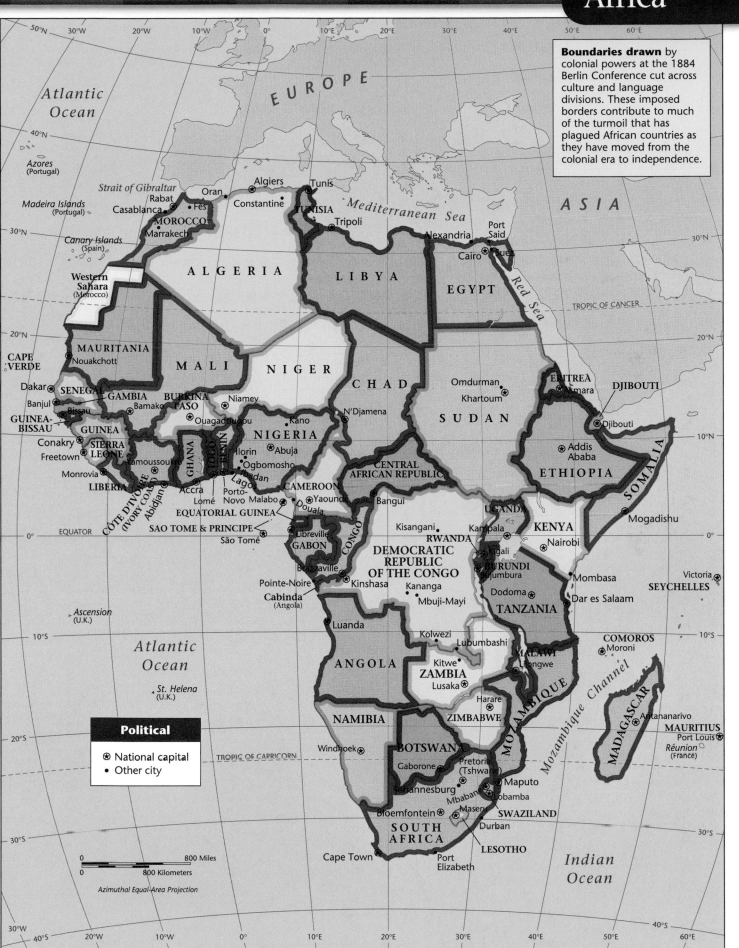

Boundaries drawn by colonial powers at the 1884 Berlin Conference cut across culture and language divisions. These imposed borders contribute to much of the turmoil that has plagued African countries as they have moved from the colonial era to independence.

EUROPE

ASIA

Atlantic Ocean

Mediterranean Sea

Red Sea

Azores (Portugal)

Madeira Islands (Portugal)

Strait of Gibraltar

Algiers
Oran
Tunis
Constantine
TUNISIA
Tripoli
Alexandria
Port Said
Cairo
Suez

Rabat
Casablanca
Fès
MOROCCO
Marrakech

Canary Islands (Spain)

Western Sahara (Morocco)

ALGERIA

LIBYA

EGYPT

TROPIC OF CANCER

MAURITANIA
Nouakchott

MALI

NIGER

CHAD

SUDAN

CAPE VERDE

Dakar
SENEGAL
GAMBIA
Banjul
Bissau
GUINEA-BISSAU
GUINEA
Conakry
Freetown
SIERRA LEONE
Monrovia
LIBERIA

BURKINA FASO
Bamako
Niamey

Ouagadougou
Kano
Yamoussoukro
CÔTE D'IVOIRE (IVORY COAST)
Abidjan
GHANA
TOGO
BENIN
Ilorin
Ogbomosho
Ibadan
Lagos
Accra
Lomé
Porto-Novo
NIGERIA
Abuja

N'Djamena

CENTRAL AFRICAN REPUBLIC

Omdurman
Khartoum

Bangui

ERITREA
Asmara
DJIBOUTI
Djibouti

Addis Ababa

ETHIOPIA

SOMALIA

Mogadishu

CAMEROON
Malabo
Douala
Yaoundé
EQUATORIAL GUINEA
SAO TOME & PRINCIPE
São Tomé
GABON
Libreville
CONGO

EQUATOR

Kisangani

UGANDA
Kampala

RWANDA
Kigali
BURUNDI
Bujumbura

KENYA
Nairobi

SEYCHELLES

Mombasa

Victoria

DEMOCRATIC REPUBLIC OF THE CONGO

Brazzaville
Pointe-Noire
Kinshasa
Kananga
Mbuji-Mayi

Cabinda (Angola)

Luanda

Kolwezi
Lubumbashi
Kitwe
ZAMBIA
Lusaka

Dodoma
TANZANIA
Dar es Salaam

COMOROS
Moroni

Atlantic Ocean

Ascension (U.K.)

St. Helena (U.K.)

ANGOLA

NAMIBIA

MALAWI
Lilongwe

Harare
ZIMBABWE

MOZAMBIQUE

Mozambique Channel

MADAGASCAR
Antananarivo

MAURITIUS
Port Louis
Réunion (France)

TROPIC OF CAPRICORN

Windhoek

BOTSWANA

Gaborone
Pretoria (Tshwane)
Johannesburg
Maputo
Mbabane
Lobamba
SWAZILAND
Maseru
LESOTHO
Durban
Bloemfontein
SOUTH AFRICA
Cape Town
Port Elizabeth

Indian Ocean

Political

⊛ National capital
• Other city

0 — 800 Miles
0 — 800 Kilometers

Azimuthal Equal-Area Projection

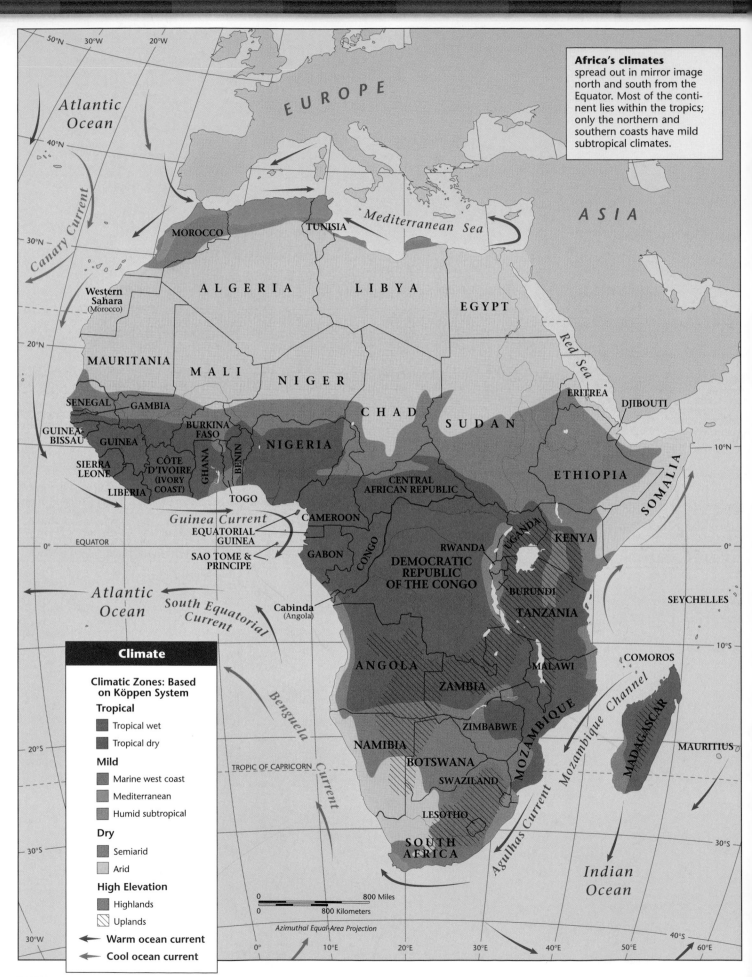

EUROPE

Atlantic Ocean

ASIA

Mediterranean Sea

Canary Current

MOROCCO

TUNISIA

ALGERIA

LIBYA

EGYPT

Western Sahara (Morocco)

Red Sea

MAURITANIA

MALI

NIGER

CHAD

SUDAN

ERITREA

DJIBOUTI

SENEGAL

GAMBIA

BURKINA FASO

NIGERIA

GUINEA-BISSAU

GUINEA

SIERRA LEONE

CÔTE D'IVOIRE (IVORY COAST)

GHANA

BENIN

TOGO

LIBERIA

CENTRAL AFRICAN REPUBLIC

ETHIOPIA

SOMALIA

10°N

Guinea Current

CAMEROON

EQUATORIAL GUINEA

SAO TOME & PRINCIPE

GABON

CONGO

DEMOCRATIC REPUBLIC OF THE CONGO

UGANDA

RWANDA

KENYA

EQUATOR

0°

BURUNDI

Atlantic Ocean

South Equatorial Current

Cabinda (Angola)

TANZANIA

SEYCHELLES

10°S

COMOROS

ANGOLA

MALAWI

ZAMBIA

Benguela Current

ZIMBABWE

MOZAMBIQUE

Mozambique Channel

MADAGASCAR

MAURITIUS

20°S

NAMIBIA

TROPIC OF CAPRICORN

BOTSWANA

SWAZILAND

Agulhas Current

Indian Ocean

LESOTHO

SOUTH AFRICA

30°S

Climate

Climatic Zones: Based on Köppen System

Tropical
- Tropical wet
- Tropical dry

Mild
- Marine west coast
- Mediterranean
- Humid subtropical

Dry
- Semiarid
- Arid

High Elevation
- Highlands
- Uplands

← Warm ocean current
← Cool ocean current

800 Miles
800 Kilometers

Azimuthal Equal-Area Projection

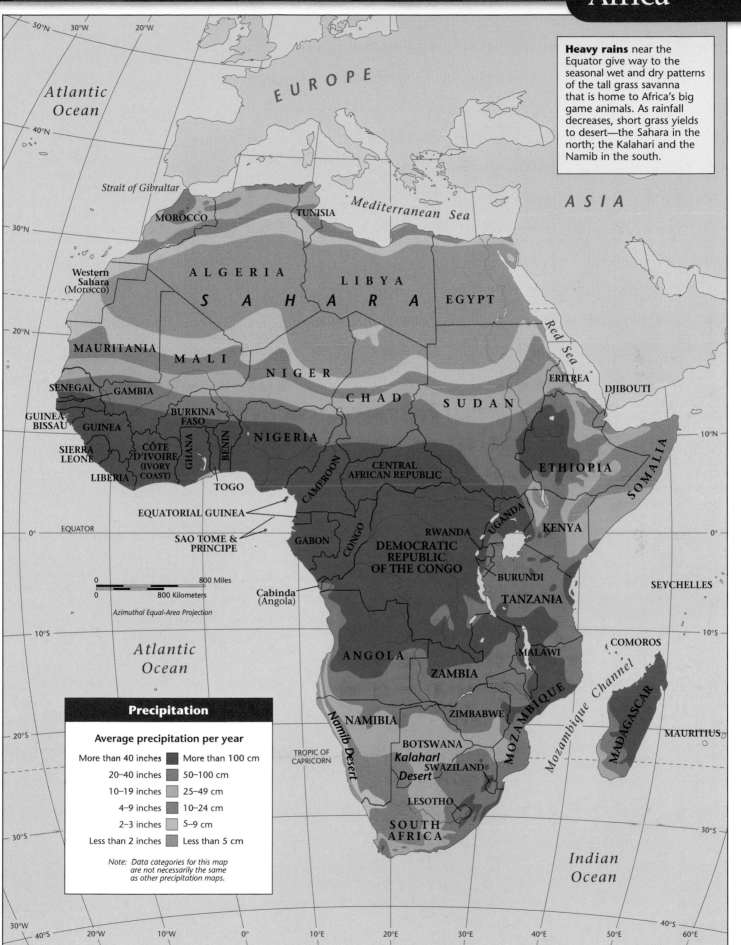

Heavy rains near the Equator give way to the seasonal wet and dry patterns of the tall grass savanna that is home to Africa's big game animals. As rainfall decreases, short grass yields to desert—the Sahara in the north; the Kalahari and the Namib in the south.

Atlantic Ocean

EUROPE

Mediterranean Sea

ASIA

Strait of Gibraltar

MOROCCO

TUNISIA

Western Sahara (Morocco)

ALGERIA

LIBYA

EGYPT

S A H A R A

Red Sea

MAURITANIA

MALI

NIGER

ERITREA

DJIBOUTI

SENEGAL

GAMBIA

CHAD

SUDAN

GUINEA-BISSAU

BURKINA FASO

GUINEA

NIGERIA

SIERRA LEONE

CÔTE D'IVOIRE (IVORY COAST)

GHANA

BENIN

LIBERIA

TOGO

CAMEROON

CENTRAL AFRICAN REPUBLIC

ETHIOPIA

SOMALIA

EQUATORIAL GUINEA

SAO TOME & PRINCIPE

GABON

CONGO

DEMOCRATIC REPUBLIC OF THE CONGO

UGANDA

RWANDA

KENYA

EQUATOR

BURUNDI

SEYCHELLES

0   800 Miles
0   800 Kilometers

Azimuthal Equal-Area Projection

TANZANIA

Cabinda (Angola)

COMOROS

Atlantic Ocean

ANGOLA

ZAMBIA

MALAWI

MOZAMBIQUE

MADAGASCAR

MAURITIUS

Mozambique Channel

Namib Desert

NAMIBIA

ZIMBABWE

Precipitation

Average precipitation per year

More than 40 inches	More than 100 cm
20–40 inches	50–100 cm
10–19 inches	25–49 cm
4–9 inches	10–24 cm
2–3 inches	5–9 cm
Less than 2 inches	Less than 5 cm

TROPIC OF CAPRICORN

BOTSWANA

Kalahari Desert

SWAZILAND

LESOTHO

SOUTH AFRICA

Note: Data categories for this map are not necessarily the same as other precipitation maps.

Indian Ocean

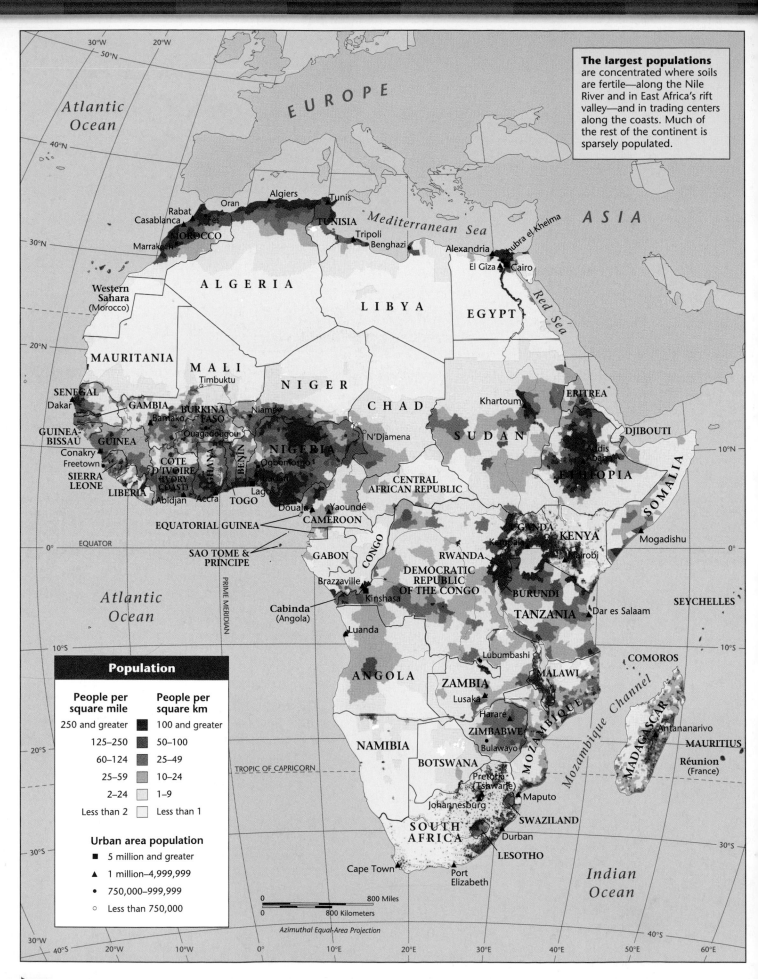

The largest populations are concentrated where soils are fertile—along the Nile River and in East Africa's rift valley—and in trading centers along the coasts. Much of the rest of the continent is sparsely populated.

EUROPE

ASIA

Atlantic Ocean

Mediterranean Sea

Algiers
Tunis
Oran
TUNISIA
Rabat
Casablanca
Fès
MOROCCO
Tripoli
Benghazi
Alexandria
Shubra el Kheima
Marrakech

El Giza
Cairo
Red Sea

Western Sahara (Morocco)

ALGERIA
LIBYA
EGYPT

MAURITANIA
MALI
NIGER
CHAD
Timbuktu
Khartoum
ERITREA
SUDAN
DJIBOUTI

SENEGAL
Dakar
GAMBIA
BURKINA FASO
Niamey
GUINEA-BISSAU
Bamako
Ouagadougou
N'Djamena
Addis Ababa
GUINEA
Conakry
Freetown
SIERRA LEONE
CÔTE D'IVOIRE (IVORY COAST)
GHANA
BENIN
TOGO
NIGERIA
Ogbomosho
Ibadan
Lagos
CENTRAL AFRICAN REPUBLIC
ETHIOPIA
SOMALIA
LIBERIA
Abidjan
Accra

Douala
Yaoundé
CAMEROON
EQUATORIAL GUINEA
SAO TOME & PRINCIPE

GABON
CONGO
Brazzaville
Kinshasa
Cabinda (Angola)
Luanda

UGANDA
Kampala
KENYA
Nairobi
Mogadishu
RWANDA
DEMOCRATIC REPUBLIC OF THE CONGO
BURUNDI
TANZANIA
Dar es Salaam
SEYCHELLES

EQUATOR

PRIME MERIDIAN

Atlantic Ocean

Lubumbashi

COMOROS

ANGOLA
ZAMBIA
Lusaka
MALAWI
Harare
ZIMBABWE
Bulawayo
NAMIBIA
BOTSWANA
MOZAMBIQUE
Mozambique Channel
MADAGASCAR
Antananarivo
MAURITIUS
Réunion (France)

TROPIC OF CAPRICORN

Pretoria (Tshwane)
Maputo
Johannesburg
SWAZILAND
Durban
SOUTH AFRICA
LESOTHO
Cape Town
Port Elizabeth

Indian Ocean

Population

People per square mile	**People per square km**
250 and greater	100 and greater
125–250	50–100
60–124	25–49
25–59	10–24
2–24	1–9
Less than 2	Less than 1

Urban area population
- ■ 5 million and greater
- ▲ 1 million–4,999,999
- • 750,000–999,999
- ○ Less than 750,000

0 — 800 Miles
0 — 800 Kilometers

Azimuthal Equal-Area Projection

Africa

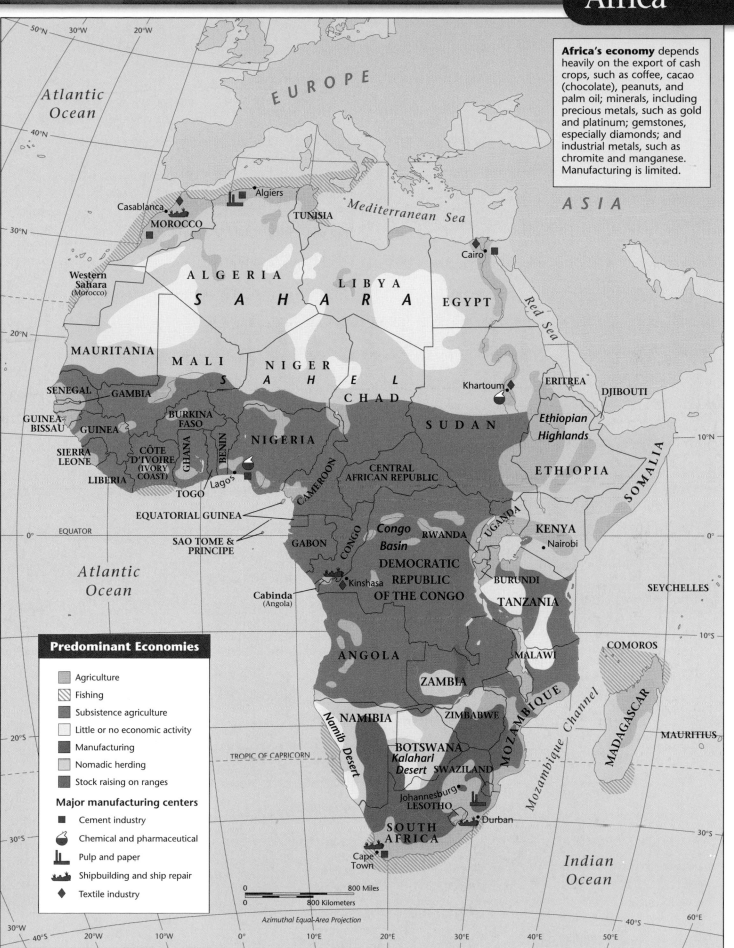

Atlantic Ocean

EUROPE

Mediterranean Sea

ASIA

Casablanca
Algiers
MOROCCO
TUNISIA

Cairo

Western Sahara (Morocco)

ALGERIA
SAHARA
LIBYA
EGYPT

Red Sea

MAURITANIA
MALI
NIGER
SAHEL
CHAD
SUDAN
ERITREA
DJIBOUTI

SENEGAL
GAMBIA
GUINEA-BISSAU
GUINEA
SIERRA LEONE
LIBERIA
BURKINA FASO
CÔTE D'IVOIRE (IVORY COAST)
GHANA
BENIN
TOGO
NIGERIA
Lagos
CAMEROON
CENTRAL AFRICAN REPUBLIC

Khartoum

Ethiopian Highlands
ETHIOPIA
SOMALIA

EQUATORIAL GUINEA
SAO TOME & PRINCIPE
GABON
CONGO
Congo Basin
DEMOCRATIC REPUBLIC OF THE CONGO
RWANDA
UGANDA
KENYA
Nairobi

EQUATOR

Atlantic Ocean

Cabinda (Angola)
Kinshasa
BURUNDI
TANZANIA
SEYCHELLES

ANGOLA
ZAMBIA
MALAWI
COMOROS

Namib Desert
NAMIBIA
ZIMBABWE
MOZAMBIQUE
Mozambique Channel
MADAGASCAR
MAURITIUS

TROPIC OF CAPRICORN
BOTSWANA
Kalahari Desert
SWAZILAND

Johannesburg
LESOTHO
SOUTH AFRICA
Durban
Cape Town

Indian Ocean

Predominant Economies

- Agriculture
- Fishing
- Subsistence agriculture
- Little or no economic activity
- Manufacturing
- Nomadic herding
- Stock raising on ranges

Major manufacturing centers

- Cement industry
- Chemical and pharmaceutical
- Pulp and paper
- Shipbuilding and ship repair
- Textile industry

0   800 Miles
0   800 Kilometers

Azimuthal Equal-Area Projection

Tectonics at Work
The Rift Valley's Geologic History

30 million years before present

The Arabian Peninsula and Africa were joined as one landmass 30 million years ago.

7 million years before present

ASIA

AFRICA

Fiery-hot magma rising from within Earth caused rifting that began to push apart the land along what is now the Red Sea.

30 million years in the future

ASIA

AFRICA

Long, narrow lakes could become a single channel if rifting continues and causes the Somali Plate to break away.

Great Rift Valley

More than a hundred million years ago, Gondwana, the southern part of the supercontinent Pangaea, began to break apart. Landmasses that we know today as South America, Antarctica, Australia, and the Indian subcontinent slowly moved away, propelled by tectonic forces originating deep within Earth (see map page 14). The part of Gondwana that was left behind is what we know as Africa.

The forces that tore apart Gondwana continue today, especially in East Africa where the Great Rift Valley marks the boundary of what many earth scientists believe eventually will be a new sea that will separate part of eastern and southern Africa from the rest of the continent.

▶ **Volcanic cones** in the tiny country of Djibouti mark the area where active tectonic rifting may someday result in the formation of a new ocean.

▼ **Colorful flamingos** are attracted to rift valley lakes, where high evaporation rates help create alkaline waters. The birds feed on brine shrimp and various kinds of algae.

▶ **Subsistence farmers,** many of them women, grow staple crops of maize (corn) and beans in the fertile volcanic soils. Large commercial farms produce cash crops, such as coffee and sisal.

Web Link for information on Great Rift Valley: http://4dw.net/geolor/EastAfrican_Rift_Valley_geolor.htm

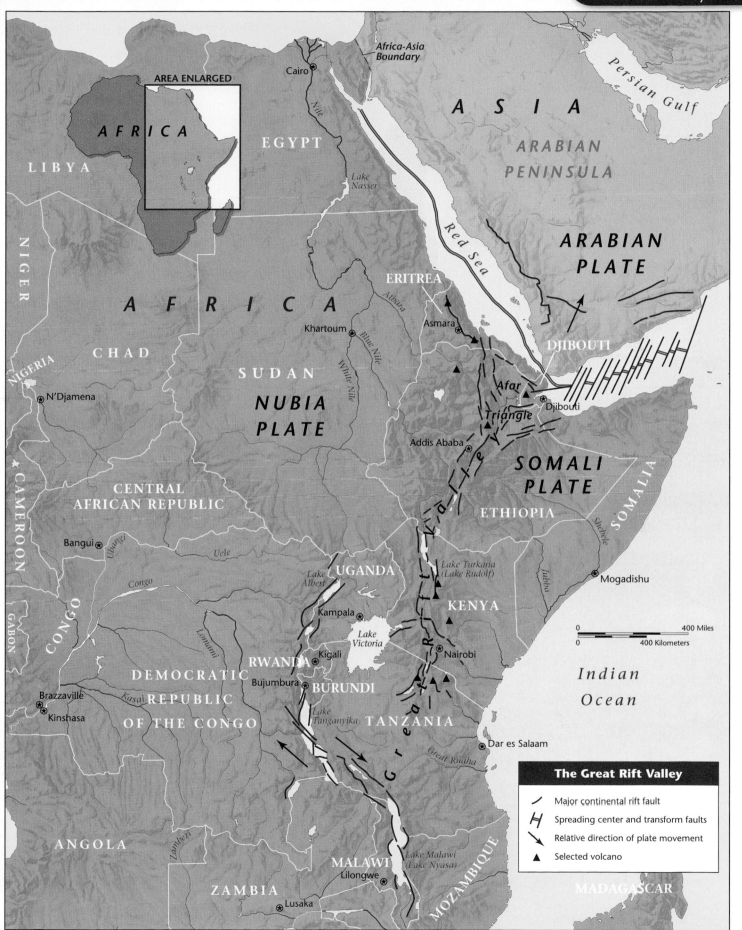

AREA ENLARGED

AFRICA

LIBYA

NIGER

CHAD

N'Djamena ⊛

NIGERIA

CAMEROON

CONGO

GABON

Brazzaville ⊛
Kinshasa ⊛

ANGOLA

ZAMBIA

Lusaka ⊛

EGYPT

Cairo ⊛

Lake Nasser

A F R I C A

Khartoum ⊛

S U D A N

NUBIA PLATE

CENTRAL AFRICAN REPUBLIC

Bangui ⊛

Uele

Ubangi

Congo

Lomami

Kasai

Zambezi

DEMOCRATIC REPUBLIC OF THE CONGO

UGANDA

Lake Albert

Kampala ⊛

RWANDA

Kigali ⊛

Bujumbura ⊛

BURUNDI

Lake Tanganyika

Lake Victoria

MALAWI

Lilongwe ⊛

Lake Malawi (Lake Nyasa)

Africa-Asia Boundary

ERITREA

Asmara ⊛

Athana

Blue Nile

White Nile

A S I A

ARABIAN PENINSULA

ARABIAN PLATE

Red Sea

Nile

Persian Gulf

DJIBOUTI

Afar Triangle

Djibouti ⊛

Addis Ababa ⊛

SOMALI PLATE

ETHIOPIA

SOMALIA

Shebele

Jubba

Mogadishu ⊛

Lake Turkana (Lake Rudolf)

KENYA

Nairobi ⊛

G r e a t   R i f t   V a l l e y

TANZANIA

Great Ruaha

Dar es Salaam ⊛

Indian Ocean

MOZAMBIQUE

MADAGASCAR

| | 0 | | 400 Miles |
| 0 | | 400 Kilometers |

The Great Rift Valley

⟋   Major continental rift fault

H   Spreading center and transform faults

↘   Relative direction of plate movement

▲   Selected volcano

Asia

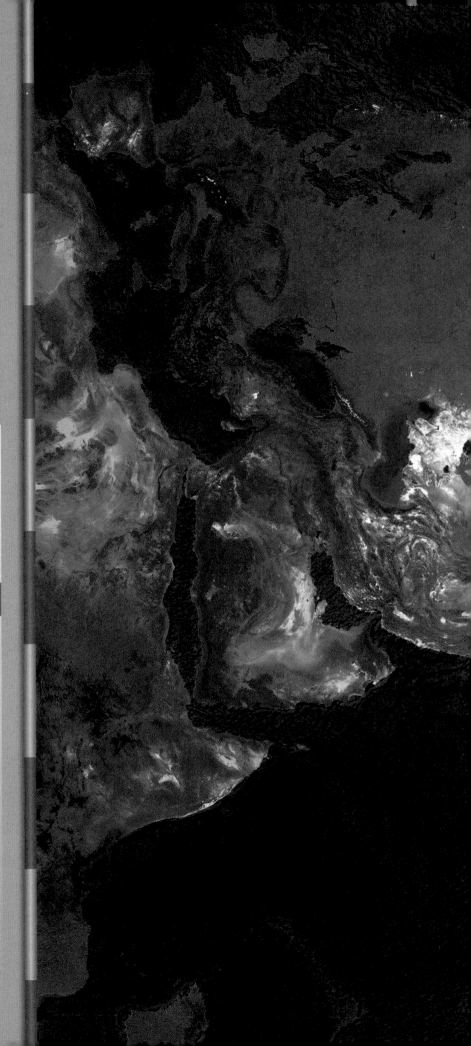

From the frozen shores of the Arctic Ocean to the equatorial islands of Indonesia, Asia stretches across 90 degrees of latitude. From the Ural Mountains to the Pacific Ocean it covers more than 150 degrees of longitude. Here, three of history's great culture hearths emerged in the valleys of the Tigris and Euphrates, the Indus, and the Yellow (Huang) Rivers. Today, Asia is home to more than 60 percent of Earth's people and some of the world's fastest growing economies.

Facts & Figures

▶ **Land area:** 17,213,300 sq mi (44,579,000 sq km)

▶ **Population:** 3,874,984,000

▶ **Highest point:** Mount Everest, China-Nepal: 29,035 ft (8,850 m)

▶ **Lowest point:** Dead Sea, Israel-Jordan: 1,365 ft (416 m) below sea level

▶ **Longest river:** Yangtze (Chang), China: 3,964 mi (6,380 km)

▶ **Largest lake entirely in Asia:** Baikal, Russia: 12,163 sq mi (31,500 sq km)

▶ **Number of independent countries:** 46 (excluding Russia)

▶ **Largest country entirely in Asia:** China: 3,705,405 sq mi (9,596,960 sq km)

▶ **Smallest country:** Maldives: 115 sq mi (298 sq km)

▶ **Most populous country:** China: Pop. 1,300,060,000

▶ **Least populous country:** Maldives: Pop. 298,000

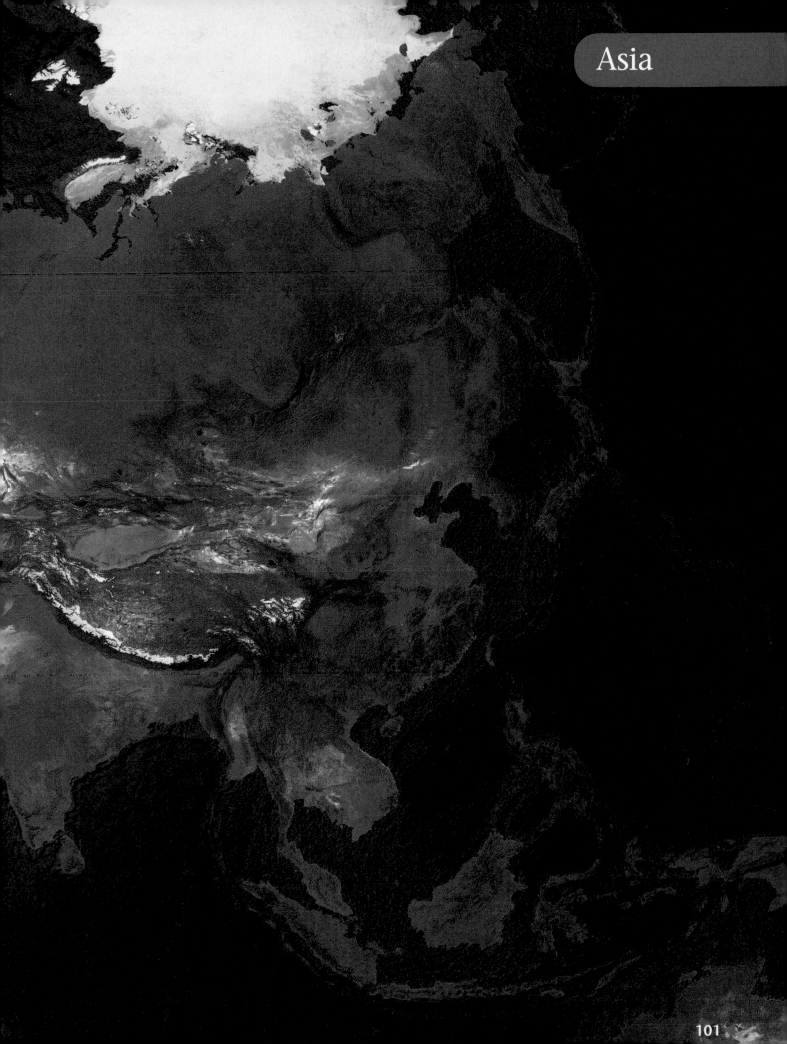

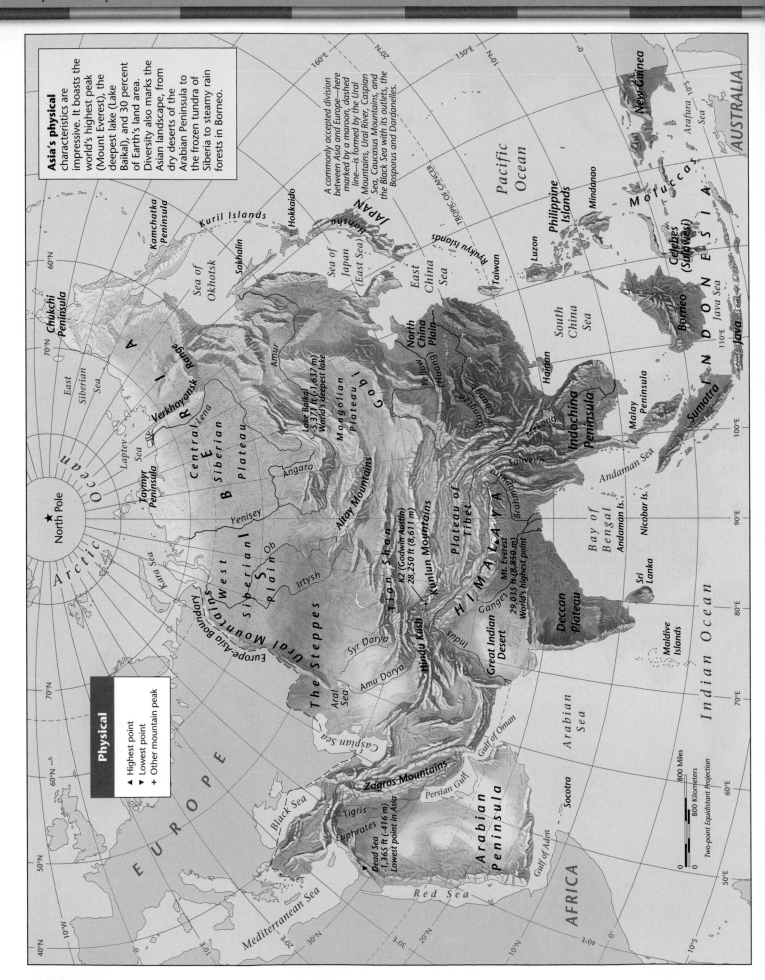

Asia's physical characteristics are impressive. It boasts the world's highest peak (Mount Everest), the deepest lake (Lake Baikal), and 30 percent of Earth's land area. Diversity also marks the Asian landscape, from dry deserts of the Arabian Peninsula to the frozen tundra of Siberia to steamy rain forests in Borneo.

A commonly accepted division between Asia and Europe—here marked by a maroon, dashed line—is formed by the Ural Mountains, Ural River, Caspian Sea, Caucasus Mountains, and the Black Sea with its outlets, the Bosporus and Dardanelles.

Physical

▲ Highest point
▼ Lowest point
+ Other mountain peak

North Pole

Arctic Ocean

Chukchi Peninsula

East Siberian Sea

Laptev Sea

Kara Sea

Taymyr Peninsula

Kamchatka Peninsula

Kuril Islands

Sea of Okhotsk

Sakhalin

Hokkaido

Verkhoyansk Range

Lena

Central Siberian Plateau

Amur

Sea of Japan (East Sea)

JAPAN

Honshu

Kyushu

Ryukyu Islands

East China Sea

North China Plain

Angara

Yenisey

West Siberian Plain

Ob

Irtysh

Lake Baikal -5,371 ft (1,637 m) World's deepest lake

Mongolian Plateau

Gobi

Yellow (Huang)

Yangtze (Chang)

Taiwan

Luzon

Philippine Islands

Mindanao

Pacific Ocean

TROPIC OF CANCER

Haikan

South China Sea

Altay Mountains

Tian Shan

K2 (Godwin Austen) 28,250 ft (8,611 m)

Kunlun Mountains

Plateau of Tibet

Mekong

Salween

Indochina Peninsula

Malay Peninsula

Borneo

Celebes (Sulawesi)

Moluccas

I N D O N E S I A

Sumatra

Java Sea

Java

New Guinea

Arafura Sea

AUSTRALIA

Ural Mountains

The Steppes

Syr Darya

Amu Darya

Aral Sea

Hindu Kush

Indus

H I M A L A Y A

Brahmaputra

Ganges

Mt. Everest 29,035 ft (8,850 m) World's highest point

Great Indian Desert

Deccan Plateau

Bay of Bengal

Andaman Is.

Nicobar Is.

Sri Lanka

Maldive Islands

Andaman Sea

Indian Ocean

Europe-Asia boundary

EUROPE

Caspian Sea

Black Sea

Zagros Mountains

Tigris

Euphrates

Dead Sea -1,365 ft (-416 m) Lowest point in Asia

Persian Gulf

Gulf of Oman

Arabian Peninsula

Arabian Sea

Socotra

Gulf of Aden

Red Sea

Mediterranean Sea

AFRICA

800 Miles
800 Kilometers
Two-point Equidistant Projection

Asia

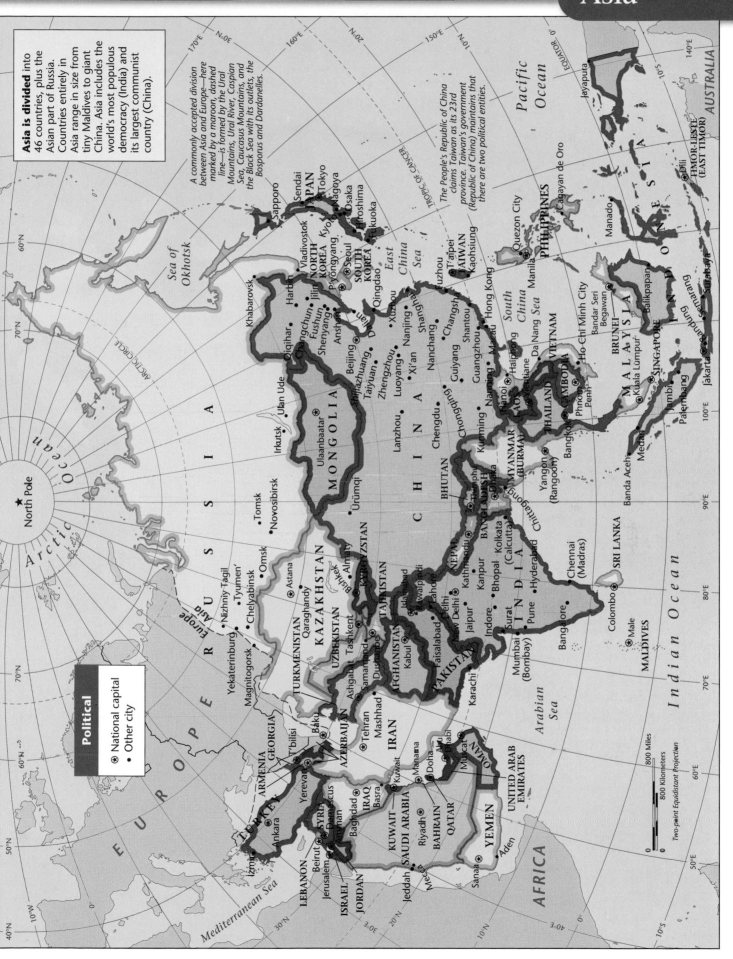

Asia is divided into 46 countries, plus the Asian part of Russia. Countries entirely in Asia range in size from tiny Maldives to giant China. Asia includes the world's most populous democracy (India) and its largest communist country (China).

A commonly accepted division between Asia and Europe—here marked by a maroon, dashed line—is formed by the Ural Mountains, Ural River, Caspian Sea, Caucasus Mountains, and the Black Sea with its outlets, the Bosporus and Dardanelles.

The People's Republic of China claims Taiwan as its 23rd province. Taiwan's government (Republic of China) maintains that there are two political entities.

Political

⊛ National capital
• Other city

North Pole

Arctic Ocean

EUROPE

Europe
Asia

R U S S I A

Sea of Okhotsk

Nizhniy Tagil
Yekaterinburg
Tyumen'
Magnitogorsk
Chelyabinsk
Omsk
Tomsk
Novosibirsk
Irkutsk
Ulan Ude
Khabarovsk
Vladivostok

Astana
Qaraghandy
KAZAKHSTAN
Qaraghandy

TURKMENISTAN
Ashgabat
UZBEKISTAN
Tashkent
Samarqand
Dushanbe
TAJIKISTAN
Bishkek
KYRGYZSTAN
Almaty
Ürümqi

MONGOLIA
Ulaanbaatar

Qiqihar
Changchun
Harbin
Jilin
Fushun
Shenyang
Anshan
NORTH KOREA
Pyongyang
Dalian
Beijing
Ujon
Sendai
Sapporo
JAPAN
Tokyo
Nagoya
Kyoto
Osaka
Hiroshima
Fukuoka
SOUTH KOREA
Seoul
Qingdao

Shijiazhuang
Taiyuan
Zhengzhou
Luoyang
Xi'an
Nanjing
Xuzhou
Shanghai
Nanchang
East China Sea
Fuzhou
T'aipei
TAIWAN
Kaohsiung

C H I N A

Lanzhou
Chengdu
Chongqing
Guiyang
Changsha
Kunming
Guangzhou
Guilin
Nanning
Hong Kong
Macau
Shantou
South China Sea

TROPIC OF CANCER

Pacific Ocean

EQUATOR 0°

Jayapura

PHILIPPINES
Quezon City
Manila
Cagayan de Oro

BRUNEI
Bandar Seri Begawan

M A L A Y S I A
Kuala Lumpur
SINGAPORE

I N D O N E S I A
Manado
Balikpapan
Jambi
Jakarta
Bandung
Semarang
Surabaya
Banda Aceh
Medan
Palembang
Gunungsitoli

TIMOR-LESTE
(EAST TIMOR)
Dili

AUSTRALIA

AFGHANISTAN
Kabul

PAKISTAN
Faisalabad
Rawalpindi
Lahore
Islamabad
Karachi

NEPAL
Kathmandu
BHUTAN
Thimphu

Delhi
New Delhi
Jaipur
Kanpur
Indore
Bhopal
Surat
I N D I A
Pune
Hyderabad
Mumbai
(Bombay)
Bangalore
Chennai
(Madras)

BANGLADESH
Dhaka
Chittagong
Kolkata
(Calcutta)

MYANMAR
(BURMA)
Yangon
(Rangoon)

LAOS
Vientiane
THAILAND
Bangkok
CAMBODIA
Phnom Penh
VIETNAM
Hanoi
Haiphong
Da Nang
Ho Chi Minh City

SRI LANKA
Colombo

Male
MALDIVES

Indian Ocean

Arabian Sea

TURKEY
Ankara
Izmir
GEORGIA
Tbilisi
ARMENIA
Yerevan
AZERBAIJAN
Baku

LEBANON
Beirut
SYRIA
Damascus
Jerusalem
ISRAEL
Amman
JORDAN

IRAQ
Baghdad
Basra

IRAN
Tehran
Mashhad

KUWAIT
Kuwait
SAUDI ARABIA
Riyadh
Mecca
Jeddah
BAHRAIN
Manama
QATAR
Doha
Abu Dhabi
UNITED ARAB EMIRATES
OMAN
Muscat

YEMEN
Sanaa
Aden

AFRICA

Mediterranean Sea

ARCTIC CIRCLE

800 Miles
800 Kilometers
Two-point Equidistant Projection

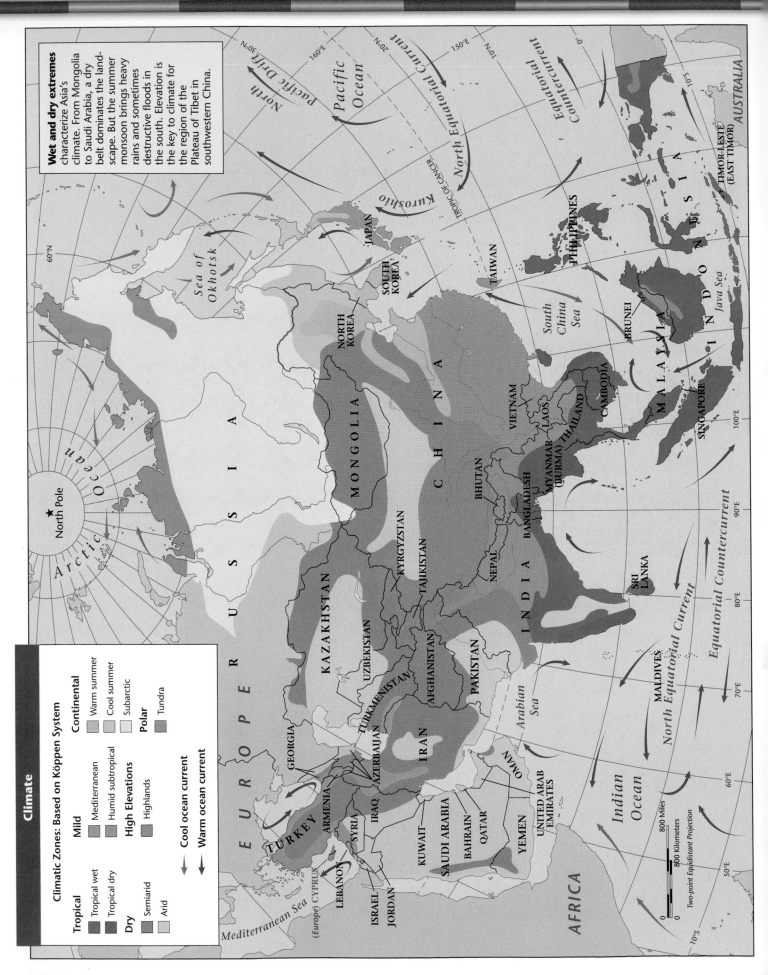

Climate

Climatic Zones: Based on Köppen System

Tropical
- Tropical wet
- Tropical dry

Dry
- Semiarid
- Arid

Mild
- Mediterranean
- Humid subtropical

High Elevations
- Highlands

Continental
- Warm summer
- Cool summer
- Subarctic

Polar
- Tundra

→ Cool ocean current
→ Warm ocean current

Wet and dry extremes characterize Asia's climate. From Mongolia to Saudi Arabia, a dry belt dominates the landscape. But the summer monsoon brings heavy rains and sometimes destructive floods in the south. Elevation is the key to climate for the region of the Plateau of Tibet in southwestern China.

Asia

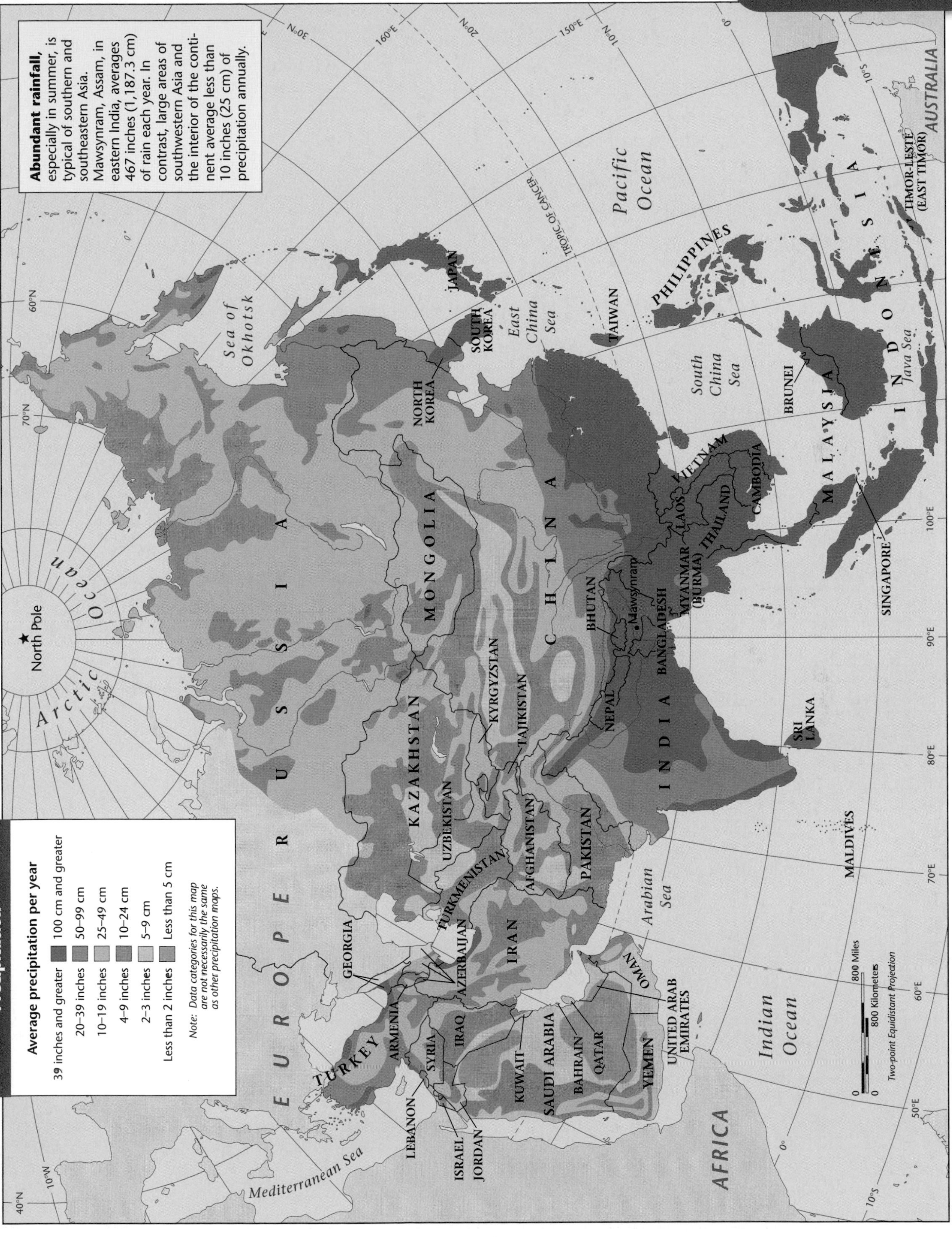

Precipitation
Average precipitation per year
39 inches and greater 100 cm and greater
20–39 inches 50–99 cm
10–19 inches 25–49 cm
4–9 inches 10–24 cm
2–3 inches 5–9 cm
Less than 2 inches Less than 5 cm
Note: Data categories for this map are not necessarily the same as other precipitation maps.
Abundant rainfall, especially in summer, is typical of southern and southeastern Asia. Mawsynram, Assam, in eastern India, averages 467 inches (1,187.3 cm) of rain each year. In contrast, large areas of southwestern Asia and the interior of the continent average less than 10 inches (25 cm) of precipitation annually.
North Pole
Arctic Ocean
Sea of Okhotsk
Pacific Ocean
East China Sea
South China Sea
Java Sea
Arabian Sea
Indian Ocean
Mediterranean Sea
TROPIC OF CANCER
EUROPE
AFRICA
AUSTRALIA
RUSSIA
MONGOLIA
CHINA
KAZAKHSTAN
UZBEKISTAN
TURKMENISTAN
KYRGYZSTAN
TAJIKISTAN
AFGHANISTAN
PAKISTAN
INDIA
NEPAL
BHUTAN
BANGLADESH
Mawsynram
MYANMAR (BURMA)
LAOS
THAILAND
VIETNAM
CAMBODIA
MALAYSIA
SINGAPORE
BRUNEI
INDONESIA
PHILIPPINES
TAIWAN
JAPAN
NORTH KOREA
SOUTH KOREA
TIMOR-LESTE (EAST TIMOR)
SRI LANKA
MALDIVES
TURKEY
GEORGIA
ARMENIA
AZERBAIJAN
IRAN
IRAQ
SYRIA
LEBANON
ISRAEL
JORDAN
KUWAIT
SAUDI ARABIA
BAHRAIN
QATAR
UNITED ARAB EMIRATES
OMAN
YEMEN
800 Miles
800 Kilometers
Two-point Equidistant Projection
40°N
30°N
20°N
10°N
0°
10°S
60°N
70°N
10°W
50°E
60°E
70°E
80°E
90°E
100°E
150°E
160°E

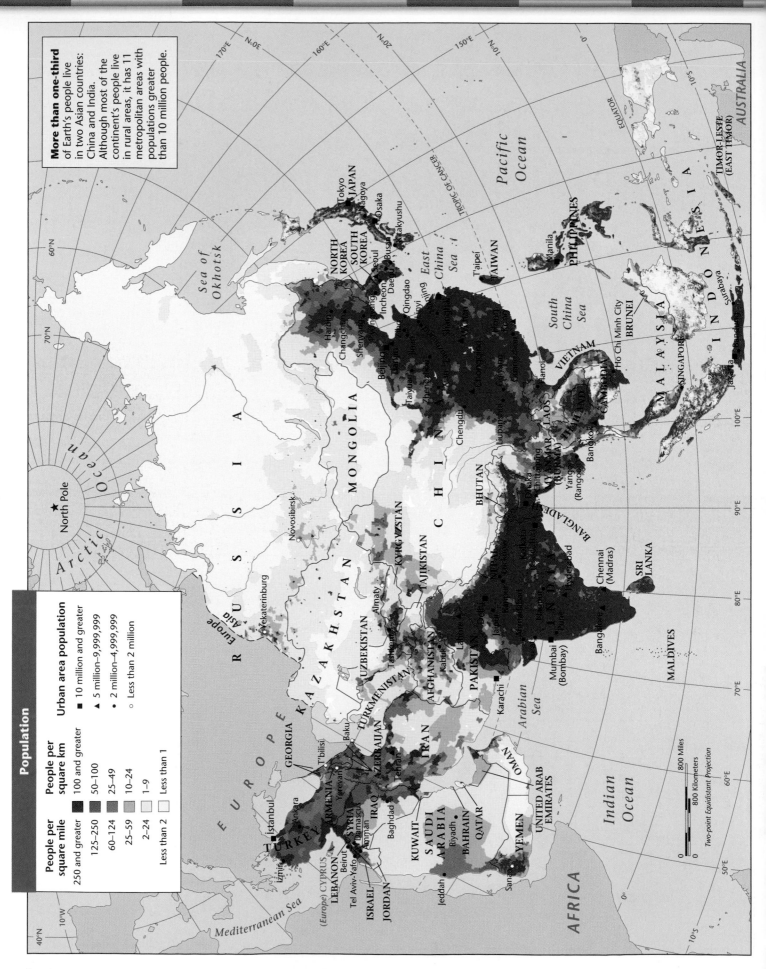

Population

More than one-third of Earth's people live in two Asian countries: China and India. Although most of the continent's people live in rural areas, it has 11 metropolitan areas with populations greater than 10 million people.

People per square mile	People per square km
250 and greater	100 and greater
125–250	50–100
60–124	25–49
25–59	10–24
2–24	1–9
Less than 2	Less than 1

Urban area population
- ■ 10 million and greater
- ▲ 5 million–9,999,999
- ● 2 million–4,999,999
- ○ Less than 2 million

North Pole

Arctic Ocean

Sea of Okhotsk

R U S S I A

Ekaterinburg
Novosibirsk

Europe
Asia

Pacific Ocean

Tokyo
JAPAN
Nagoya
Osaka
Kitakyushu

NORTH KOREA
SOUTH KOREA
Seoul
Incheon
Busan
Daegu

Harbin
Changchun
Shenyang
Beijing
Tianjin
Taiyuan
Zhengzhou
Qingdao
Jinan

TAIWAN
Taipei

East China Sea

C H I N A

M O N G O L I A

K A Z A K H S T A N

Almaty
Tashkent
UZBEKISTAN
TURKMENISTAN
KYRGYZSTAN
TAJIKISTAN

Xi'an
Chengdu
Chongqing
Wuhan
Shanghai

TROPIC OF CANCER

South China Sea

VIETNAM
Hanoi
Ho Chi Minh City

LAOS
MYANMAR (BURMA)
Yangon (Rangoon)
THAILAND
Bangkok
CAMBODIA

BHUTAN
NEPAL
Kathmandu

BANGLADESH
Dhaka
Chittagong
Kolkata (Calcutta)

I N D I A
New Delhi
Jaipur
Kanpur
Ahmadabad
Surat
Pune
Hyderabad
Bangalore
Chennai (Madras)

SRI LANKA

AFGHANISTAN
Kabul
PAKISTAN
Lahore
Karachi
Mumbai (Bombay)

Arabian Sea

IRAN
Tehran
AZERBAIJAN
Baku
ARMENIA
Yerevan
GEORGIA
T'bilisi

IRAQ
Baghdad
SYRIA
Damascus
Amman
JORDAN
LEBANON
Beirut
Tel Aviv-Yafo
ISRAEL
(Europe) CYPRUS

TURKEY
Istanbul
Ankara
İzmir

Mediterranean Sea

KUWAIT
SAUDI ARABIA
Riyadh
BAHRAIN
QATAR
UNITED ARAB EMIRATES
OMAN
YEMEN
Sanaa
Jeddah

Indian Ocean

AFRICA

MALAYSIA
SINGAPORE
BRUNEI
Jakarta
Surabaya
I N D O N E S I A
PHILIPPINES
Manila

TIMOR-LESTE (EAST TIMOR)

AUSTRALIA

MALDIVES

EQUATOR

800 Miles
800 Kilometers
Two-point Equidistant Projection

Asia

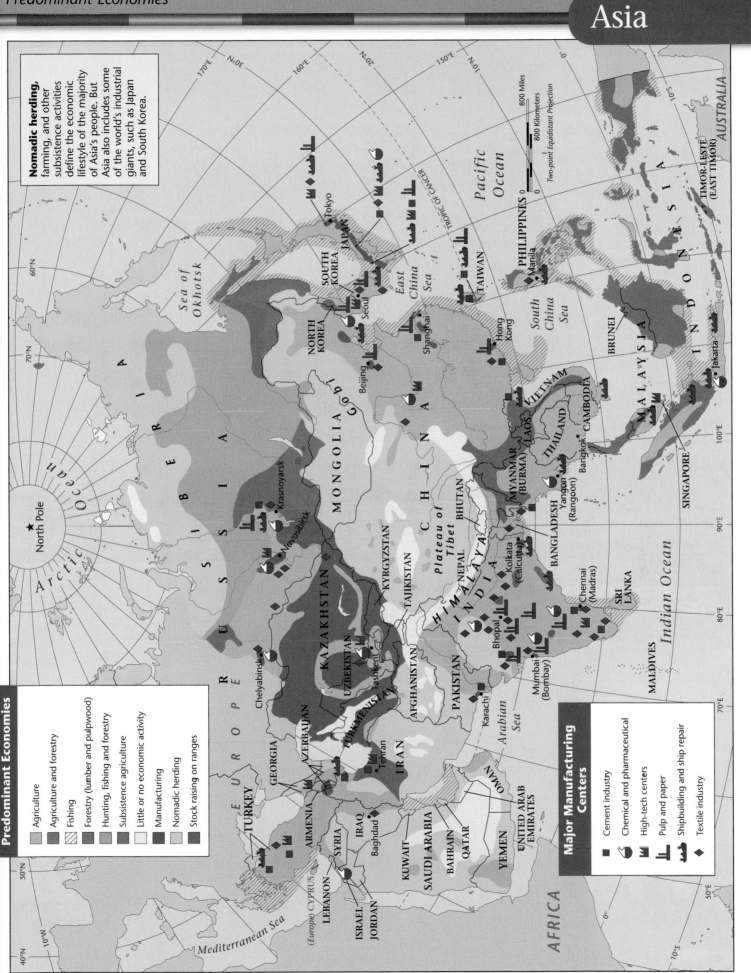

Nomadic herding, farming, and other subsistence activities define the economic lifestyle of the majority of Asia's people. But Asia also includes some of the world's industrial giants, such as Japan and South Korea.

Predominant Economies

- Agriculture
- Agriculture and forestry
- Fishing
- Forestry (lumber and pulpwood)
- Hunting, fishing and forestry
- Subsistence agriculture
- Little or no economic activity
- Manufacturing
- Nomadic herding
- Stock raising on ranges

Major Manufacturing Centers

- Cement industry
- Chemical and pharmaceutical
- High-tech centers
- Pulp and paper
- Shipbuilding and ship repair
- Textile industry

North Pole

Arctic Ocean

S I B E R I A

R U S S I A

E U R O P E

Sea of Okhotsk

MONGOLIA

Gobi

KAZAKHSTAN

UZBEKISTAN

TURKMENISTAN

KYRGYZSTAN

TAJIKISTAN

AFGHANISTAN

PAKISTAN

C H I N A

Plateau of Tibet

H I M A L A Y A

NEPAL

BHUTAN

I N D I A

BANGLADESH

MYANMAR (BURMA)

LAOS

THAILAND

VIETNAM

CAMBODIA

SRI LANKA

MALDIVES

Indian Ocean

Arabian Sea

IRAN

IRAQ

KUWAIT

SAUDI ARABIA

BAHRAIN

QATAR

UNITED ARAB EMIRATES

OMAN

YEMEN

TURKEY

GEORGIA

ARMENIA

AZERBAIJAN

SYRIA

LEBANON

ISRAEL

JORDAN

(Europe) CYPRUS

Mediterranean Sea

AFRICA

NORTH KOREA

SOUTH KOREA

JAPAN

Tokyo

Seoul

Beijing

Shanghai

Hong Kong

East China Sea

South China Sea

Pacific Ocean

TAIWAN

PHILIPPINES

Manila

BRUNEI

M A L A Y S I A

SINGAPORE

I N D O N E S I A

Jakarta

TIMOR-LESTE (EAST TIMOR)

AUSTRALIA

Krasnoyarsk

Novosibirsk

Chelyabinsk

Tashkent

Tehran

Baghdad

Karachi

Mumbai (Bombay)

Bhopal

Chennai (Madras)

Kolkata (Calcutta)

Yangon (Rangoon)

Bangkok

800 Miles

800 Kilometers

Two-point Equidistant Projection

TROPIC OF CANCER

107

World Heritage Sites

In 1972, the United Nations Educational, Scientific and Cultural Organization (UNESCO) adopted a treaty, signed by more than 150 countries, dedicated to the preservation of cultural and natural sites of "outstanding universal value" that are "testimonies to an enduring past." These sites are designated as World Heritage Sites because they are part of the universal heritage of people everywhere.

Since much of human history is rooted in Asia, the continent is home to many of the best known World Heritage Sites, including the Taj Mahal, in India, and the temple complex at Angkor in Cambodia. Some of the world's endangered and vulnerable animals, such as the tiger and the komodo dragon, are native to Asia, and their habitats also are preserved as World Heritage Sites.

In July 2004, the World Heritage List included 788 sites in 134 countries. Among these, 163 sites are in Asian countries, including five in the part of Russia that lies east of the Ural Mountains.

▲ **Cappadocia,** a centuries-old complex of caves, dwellings, and Christian churches carved into ancient volcanic rock in central Turkey, is an example of a mixed World Heritage Site.

World Heritage Sites

These sites are chosen for their universal value. Cultural sites reflect unusual human ingenuity or represent the traditions or values of an established culture or civilization. Natural sites are often examples of important geological processes or the habitats of endangered species. A few sites are selected because they combine cultural and natural characteristics.

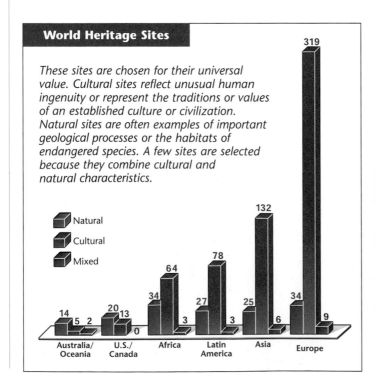

Legend:
- Natural
- Cultural
- Mixed

	Australia/Oceania	U.S./Canada	Africa	Latin America	Asia	Europe
Natural	14	20	34	27	25	34
Cultural	5	13	64	78	132	319
Mixed	2	0	3	3	6	9

▲ **Angkor Wat,** which is part of a cultural site in Cambodia, honors the Hindu god Vishnu. Nearby temples at Angkor Thom are Buddhist.

Web Link for information on World Heritage Sites: http://whc.unesco.org/

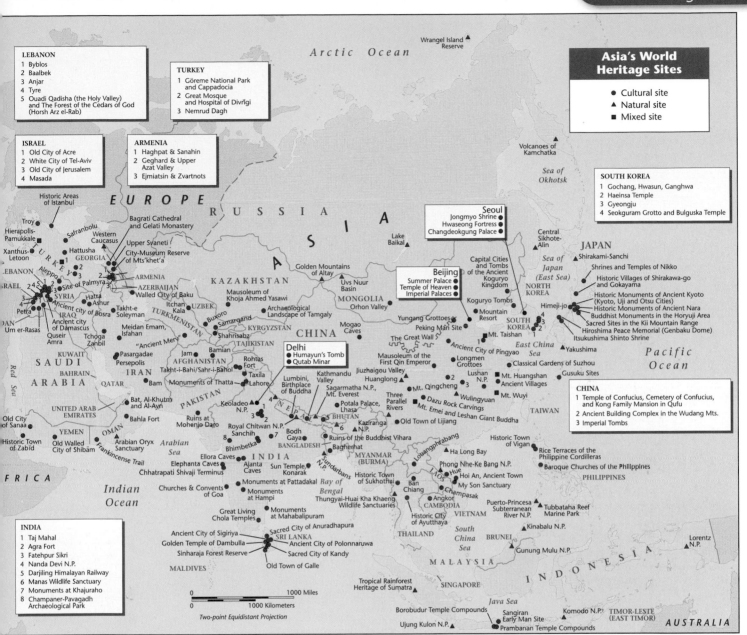

Asia's World Heritage Sites

- ● Cultural site
- ▲ Natural site
- ■ Mixed site

LEBANON
1 Byblos
2 Baalbek
3 Anjar
4 Tyre
5 Ouadi Qadisha (the Holy Valley) and The Forest of the Cedars of God (Horsh Arz el-Rab)

TURKEY
1 Göreme National Park and Cappadocia
2 Great Mosque and Hospital of Divriği
3 Nemrud Dagh

ISRAEL
1 Old City of Acre
2 White City of Tel-Aviv
3 Old City of Jerusalem
4 Masada

ARMENIA
1 Haghpat & Sanahin
2 Geghard & Upper Azat Valley
3 Ejmiatsin & Zvartnots

SOUTH KOREA
1 Gochang, Hwasun, Ganghwa
2 Haeinsa Temple
3 Gyeongju
4 Seokguram Grotto and Bulguska Temple

CHINA
1 Temple of Confucius, Cemetery of Confucius, and Kong Family Mansion in Qufu
2 Ancient Building Complex in the Wudang Mts.
3 Imperial Tombs

INDIA
1 Taj Mahal
2 Agra Fort
3 Fatehpur Sikri
4 Nanda Devi N.P.
5 Darjiling Himalayan Railway
6 Manas Wildlife Sanctuary
7 Monuments at Khajuraho
8 Champaner-Pavagadh Archaeological Park

Seoul
Jongmyo Shrine
Hwaseong Fortress
Changdeokgung Palace

Beijing
Summer Palace
Temple of Heaven
Imperial Palaces

Delhi
Humayun's Tomb
Qutab Minar

Two-point Equidistant Projection

0 — 1000 Miles
0 — 1000 Kilometers

▲ **The Taj Mahal,** *a cultural site in India, is an outstanding example of Muslim architecture in a country most often associated with Hinduism.*

▲ **Tubbataha Reef Marine Park,** *a natural site in the Philippines, is habitat for birds, sea turtles, and fish.*

Australia & Oceania

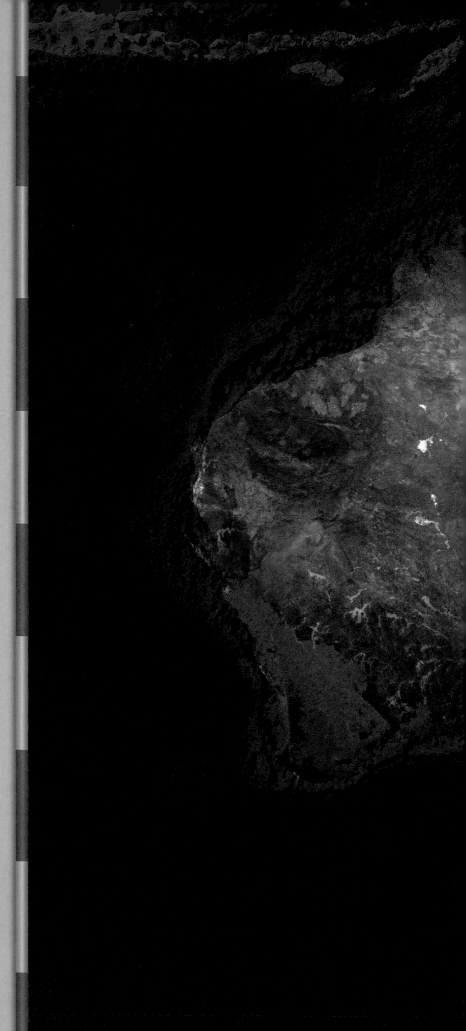

Smallest of Earth's great landmasses, Australia is the only one that is both a continent and a country. It is part of the greater region of Oceania, which includes New Zealand, the eastern part of New Guinea, and hundreds of smaller islands scattered across the Pacific Ocean. Although Hawai'i is politically part of the United States, geographically and culturally it is part of Oceania.

Facts & Figures

▶ **Land area:** 3,278,062 sq mi (8,490,180 sq km)

▶ **Population:** 32,822,000

▶ **Highest point:** Mount Wilhelm, Papua New Guinea: 14,793 ft (4,509 m)

▶ **Lowest point:** Lake Eyre, Australia: 52 ft (16 m) below sea level

▶ **Longest river:** Murray-Darling, Australia: 2,094 mi (3,370 km)

▶ **Largest lake:** Lake Eyre, Australia: 3,430 sq mi (8,884 sq km)

▶ **Number of independent countries:** 14

▶ **Largest country:** Australia: 2,969,906 sq mi (7,692,024 sq km)

▶ **Smallest country:** Nauru: 8 sq mi (21 sq km)

▶ **Most populous country:** Australia: Pop. 20,125,000

▶ **Least populous country:** Tuvalu: Pop. 9,000

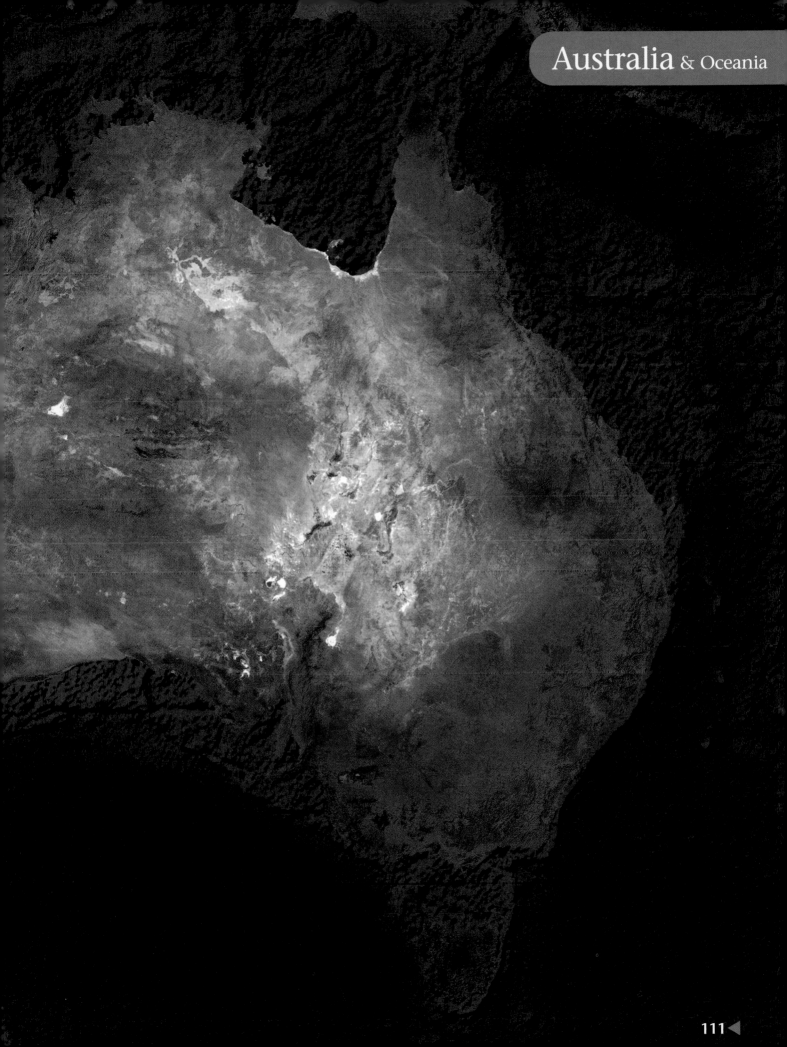

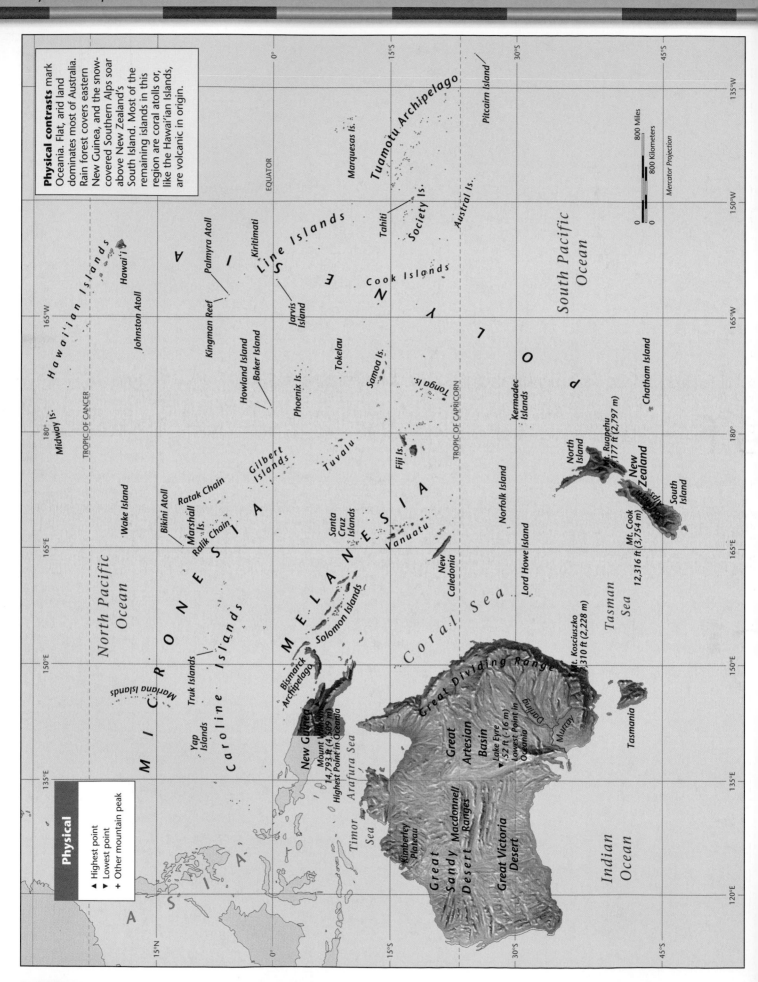

Physical contrasts mark Oceania. Flat, arid land dominates most of Australia. Rain forest covers eastern New Guinea, and the snow-covered Southern Alps soar above New Zealand's South Island. Most of the remaining islands in this region are coral atolls or, like the Hawai'ian Islands, are volcanic in origin.

Physical

▲ Highest point
▼ Lowest point
+ Other mountain peak

800 Miles
800 Kilometers

Mercator Projection

Pitcairn Island

Tuamotu Archipelago

Marquesas Is.

EQUATOR

Austral Is.

Society Is.

Tahiti

South Pacific Ocean

Cook Islands

Line Islands

Kiritimati

Palmyra Atoll

Jarvis Island

Kingman Reef

Baker Island

Howland Island

Johnston Atoll

Hawai'ian Islands

Hawai'i

TROPIC OF CANCER

Midway Is.

Phoenix Is.

Tokelau

Samoa Is.

Tonga Is.

TROPIC OF CAPRICORN

Kermadec Islands

Chatham Island

North Island

Mt. Ruapehu
9,177 ft (2,797 m)

New Zealand

South Island

Mt. Cook
12,316 ft (3,754 m)

Tasman Sea

Fiji Is.

Tuvalu

Gilbert Islands

Ratak Chain

Marshall Is.

Ralik Chain

Bikini Atoll

Wake Island

North Pacific Ocean

MICRONESIA

Caroline Islands

Yap Islands

Truk Islands

Mariana Islands

Norfolk Island

Lord Howe Island

Mt. Kosciuszko
7,310 ft (2,228 m)

Great Dividing Range

Coral Sea

New Caledonia

Vanuatu

Santa Cruz Islands

Solomon Islands

MELANESIA

Bismarck Archipelago

New Guinea

Mount Wilhelm
14,793 ft (4,509 m)
Highest Point in Oceania

Arafura Sea

Timor Sea

A S I A

Kimberley Plateau

Great Sandy Desert

Macdonnell Ranges

Great Artesian Basin

Lake Eyre
-52 ft (-16 m)
Lowest Point in Oceania

Great Victoria Desert

Darling

Murray

Tasmania

Indian Ocean

15°N

0°

15°S

30°S

45°S

120°E

135°E

150°E

165°E

180°

165°W

150°W

135°W

Australia & Oceania

Oceania is made up of more than two dozen countries and dependencies. In the early years of the 20th century, most of the islands were under the control of the United Kingdom, France, or the United States. Independence has been a slow and sometimes difficult process.

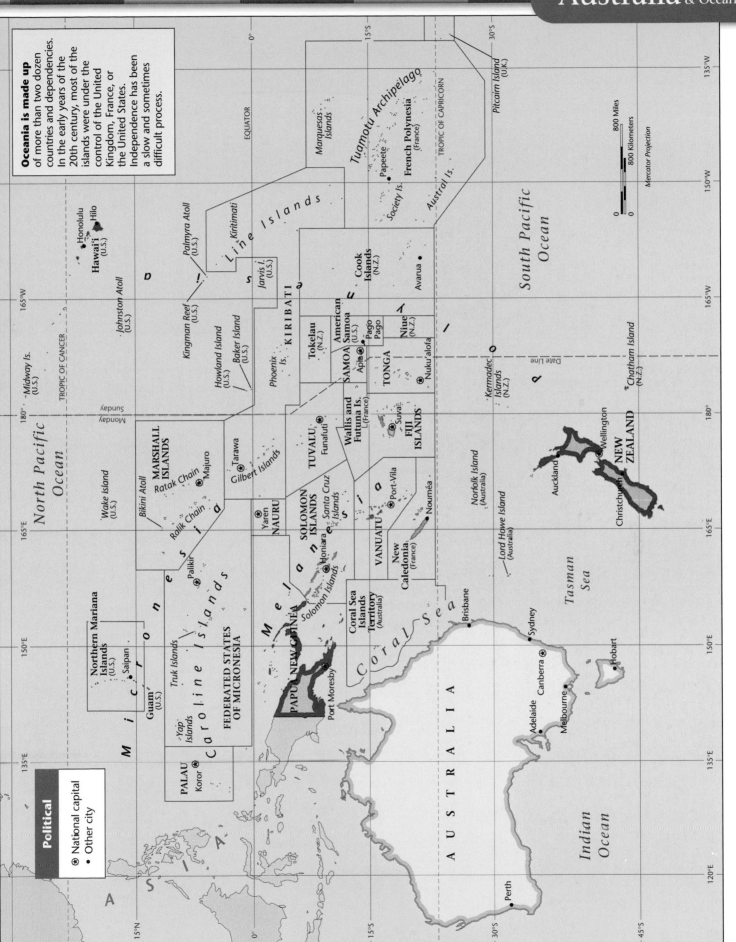

Political
⊛ National capital
• Other city

North Pacific Ocean

South Pacific Ocean

Indian Ocean

Tasman Sea

Coral Sea

EQUATOR

TROPIC OF CANCER

TROPIC OF CAPRICORN

Date Line

Mercator Projection

800 Miles
800 Kilometers

Marquesas Islands

Tuamotu Archipelago

Papeete
Society Is.
French Polynesia (France)
Austral Is.

Pitcairn Island (U.K.)

Honolulu
Hilo
Hawai'i (U.S.)

Johnston Atoll (U.S.)

Palmyra Atoll (U.S.)

Kiritimati

Line Islands

Cook Islands (N.Z.)
Avarua

Midway Is. (U.S.)

Kingman Reef (U.S.)
Jarvis I. (U.S.)

Niue (N.Z.)

Wake Island (U.S.)

Howland Island (U.S.)
Baker Island (U.S.)

KIRIBATI

Phoenix Is.

Tokelau (N.Z.)
American Samoa (U.S.)
Pago Pago

SAMOA
Apia

TONGA
Nuku'alofa

Sunday
Monday

MARSHALL ISLANDS
Bikini Atoll
Ratak Chain
Majuro
Ralik Chain

Tarawa
Gilbert Islands

TUVALU
Funafuti

Wallis and Futuna Is. (France)

Suva
FIJI ISLANDS

Kermadec Islands (N.Z.)

Chatham Island (N.Z.)

Palikir

Yaren **NAURU**

SOLOMON ISLANDS
Honiara
Santa Cruz Islands

Port-Vila

Norfolk Island (Australia)

Wellington
Auckland
NEW ZEALAND
Christchurch

VANUATU

New Caledonia (France)
Nouméa

Lord Howe Island (Australia)

Solomon Islands

Northern Mariana Islands (U.S.)
Saipan

Truk Islands

FEDERATED STATES OF MICRONESIA

Guam (U.S.)

PAPUA NEW GUINEA
Port Moresby

Coral Sea Islands Territory (Australia)

Brisbane
Sydney
Canberra ⊛
Melbourne
Adelaide
Hobart

Perth

AUSTRALIA

Yap Islands

Caroline Islands

PALAU
Koror ⊛

Micronesia
Melanesia
Polynesia

A S I A

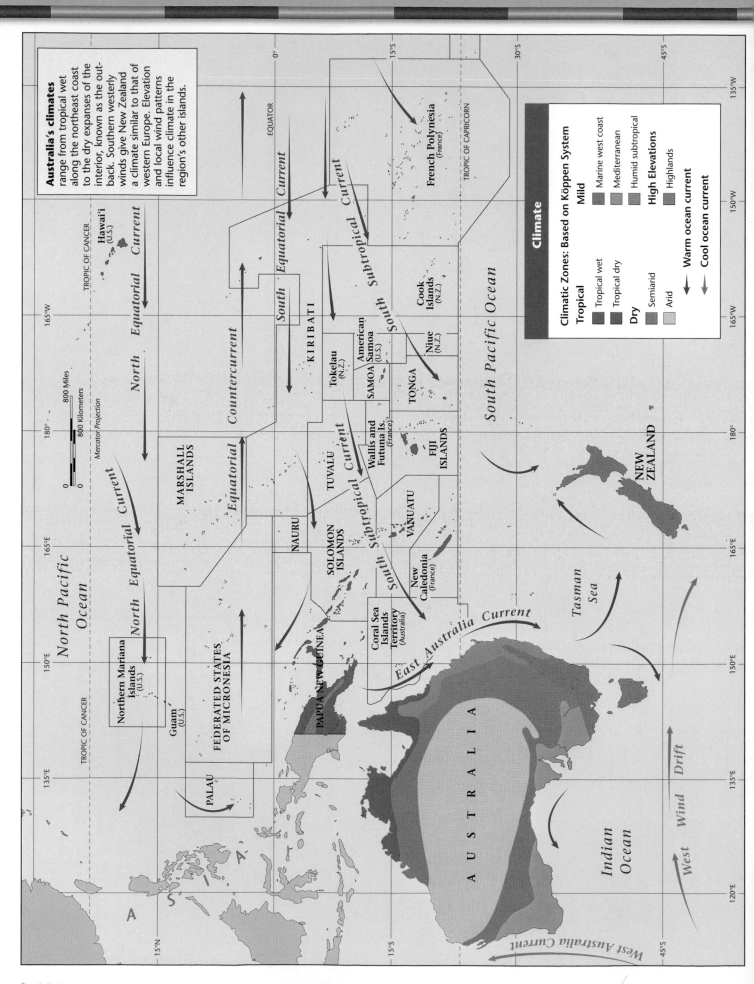

Australia's climates range from tropical wet along the northeast coast to the dry expanses of the interior, known as the outback. Southern westerly winds give New Zealand a climate similar to that of western Europe. Elevation and local wind patterns influence climate in the region's other islands.

Hawai'i (U.S.)

French Polynesia (France)

TROPIC OF CANCER

TROPIC OF CAPRICORN

EQUATOR

North Pacific Ocean

North Equatorial Current

North Equatorial Current

North Equatorial Current

Equatorial Countercurrent

South Equatorial Current

South Subtropical Current

South

South Pacific Ocean

Cook Islands (N.Z.)

Niue (N.Z.)

KIRIBATI

American Samoa (U.S.)

Tokelau (N.Z.)

SAMOA

TONGA

Wallis and Futuna Is. (France)

TUVALU

FIJI ISLANDS

South Subtropical Current

MARSHALL ISLANDS

NAURU

VANUATU

SOLOMON ISLANDS

New Caledonia (France)

Northern Mariana Islands (U.S.)

Guam (U.S.)

FEDERATED STATES OF MICRONESIA

PALAU

A S I A

PAPUA NEW GUINEA

Coral Sea Islands Territory (Australia)

East Australia Current

Tasman Sea

NEW ZEALAND

A U S T R A L I A

Indian Ocean

West Wind Drift

West Australia Current

800 Miles
800 Kilometers
0
0
Mercator Projection

Climate

Climatic Zones: Based on Köppen System

Tropical
Tropical wet
Tropical dry

Dry
Semiarid
Arid

Mild
Marine west coast
Mediterranean
Humid subtropical

High Elevations
Highlands

Warm ocean current
Cool ocean current

15°N

TROPIC OF CANCER

135°E

150°E

165°E

180°

165°W

15°S

45°S

120°E

135°E

150°E

165°E

180°

135°W

150°W

165°W

0°

15°S

30°S

45°S

Precipitation varies greatly throughout Oceania, with some islands receiving heavy rainfall all year and others frequently suffering water shortages. Australia's dry interior lies in sharp contrast to its well-watered coastal areas. New Zealand has year-round precipitation.

Hawai'i (U.S.)

EQUATOR

TROPIC OF CAPRICORN

French Polynesia (France)

KIRIBATI

Cook Islands (N.Z.)

Tokelau (N.Z.)

American Samoa (U.S.)

Niue (N.Z.)

SAMOA

TONGA

Wallis and Futuna Is. (France)

FIJI ISLANDS

North Pacific Ocean

MARSHALL ISLANDS

TUVALU

South Pacific Ocean

NEW ZEALAND

NAURU

VANUATU

SOLOMON ISLANDS

New Caledonia (France)

Coral Sea Islands Territory (Australia)

Tasman Sea

Northern Mariana Islands (U.S.)

Guam (U.S.)

FEDERATED STATES OF MICRONESIA

PAPUA NEW GUINEA

A U S T R A L I A

PALAU

TROPIC OF CANCER

A S I A

Indian Ocean

800 Miles

800 Kilometers

Mercator Projection

Precipitation

Average precipitation per year

More than 80 inches	More than 200 cm
60–80 inches	150–200 cm
40–59 inches	100–149 cm
20–39 inches	50–99 cm
10–19 inches	25–49 cm
Less than 10 inches	Less than 25 cm

Note: Data categories for this map are not necessarily the same as other precipitation maps.

15°N

0°

15°S

45°S

165°W

180°

165°E

150°E

135°E

120°E

15°S

30°S

45°S

0°

165°W

180°

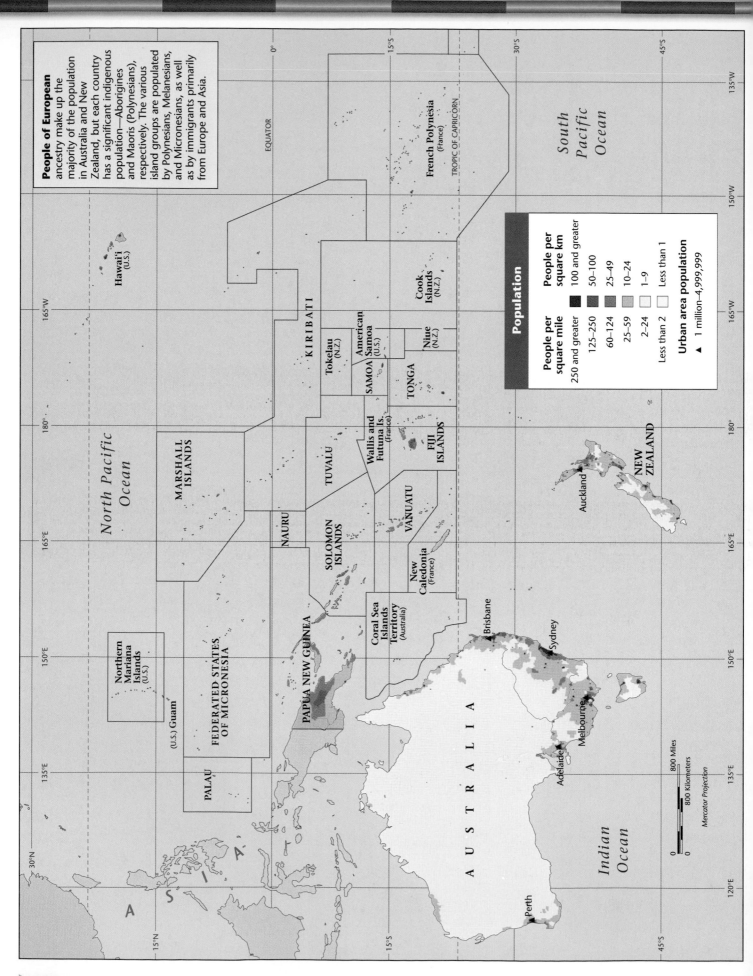

People of European ancestry make up the majority of the population in Australia and New Zealand, but each country has a significant indigenous population—Aborigines and Maoris (Polynesians), respectively. The various island groups are populated by Polynesians, Melanesians, and Micronesians, as well as by immigrants primarily from Europe and Asia.

EQUATOR

TROPIC OF CAPRICORN

North Pacific Ocean

South Pacific Ocean

Indian Ocean

Hawaiʻi (U.S.)

KIRIBATI

Tokelau (N.Z.)

American Samoa (U.S.)

SAMOA

Niue (N.Z.)

TONGA

Cook Islands (N.Z.)

French Polynesia (France)

MARSHALL ISLANDS

Wallis and Futuna Is. (France)

FIJI ISLANDS

TUVALU

NAURU

VANUATU

SOLOMON ISLANDS

New Caledonia (France)

Coral Sea Islands Territory (Australia)

PAPUA NEW GUINEA

FEDERATED STATES OF MICRONESIA

Northern Mariana Islands (U.S.)

(U.S.) Guam

PALAU

A S I A

A U S T R A L I A

Perth

Adelaide

Melbourne

Sydney

Brisbane

NEW ZEALAND

Auckland

Population

People per square mile
- 250 and greater
- 125–250
- 60–124
- 25–59
- 2–24
- Less than 2

People per square km
- 100 and greater
- 50–100
- 25–49
- 10–24
- 1–9
- Less than 1

▲ Urban area population
1 million–4,999,999

800 Miles
800 Kilometers

Mercator Projection

Australia & Oceania

Primary economic products make up much of the market in Oceania. New Zealand and Australia account for almost two-thirds of world wool exports and more than one-fifth of beef exports. Plantation agriculture, fishing, tourism, or mining form the economic base in most of the small island countries. For example, New Caledonia is a leading exporter of nickel, and Fiji exports sugar and gold.

EQUATOR

0°

15°S

30°S

135°W

TROPIC OF CAPRICORN

French Polynesia
(France)

Hawai'i
(U.S.)

165°W

180°

Cook
Islands
(N.Z.)

Niue
(N.Z.)

K I R I B A T I

American
Samoa
(U.S.)

Tokelau
(N.Z.)

SAMOA

TONGA

South Pacific Ocean

*North Pacific
Ocean*

MARSHALL
ISLANDS

165°E

180°

NEW
ZEALAND

Auckland

Wellington

Wallis and
Futuna Is.
(France)

FIJI
ISLANDS

TUVALU

NAURU

SOLOMON
ISLANDS

VANUATU

New
Caledonia
(France)

*Tasman
Sea*

Northern
Mariana
Islands
(U.S.)

TROPIC OF CANCER

150°E

Guam
(U.S.)

FEDERATED STATES
OF MICRONESIA

135°E

PALAU

PAPUA NEW GUINEA

Port Moresby

Coral Sea
Islands
Territory
(Australia)

Brisbane

Sydney

Canberra

Melbourne

Adelaide

A U S T R A L I A

15°N

A   S   I   A

*Indian
Ocean*

Perth

120°E

135°E

150°E

165°E

180°

15°S

45°S

800 Miles

800 Kilometers

0

0

Mercator Projection

Predominant Economies

- Agriculture
- Fishing
- Hunting, fishing and forestry
- Subsistence agriculture
- Little or no economic activity
- Manufacturing
- Stock raising on ranges

Major manufacturing centers

- High-tech centers
- Pulp and paper
- Shipbuilding and ship repair

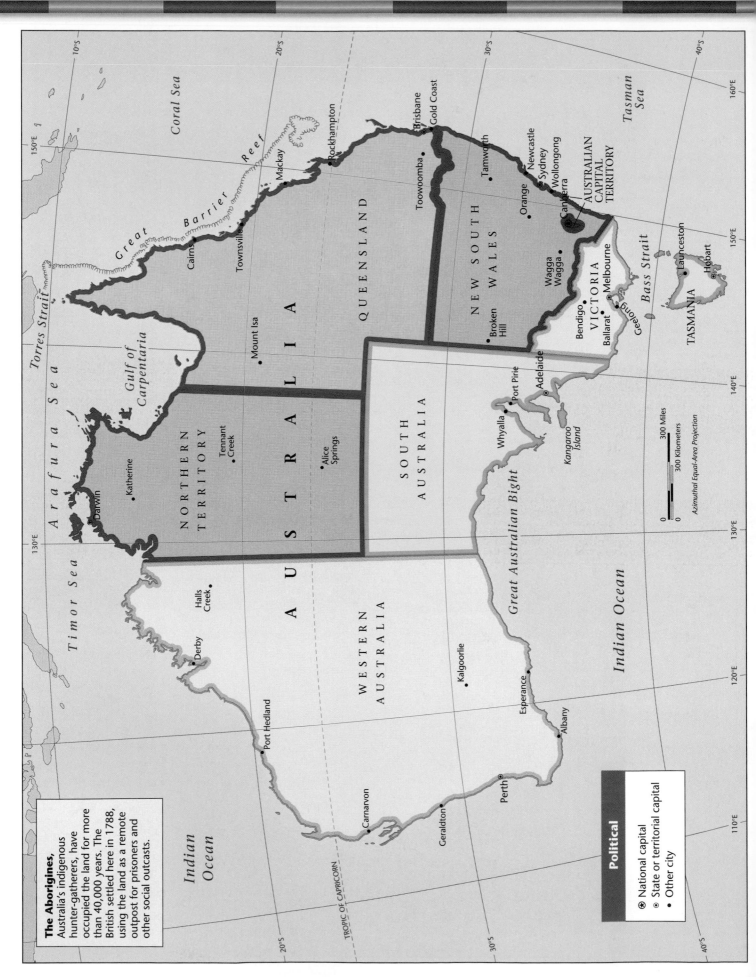

The Aborigines, Australia's indigenous hunter-gatherers, have occupied the land for more than 40,000 years. The British settled here in 1788, using the land as a remote outpost for prisoners and other social outcasts.

Political

⊗ National capital
◉ State or territorial capital
• Other city

300 Miles
300 Kilometers

Azimuthal Equal-Area Projection

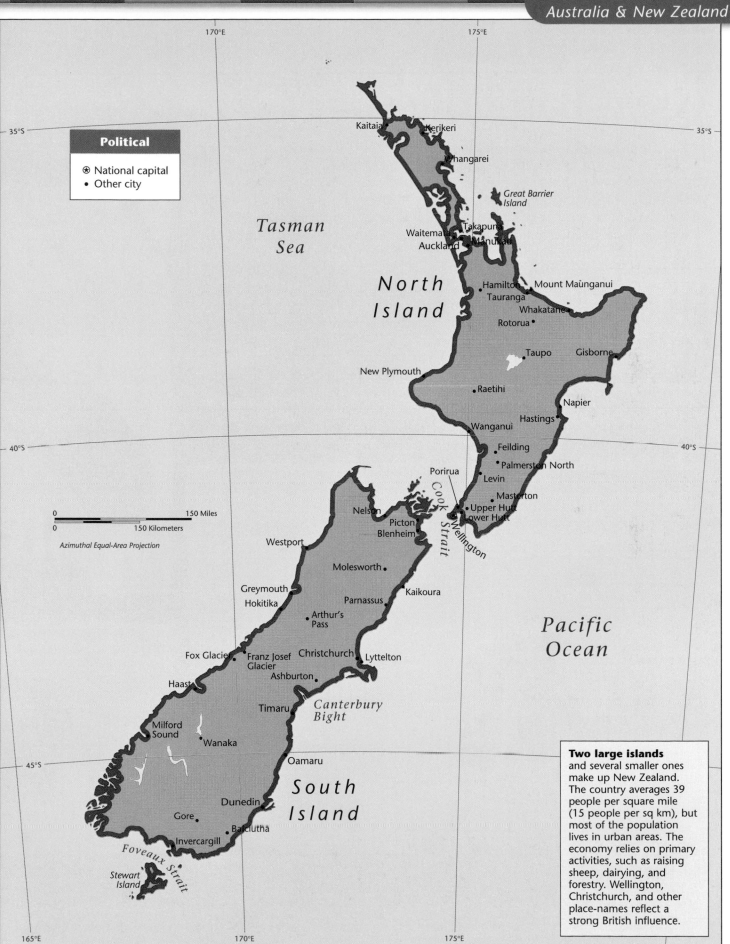

Political

⊗ National capital
• Other city

Tasman
Sea

North
Island

Kaitaia
Kerikeri
Whangarei
Great Barrier
Island
Takapuna
Waitemata
Auckland
Manukau
Hamilton
Mount Maùnganui
Tauranga
Whakatane
Rotorua
Taupo
Gisborne
New Plymouth
Raetihi
Napier
Hastings
Wanganui
Feilding
Palmerston North
Porirua
Levin
Masterton
Nelson
Upper Hutt
Lower Hutt
Picton
Wellington
Blenheim

Cook
Strait

150 Miles
150 Kilometers
Azimuthal Equal-Area Projection

Westport
Molesworth
Kaikoura
Greymouth
Hokitika
Parnassus
Arthur's
Pass
Fox Glacier
Franz Josef
Glacier
Christchurch
Lyttelton
Haast
Ashburton
Timaru
Canterbury
Bight
Milford
Sound
Wanaka
Oamaru
Gore
Dunedin
South
Island
Balclutha
Invercargill
Foveaux Strait
Stewart
Island

Pacific
Ocean

Two large islands
and several smaller ones
make up New Zealand.
The country averages 39
people per square mile
(15 people per sq km), but
most of the population
lives in urban areas. The
economy relies on primary
activities, such as raising
sheep, dairying, and
forestry. Wellington,
Christchurch, and other
place-names reflect a
strong British influence.

Great Barrier Reef

Stretching like intricate necklaces along the edges of landmasses in the warm ocean waters of the tropics, coral reefs form one of nature's most complex ecosystems. Corals are tiny marine animals that thrive in shallow coastal waters of the tropics. One type of coral, called a "hard coral," produces a limestone skeleton. When the tiny animal dies, its stonelike skeleton is left behind. The accumulation of millions of these skeletons over thousands of years has produced the large reef formations found in many coastal waters of the tropics.

Most coral reefs are formed between 30 degrees N and 30 degrees S latitude in waters with a temperature between 70 and 85 degrees Fahrenheit (21 and 29 degrees Celsius). It is estimated that Earth's coral reefs cover 110,000 square miles (284,300 sq km). Coral reefs are important because they form a habitat for marine animals such as fish, sea turtles, lobsters, and starfish. They also protect fragile coastlines from damaging ocean waves and may be a source of medicines.

The largest coral reef in the world, the Great Barrier Reef, lies off the northeast coast of Australia (see large map). This reef, which is made up of more than 400 different types of coral and home to more than 1,500 species of fish, is a popular tourist destination. People visit to snorkel and dive along the reef and view the great diversity of marine life living among the corals.

▼ *An anemone fish* is specially adapted to live among the venomous tentacles of one of the reef's sea anemones.

▲ *Brilliantly colored corals* and the fish that live among them attract divers and snorkelers to the Great Barrier Reef every year.

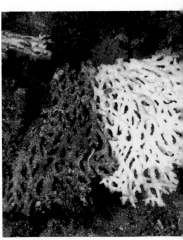

▲ *Corals are at risk* due to environmental hazards, such as storms and changes in water temperature and salinity as well as pollution and other human-related factors.

Web Link for information on coral reefs: http://www.coralreef.noaa.gov/

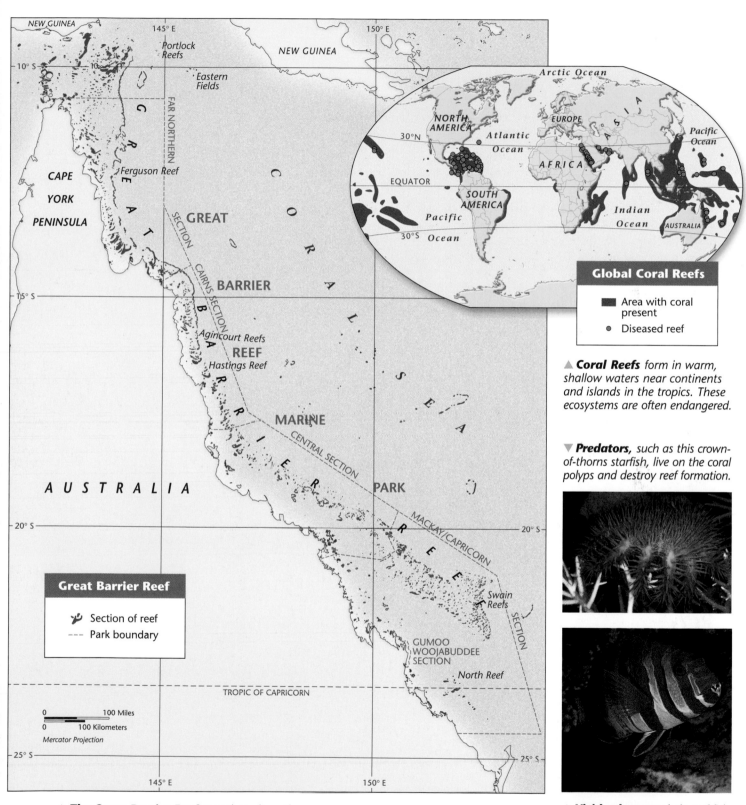

NEW GUINEA

145° E

Portlock
Reefs

NEW GUINEA

150° E

10° S

Eastern
Fields

CAPE

YORK

PENINSULA

Ferguson Reef

FAR NORTHERN SECTION

GREAT

G R E A T

SECTION

CAIRNS SECTION

BARRIER

C O R A L

15° S

Agincourt Reefs

REEF

Hastings Reef

MARINE

CENTRAL SECTION

B A R R I E R

S E A

AUSTRALIA

PARK

20° S

MACKAY/CAPRICORN

R E E F

20° S

Great Barrier Reef

🐚 Section of reef

--- Park boundary

Swain
Reefs

SECTION

GUMOO
WOOJABUDDEE
SECTION

North Reef

0   100 Miles

0   100 Kilometers

Mercator Projection

TROPIC OF CAPRICORN

25° S

25° S

145° E

150° E

Arctic Ocean

NORTH
AMERICA

EUROPE

ASIA

30°N

Atlantic
Ocean

Pacific
Ocean

EQUATOR

AFRICA

SOUTH
AMERICA

Pacific

Indian
Ocean

AUSTRALIA

30°S

Ocean

Global Coral Reefs

■ Area with coral
present

● Diseased reef

▲ **Coral Reefs** form in warm,
shallow waters near continents
and islands in the tropics. These
ecosystems are often endangered.

▼ **Predators,** such as this crown-
of-thorns starfish, live on the coral
polyps and destroy reef formation.

▲ **The Great Barrier Reef** stretches along the
northeast coast of Australia for 1,429 miles
(2,300 km), from the tip of the Cape York Peninsula
to just north of Brisbane in the state of Queensland.

▲ **Vivid colors** may help reef fish
recognize others of their species.
The colors of this harlequin fish
darken with age.

Antarctica

A bout 180 million years ago Antarctica broke away from the ancient supercontinent Gondwana. Slowly the continent drifted to its present location at the southernmost point on Earth. Approximately 98 percent of the continent lies under permanent ice sheets that are nearly 3 miles (5 km) thick in places. It is estimated that if all of Antarctica's ice were to melt, the global ocean level would rise more than 200 feet (60 m).

Facts & Figures

▶ **Land area:** 5,100,400 sq mi (13,209,000 sq km)

▶ **Population:** no permanent residents

▶ **Highest point:** Vinson Massif: 16,067 ft (4,897 m)

▶ **Lowest point:** Bentley Subglacial Trench: 8,366 ft (2,550 m) below sea level

▶ **Number of independent countries:** 0

▶ **Number of countries claiming land:** 7

▶ **Number of countries operating year-round research stations:** 19

▶ **Number of year-round research stations:** 46

▶ **Coldest place:** Plateau Station; average annual temperature: -70°F (-56.7°C)

▶ **Average precipitation on the polar plateau:** less than 2 in (5 cm) per year

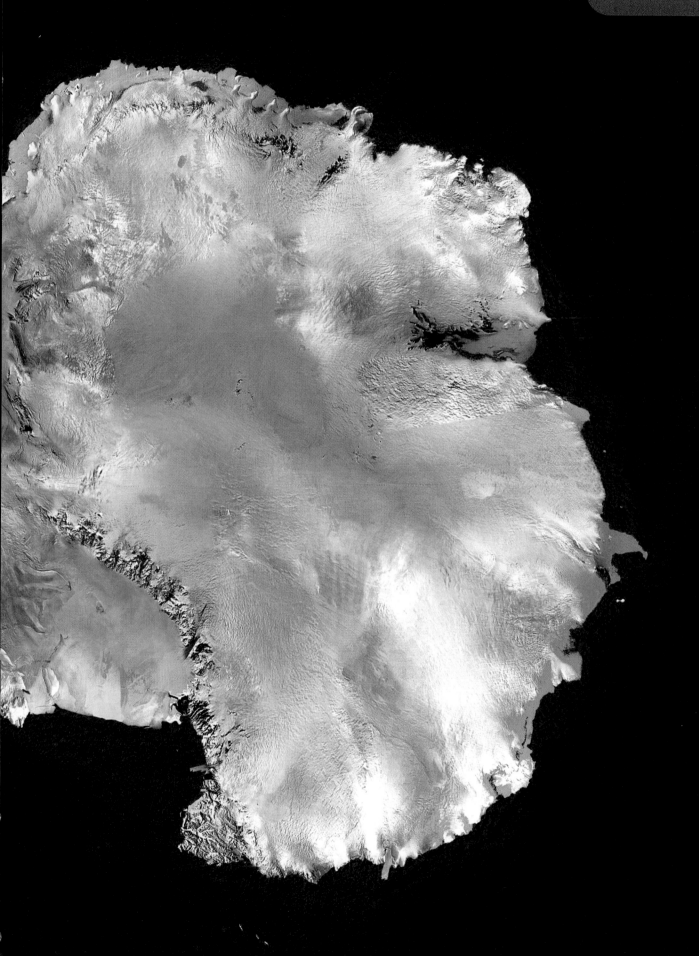

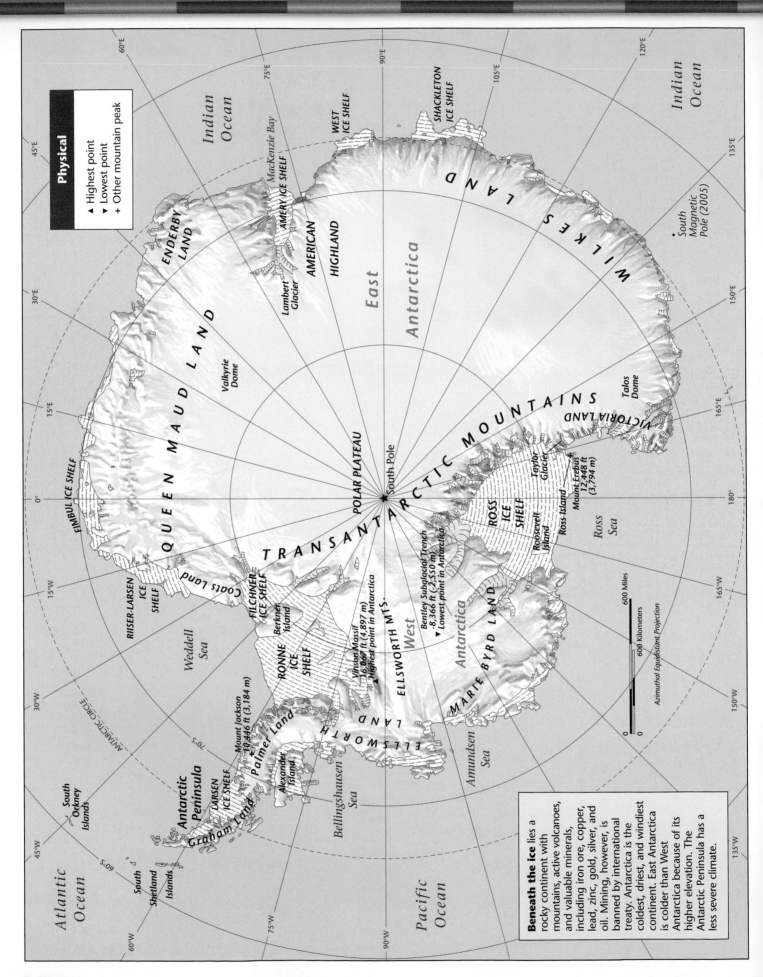

Physical
- ▲ Highest point
- ▼ Lowest point
- + Other mountain peak

Indian Ocean

60°E

75°E

90°E

105°E

120°E

Indian Ocean

135°E

SHACKLETON ICE SHELF

WEST ICE SHELF

MacKenzie Bay

AMERY ICE SHELF

W I L K E S   L A N D

South Magnetic Pole (2005)

45°E

ENDERBY LAND

AMERICAN HIGHLAND

Lambert Glacier

East Antarctica

150°E

30°E

Q U E E N   M A U D   L A N D

Valkyrie Dome

Talos Dome

VICTORIA LAND

165°E

15°E

T R A N S A N T A R C T I C   M O U N T A I N S

Taylor Glacier

Mount Erebus 12,448 ft (3,794 m)

FIMBUL ICE SHELF

0°

Polar Plateau

South Pole

ROSS ICE SHELF

Roosevelt Island

Ross Island

Ross Sea

180°

RIISER-LARSEN ICE SHELF

Coats Land

FILCHNER ICE SHELF

Berkner Island

Bentley Subglacial Trench -8,366 ft (-2,550 m) ▼ Lowest point in Antarctica

15°W

RONNE ICE SHELF

Vinson Massif 16,067 ft (4,897 m) ▲ Highest point in Antarctica

ELLSWORTH MTS.

West Antarctica

MARIE BYRD LAND

165°W

Weddell Sea

ELLSWORTH LAND

30°W

ANTARCTIC CIRCLE

70°S

Mount Jackson 10,446 ft (3,184 m)

Palmer Land

150°W

Amundsen Sea

South Orkney Islands

Antarctic Peninsula

LARSEN ICE SHELF

Alexander Island

Graham Land

Bellingshausen Sea

45°W

60°S

South Shetland Islands

135°W

Atlantic Ocean

75°W

Pacific Ocean

90°W

600 Miles

600 Kilometers

Azimuthal Equidistant Projection

Beneath the ice lies a rocky continent with mountains, active volcanoes, and valuable minerals, including iron ore, copper, lead, zinc, gold, silver, and oil. Mining, however, is banned by international treaty. Antarctica is the coldest, driest, and windiest continent. East Antarctica is colder than West Antarctica because of its higher elevation. The Antarctic Peninsula has a less severe climate.

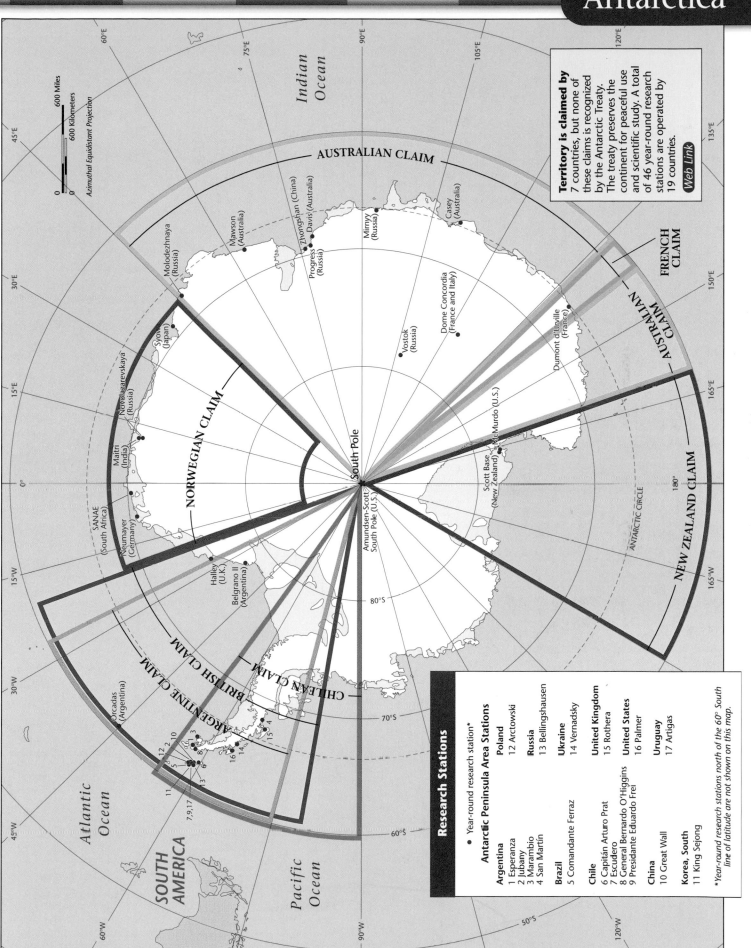

60°E

75°E

90°E

Indian Ocean

105°E

45°E

120°E

600 Miles
600 Kilometers

Azimuthal Equidistant Projection

30°E

AUSTRALIAN CLAIM

135°E

Mawson (Australia)

Zhongshan (China)

Davis (Australia)

Progress (Russia)

Mirnyy (Russia)

Casey (Australia)

Molodezhnaya (Russia)

Dome Concordia (France and Italy)

FRENCH CLAIM

15°E

Syowa (Japan)

Vostok (Russia)

150°E

Novolazarevskaya (Russia)

AUSTRALIAN CLAIM

NORWEGIAN CLAIM

Dumont d'Urville (France)

0°

Maitri (India)

McMurdo (U.S.)

Scott Base (New Zealand)

165°E

SANAE (South Africa)

South Pole

180°

Neumayer (Germany)

Amundsen-Scott South Pole (U.S.)

NEW ZEALAND CLAIM

15°W

Halley (U.K.)

Belgrano II (Argentina)

ANTARCTIC CIRCLE

165°W

80°S

ARGENTINE CLAIM

BRITISH CLAIM

30°W

Orcadas (Argentina)

CHILEAN CLAIM

70°S

12 2 10
5 3
16 14
4
15

Territory is claimed by 7 countries, but none of these claims is recognized by the Antarctic Treaty. The treaty preserves the continent for peaceful use and scientific study. A total of 46 year-round research stations are operated by 19 countries.

Web Link

Research Stations

• Year-round research station*

Antarctic Peninsula Area Stations

Argentina	**Poland**
1 Esperanza	12 Arctowski
2 Jubany	
3 Marambio	**Russia**
4 San Martín	13 Bellingshausen
Brazil	**Ukraine**
5 Comandante Ferraz	14 Vernadsky
Chile	**United Kingdom**
6 Capitán Arturo Prat	15 Rothera
7 Escudero	
8 General Bernardo O'Higgins	**United States**
9 Presidante Eduardo Frei	16 Palmer
China	**Uruguay**
10 Great Wall	17 Artigas
Korea, South	
11 King Sejong	

*Year-round research stations north of the 60° South line of latitude are not shown on this map.

45°W

Atlantic Ocean

7,9,17
11

SOUTH AMERICA

Pacific Ocean

60°W

90°W

60°S

120°W

50°S

The flags and fact boxes below represent the world's 192 independent countries—those with national governments that are recognized as having the highest legal authority over the land and people within their boundaries. The flags shown are national flags recognized by the United Nations. Area figures include land and surface areas for inland bodies of water. Population figures are for the year 2004 as provided by the Population Reference Bureau of the United States. The languages listed are either the ones most commonly spoken within a country or official languages of a country.

NORTH AMERICA

Antigua and Barbuda
Area: 171 sq mi (442 sq km)
Population: 76,000
Capital: St. John's
Languages: English (official), local dialects

Bahamas
Area: 5,382 sq mi (13,939 sq km)
Population: 317,000
Capital: Nassau
Languages: English (official), Creole

Barbados
Area: 166 sq mi (430 sq km)
Population: 256,000
Capital: Bridgetown
Language: English

Belize
Area: 8,867 sq mi (22,965 sq km)
Population: 276,000
Capital: Belmopan
Languages: English (official), Spanish, Mayan, Garifuna, Creole

Canada
Area: 3,855,101 sq mi (9,984,670 sq km)
Population: 31,892,000
Capital: Ottawa
Languages: English, French (both official)

Costa Rica
Area: 19,730 sq mi (51,100 sq km)
Population: 4,220,000
Capital: San José
Languages: Spanish (official), English

Cuba
Area: 42,803 sq mi (110,860 sq km)
Population: 11,267,000
Capital: Havana
Language: Spanish

Dominica
Area: 290 sq mi (751 sq km)
Population: 69,000
Capital: Roseau
Languages: English (official), French patois

Dominican Republic
Area: 18,704 sq mi (48,442 sq km)
Population: 8,820,000
Capital: Santo Domingo
Language: Spanish

El Salvador
Area: 8,124 sq mi (21,041 sq km)
Population: 6,706,000
Capital: San Salvador
Languages: Spanish, Nahua

Grenada
Area: 133 sq mi (344 sq km)
Population: 106,000
Capital: St. George's
Languages: English (official), French patois

Guatemala
Area: 42,042 sq mi (108,889 sq km)
Population: 12,661,000
Capital: Guatemala City
Languages: Spanish, Amerindian languages

Haiti
Area: 10,714 sq mi (27,750 sq km)
Population: 8,106,000
Capital: Port-au-Prince
Languages: French, Creole (both official)

Honduras
Area: 43,433 sq mi (112,492 sq km)
Population: 7,028,000
Capital: Tegucigalpa
Languages: Spanish, Amerindian dialects

Jamaica
Area: 4,244 sq mi (10,991 sq km)
Population: 2,643,000
Capital: Kingston
Languages: English, English patois

Mexico
Area: 758,449 sq mi (1,964,375 sq km)
Population: 106,204,000
Capital: Mexico City
Languages: Spanish, Mayan, Nahuatl, other indigenous languages

Nicaragua
Area: 50,193 sq mi (130,000 sq km)
Population: 5,626,000
Capital: Managua
Languages: Spanish (official), English, indigenous languages

Panama
Area: 29,157 sq mi (75,517 sq km)
Population: 3,172,000
Capital: Panama City
Languages: Spanish (official), English

St. Kitts and Nevis
Area: 104 sq mi (269 sq km)
Population: 47,000
Capital: Basseterre
Language: English

St. Lucia
Area: 238 sq mi (616 sq km)
Population: 164,000
Capital: Castries
Languages: English (official), French patois

St. Vincent and the Grenadines
Area: 150 sq mi (389 sq km)
Population: 110,000
Capital: Kingstown
Languages: English, French patois

Trinidad and Tobago
Area: 1,980 sq mi (5,128 sq km)
Population: 1,315,000
Capital: Port-of-Spain
Languages: English (official), Hindi, French, Spanish

United States
Area: 3,794,083 sq mi (9,826,630 sq km)
Population: 293,633,000
Capital: Washington, D.C.
Languages: English, Spanish

SOUTH AMERICA

Argentina
Area: 1,073,518 sq mi
(2,780,400 sq km)
Population: 37,880,000
Capital: Buenos Aires
Languages: Spanish
(official), English, Italian,
German, French

Bolivia
Area: 424,164 sq mi
(1,098,581 sq km)
Population: 8,766,000
Capitals: La Paz, Sucre
Languages: Spanish,
Quechua, Aymara (all official)

Brazil
Area: 3,300,169 sq mi
(8,547,403 sq km)
Population: 179,091,000
Capital: Brasília
Languages: Portuguese
(official), Spanish, English,
French

Chile
Area: 291,930 sq mi
(756,096 sq km)
Population: 15,988,000
Capital: Santiago
Language: Spanish

Colombia
Area: 440,831 sq mi
(1,141,748 sq km)
Population: 45,325,000
Capital: Bogotá
Language: Spanish

Ecuador
Area: 109,483 sq mi
(283,560 sq km)
Population: 13,402,000
Capital: Quito
Languages: Spanish
(official), Quechua

Guyana
Area: 83,000 sq mi
(214,969 sq km)
Population: 767,000
Capital: Georgetown
Languages: English,
Amerindian dialects,
Creole, Hindi, Urdu

Paraguay
Area: 157,048 sq mi
(406,752 sq km)
Population: 6,018,000
Capital: Asunción
Languages: Spanish, Guaraní
(both official)

Peru
Area: 496,224 sq mi
(1,285,216 sq km)
Population: 27,547,000
Capital: Lima
Languages: Spanish,
Quechua (both official),
Aymara

Suriname
Area: 63,037 sq mi
(163,265 sq km)
Population: 449,000
Capital: Paramaribo
Languages: Dutch (official),
English, Sranang Tongo
(Taki-Taki), Hindustani,
Javanese

Uruguay
Area: 68,037 sq mi
(176,215 sq km)
Population: 3,399,000
Capital: Montevideo
Languages: Spanish,
Portunol, Brazilero

Venezuela
Area: 352,144 sq mi
(912,050 sq km)
Population: 26,170,000
Capital: Caracas
Language: Spanish (official)

EUROPE

Albania
Area: 11,100 sq mi
(28,748 sq km)
Population: 3,232,000
Capital: Tirana
Languages: Albanian, Greek

Andorra
Area: 181 sq mi
(468 sq km)
Population: 69,000
Capital: Andorra la Vella
Languages: Catalan
(official), French, Castilian

Austria
Area: 32,378 sq mi
(83,858 sq km)
Population: 8,106,000
Capital: Vienna
Language: German

Belarus
Area: 80,153 sq mi
(207,595 sq km)
Population: 9,800,000
Capital: Minsk
Languages: Belarusian,
Russian

Belgium
Area: 11,787 sq mi
(30,528 sq km)
Population: 10,417,000
Capital: Brussels
Languages: Flemish
(Dutch), French, German
(all official)

Bosnia and
Herzegovina
Area: 19,741 sq mi
(51,129 sq km)
Population: 3,889,000
Capital: Sarajevo
Languages: Croatian,
Serbian, Bosnian

Bulgaria
Area: 42,855 sq mi
(110,994 sq km)
Population: 7,778,000
Capital: Sofia
Language: Bulgarian

Croatia
Area: 21,831 sq mi
(56,542 sq km)
Population: 4,433,000
Capital: Zagreb
Language: Croatian

Cyprus
Area: 3,572 sq mi
(9,251 sq km)
Population: 948,000
Capital: Nicosia
Languages: Greek, Turkish,
English

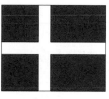

Czech Republic
Area: 30,450 sq mi
(78,866 sq km)
Population: 10,201,000
Capital: Prague
Language: Czech

Denmark
Area: 16,640 sq mi
(43,098 sq km)
Population: 5,403,000
Capital: Copenhagen
Languages: Danish,
Faroese, Greenlandic

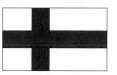

Estonia
Area: 17,462 sq mi
(45,227 sq km)
Population: 1,349,000
Capital: Tallinn
Languages: Estonian
(official), Russian, Ukrainian

Finland
Area: 130,558 sq mi
(338,145 sq km)
Population: 5,222,000
Capital: Helsinki
Languages: Finnish,
Swedish (both official)

France
Area: 210,026 sq mi
(543,965 sq km)
Population: 60,033,000
Capital: Paris
Language: French

Germany
Area: 137,847 sq mi
(357,022 sq km)
Population: 82,558,000
Capital: Berlin
Language: German

Greece
Area: 50,949 sq mi
(131,957 sq km)
Population: 11,000,000
Capital: Athens
Language: Greek

Hungary
Area: 35,919 sq mi
(93,030 sq km)
Population: 10,077,000
Capital: Budapest
Language: Hungarian

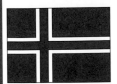

Iceland
Area: 39,769 sq mi
(103,000 sq km)
Population: 292,000
Capital: Reykjavík
Languages: Icelandic,
English, Nordic languages,
German

Ireland
Area: 27,133 sq mi
(70,273 sq km)
Population: 4,057,000
Capital: Dublin
Languages: English, Irish
(Gaelic)

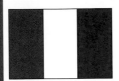

Italy
Area: 116,345 sq mi
(301,333 sq km)
Population: 57,816,000
Capital: Rome
Languages: Italian,
German, French, Slovene

Latvia
Area: 24,938 sq mi
(64,589 sq km)
Population: 2,313,000
Capital: Riga
Languages: Latvian (official),
Lithuanian, Russian

Liechtenstein
Area: 62 sq mi
(160 sq km)
Population: 34,000
Capital: Vaduz
Languages: German
(official), Alemannic dialect

Lithuania
Area: 25,212 sq mi
(65,300 sq km)
Population: 3,436,000
Capital: Vilnius
Languages: Lithuanian
(official), Polish, Russian

Luxembourg
Area: 998 sq mi
(2,586 sq km)
Population: 453,000
Capital: Luxembourg
Languages: Luxembourgish
(official), German, French

Macedonia
Area: 9,928 sq mi
(25,713 sq km)
Population: 2,038,000
Capital: Skopje
Languages: Macedonian,
Albanian

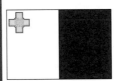

Malta
Area: 122 sq mi
(316 sq km)
Population: 399,000
Capital: Valletta
Languages: Maltese,
English (both official)

Moldova
Area: 13,050 sq mi
(33,800 sq km)
Population: 4,203,000
Capital: Chişinău
Languages: Moldovan
(official), Russian, Gagauz

Monaco
Area: 0.75 sq mi
(1.95 sq km)
Population: 33,000
Capital: Monaco
Languages: French (official),
English, Italian, Monegasque

Netherlands
Area: 16,034 sq mi
(41,528 sq km)
Population: 16,286,000
Capital: Amsterdam
Languages: Dutch, Frisian
(both official)

Norway
Area: 125,004 sq mi
(323,758 sq km)
Population: 4,590,000
Capital: Oslo
Language: Norwegian
(official)

Poland
Area: 120,728 sq mi
(312,685 sq km)
Population: 38,175,000
Capital: Warsaw
Language: Polish

Portugal
Area: 35,655 sq mi
(92,345 sq km)
Population: 10,466,000
Capital: Lisbon
Languages: Portuguese,
Mirandese (both official)

Romania
Area: 92,043 sq mi
(238,391 sq km)
Population: 21,672,000
Capital: Bucharest
Languages: Romanian
(official), Hungarian,
German

Russia
Area: 6,592,850 sq mi
(17,075,400 sq km)
Population: 144,115,000
Capital: Moscow
Language: Russian

San Marino
Area: 24 sq mi
(61 sq km)
Population: 29,000
Capital: San Marino
Language: Italian

Serbia and
Montenegro
Area: 39,450 sq mi
(102,173 sq km)
Population: 10,705,000
Capitals: Belgrade,
Podgorica
Languages: Serbian,
Albanian

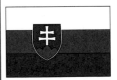

Slovakia
Area: 18,932 sq mi
(49,035 km)
Population: 5,380,000
Capital: Bratislava
Languages: Slovak (official),
Hungarian

Slovenia
Area: 7,827 sq mi
(20,273 sq km)
Population: 1,997,000
Capital: Ljubljana
Languages: Slovenian,
Serbo-Croatian

Spain
Area: 195,363 sq mi
(505,988 sq km)
Population: 42,525,000
Capital: Madrid
Languages: Castilian
Spanish, Catalan, Galician,
Basque

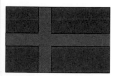

Sweden
Area: 173,732 sq mi
(449,964 sq km)
Population: 8,996,000
Capital: Stockholm
Language: Swedish

Switzerland
Area: 15,940 sq mi
(41,284 sq km)
Population: 7,404,000
Capital: Bern
Languages: German,
French, Italian, Romansch
(all official)

Ukraine
Area: 233,090 sq mi
(603,700 sq km)
Population: 47,432,000
Capital: Kiev
Languages: Ukrainian,
Russian, Romanian, Polish,
Hungarian

United Kingdom
Area: 93,788 sq mi
(242,910 sq km)
Population: 59,675,000
Capital: London
Languages: English, Welsh,
Scottish form of Gaelic

Vatican City
Area: 0.2 sq mi
(0.4 sq km)
Population: 1,000
Languages: Italian, Latin,
French

AFRICA

Algeria
Area: 919,595 sq mi
(2,381,741 sq km)
Population: 32,323,000
Capital: Algiers
Languages: Arabic (official),
French, Berber dialects

Angola
Area: 481,354 sq mi
(1,246,700 sq km)
Population: 13,294,000
Capital: Luanda
Languages: Portuguese
(official), Bantu

Benin
Area: 43,484 sq mi
(112,622 sq km)
Population: 7,250,000
Capital: Porto-Novo,
Languages: French (official),
Fon, Yoruba, other indige-
nous languages

Botswana
Area: 224,607 sq mi
(581,730 sq km)
Population: 1,684,000
Capital: Gaborone
Languages: English (official),
Setswana

Burkina Faso
Area: 105,869 sq mi
(274,200 sq km)
Population: 13,575,000
Capital: Ouagadougou
Languages: French (official),
indigenous languages

Burundi
Area: 10,747 sq mi
(27,834 sq km)
Population: 6,231,000
Capital: Bujumbura
Languages: Kirundi, French
(both official), Swahili

Cameroon
Area: 183,569 sq mi
(475,442 sq km)
Population: 16,064,000
Capital: Yaoundé
Languages: French, English
(both official), 24 major
African language groups

Cape Verde
Area: 1,558 sq mi
(4,036 sq km)
Population: 467,000
Capital: Praia
Languages: Portuguese,
Crioulo

Central African Republic
Area: 240,535 sq mi
(622,984 sq km)
Population: 3,742,000
Capital: Bangui
Languages: French (official),
Sangho, Arabic, indigenous
languages

Chad
Area: 495,755 sq mi
(1,284,000 sq km)
Population: 9,539,000
Capital: N'Djamena
Languages: French, Arabic
(both official), Sara, more
than 120 other languages
and dialects

Comoros
Area: 719 sq mi
(1,862 sq km)
Population: 652,000
Capital: Moroni
Languages: Arabic, French
(both official), Shikomoro

Congo
Area: 132,047 sq mi
(342,000 sq km)
Population: 3,818,000
Capital: Brazzaville
Languages: French (official),
Lingala, Monokutuba, many
local languages and dialects

Congo, Democratic Republic of the
Area: 905,365 sq mi
(2,344,885 sq km)
Population: 58,318,000
Capital: Kinshasa
Languages: French (official),
Lingala, Kingwana, Kikongo,
Tshiluba

Côte d'Ivoire
Area: 124,503 sq mi
(322,462 sq km)
Population: 16,897,000
Capitals: Abidjan,
Yamoussoukro
Languages: French (official),
Dioula, 60 native dialects

Djibouti
Area: 8,958 sq mi
(23,200 sq km)
Population: 712,000
Capital: Djibouti
Languages: French, Arabic
(both official), Somali, Afar

Egypt
Area: 386,874 sq mi
(1,002,000 sq km)
Population: 73,390,000
Capital: Cairo
Languages: Arabic (official),
English, French

Equatorial Guinea
Area: 10,831 sq mi
(28,051 sq km)
Population: 507,000
Capital: Malabo
Languages: Spanish,
French (both official), pidgin
English, Fang, Bubi, Ibo

Eritrea
Area: 46,774 sq mi
(121,144 sq km)
Population: 4,447,000
Capital: Asmara
Languages: Afar, Arabic,
Tigre, Kunama, Tigrinya

Ethiopia
Area: 437,600 sq mi
(1,133,380 sq km)
Population: 72,420,000
Capital: Addis Ababa
Languages: Amharic,
Tigrinya, Orominga,
Guaraginga, Somali, Arabic

Gabon
Area: 103,347 sq mi
(267,667 sq km)
Population: 1,351,000
Capital: Libreville
Languages: French, Fang,
Myene, Bateke, Bapounou/
Eschira, Bandjabi

Gambia
Area: 4,361 sq mi
(11,295 sq km)
Population: 1,547,000
Capital: Banjul
Languages: English (official),
Mandinka, Wolof, Fula

Ghana
Area: 92,100 sq mi
(238,537 sq km)
Population: 21,377,000
Capital: Accra
Languages: English (official),
African languages (including
Akan, Moshi-Dagomba,
Ewe, and Ga)

Guinea
Area: 94,926 sq mi
(245,857 sq km)
Population: 9,246,000
Capital: Conakry
Languages: French (official),
indigenous languages

Guinea-Bissau
Area: 13,948 sq mi
(36,125 sq km)
Population: 1,538,000
Capital: Bissau
Languages: Portuguese
(official), Crioulo, indigenous
languages

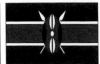

Kenya
Area: 224,081 sq mi
(580,367 sq km)
Population: 32,420,000
Capital: Nairobi
Languages: English,
Kiswahili (both official),
indigenous languages

Lesotho
Area: 11,720 sq mi
(30,355 sq km)
Population: 1,808,000
Capital: Maseru
Languages: Sesotho,
English (official), Zulu, Xhosa

Liberia
Area: 43,000 sq mi
(111,370 sq km)
Population: 3,487,000
Capital: Monrovia
Languages: English (official),
20 ethnic group languages

Libya
Area: 679,362 sq mi
(1,759,540 sq km)
Population: 5,632,000
Capital: Tripoli
Languages: Arabic, Italian,
English

Madagascar
Area: 226,658 sq mi
(587,041 sq km)
Population: 17,502,000
Capital: Antananarivo
Languages: French,
Malagasy (both official)

Malawi
Area: 45,747 sq mi
(118,484 sq km)
Population: 11,938,000
Capital: Lilongwe
Languages: English,
Chichewa (both official)

Mali
Area: 478,841 sq mi
(1,240,192 sq km)
Population: 13,409,000
Capital: Bamako
Languages: French,
Bambara (both official),
numerous African languages

Mauritania
Area: 397,955 sq mi
(1,030,700 sq km)
Population: 2,980,000
Capital: Nouakchott
Languages: Hassaniya Arabic
(official), Pulaar, Soninke,
Wolof (official), French

Mauritius
Area: 788 sq mi
(2,040 sq km)
Population: 1,235,000
Capital: Port Louis
Languages: English (official),
Creole, French (official),
Hindi, Urdu, Hakka, Bhojpuri

Morocco
Area: 274,461 sq mi
(710,850 sq km)
Population: 30,575,000
Capital: Rabat
Languages: Arabic (official),
Berber dialects, French

Mozambique
Area: 308,642 sq mi
(799,380 sq km)
Population: 19,182,000
Capital: Maputo
Languages: Portuguese
(official), indigenous dialects

Namibia
Area: 318,261 sq mi
(824,292 sq km)
Population: 1,911,000
Capital: Windhoek
Languages: English
(official), Afrikaans, German,
indigenous languages

Niger
Area: 489,191 sq mi
(1,267,000 sq km)
Population: 12,415,000
Capital: Niamey
Languages: French (official),
Hausa, Djerma

Nigeria
Area: 356,669 sq mi
(923,768 sq km)
Population: 137,253,000
Capital: Abuja
Languages: English (official),
Hausa, Yoruba, Igbo, Fulani

Rwanda
Area: 10,169 sq mi
(26,338 sq km)
Population: 8,427,000
Capital: Kigali
Languages: Kinyarwanda,
French, English (all official),
Kiswahili (Swahili)

Sao Tome and Principe
Area: 386 sq mi
(1,001 sq km)
Population: 165,000
Capital: São Tomé
Language: Portuguese
(official)

Senegal
Area: 75,955 sq mi
(196,722 sq km)
Population: 10,852,000
Capital: Dakar
Languages: French (official),
Wolof, Pulaar, Diola, Jola,
Mandinka

Seychelles
Area: 176 sq mi
(455 sq km)
Population: 80,000
Capital: Victoria
Languages: English, French
(both official), Creole

Sierra Leone
Area: 27,699 sq mi
(71,740 sq km)
Population: 5,168,000
Capital: Freetown
Languages: English (official),
Mende, Temne, Krio

Somalia
Area: 246,201 sq mi
(637,657 sq km)
Population: 8,305,000
Capital: Mogadishu
Languages: Somali (official),
Arabic, Italian, English

South Africa
Area: 470,693 sq mi (1,219,090 sq km)
Population: 46,906,000
Capitals: Pretoria (Tshwane), Cape Town, Bloemfontein
Languages: Afrikaans, English, Ndebele, Pedi, Sotho, Swazi, Tsonga, Tswana, Venda, Xhosa, Zulu (all official)

Sudan
Area: 967,500 sq mi (2,505,813 sq km)
Population: 39,148,000
Capital: Khartoum
Languages: Arabic (official), Nubian, Ta Bedawie, many local dialects

Swaziland
Area: 6,704 sq mi (17,363 sq km)
Population: 1,169,000
Capitals: Mbabane, Lobamba
Languages: English, siSwati (both official)

Tanzania
Area: 364,900 sq mi (945,087 sq km)
Population: 36,106,000
Capitals: Dar es Salaam, Dodoma
Languages: Kiswahili (Swahili), English (both official), Arabic, many local languages

Togo
Area: 21,925 sq mi (56,785 sq km)
Population: 5,557,000
Capital: Lomé
Languages: French (official), Ewe, Mina, Kabye, Dagomba

Tunisia
Area: 63,170 sq mi (163,610 sq km)
Population: 10,002,000
Capital: Tunis
Languages: Arabic (official), French

Uganda
Area: 93,104 sq mi (241,139 sq km)
Population: 26,083,000
Capital: Kampala
Languages: English (official), Ganda or Luganda, many local languages

Zambia
Area: 290,586 sq mi (752,614 sq km)
Population: 10,920,000
Capital: Lusaka
Languages: English (official), indigenous languages

Zimbabwe
Area: 150,872 sq mi (390,757 sq km)
Population: 12,672,000
Capital: Harare
Languages: English (official), Shona, Sindebele

ASIA

Afghanistan
Area: 251,773 sq mi (652,090 sq km)
Population: 28,514,000
Capital: Kabul
Languages: Pashtu, Afghan Persian (Dari), Uzbek, Turkman, 30 minor languages

Armenia
Area: 11,484 sq mi (29,743 sq km)
Population: 3,206,000
Capital: Yerevan
Languages: Armenian, Russian

Azerbaijan
Area: 33,436 sq mi (86,600 sq km)
Population: 8,295,000
Capital: Baku
Languages: Azerbaijani (Azeri), Russian, Armenian

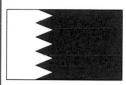

Bahrain
Area: 277 sq mi (717 sq km)
Population: 723,000
Capital: Manama
Languages: Arabic, English, Farsi, Urdu

Bangladesh
Area: 56,977 sq mi (147,570 sq km)
Population: 141,340,000
Capital: Dhaka
Languages: Bangla (Bengali) (official), English

Bhutan
Area: 17,954 sq mi (46,500 sq km)
Population: 967,000
Capital: Thimphu
Languages: Dzongkha (official), Tibetan, Nepali dialects

Brunei
Area: 2,226 sq mi (5,765 sq km)
Population: 370,000
Capital: Bandar Seri Begawan
Languages: Malay (official), English, Chinese

Cambodia
Area: 69,898 sq mi (181,035 sq km)
Population: 13,107,000
Capital: Phnom Penh
Languages: Khmer (official), French, English

China
Area: 3,705,405 sq mi (9,596,960 sq km)
Population: 1,300,060,000
Capital: Beijing
Languages: Chinese (Mandarin), Cantonese, other dialects and minority languages

East Timor (Timor-Leste)
Area: 5,640 sq mi (14,609 sq km)
Population: 820,000
Capital: Dili
Languages: Tetum, Portuguese, Bahasa Indonesian

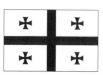

Georgia
Area: 26,911 sq mi (69,700 sq km)
Population: 4,526,000
Capital: T'bilisi
Languages: Georgian, Russian, Armenian, Azeri

India
Area: 1,269,221 sq mi (3,287,270 sq km)
Population: 1,086,640,000
Capital: New Delhi
Languages: Hindi, English, 14 other official languages

Indonesia
Area: 742,308 sq mi (1,922,570 sq km)
Population: 218,746,000
Capital: Jakarta
Languages: Bahasa Indonesian, English, Dutch, Javanese and other local dialects

Iran
Area: 636,296 sq mi (1,648,000 sq km)
Population: 67,433,000
Capital: Tehran
Languages: Persian, Turkic, Kurdish, various local dialects

Iraq
Area: 168,754 sq mi (437,072 sq km)
Population: 25,856,000
Capital: Baghdad
Languages: Arabic, Kurdish (official in Kurdish regions), Assyrian, Armenian

Israel
Area: 8,550 sq mi (22,145 sq km)
Population: 6,807,000
Capital: Jerusalem
Languages: Hebrew, Arabic, English

Japan
Area: 145,902 sq mi
(377,887 sq km)
Population: 127,635,000
Capital: Tokyo
Language: Japanese

Jordan
Area: 34,495 sq mi
(89,342 sq km)
Population: 5,635,000
Capital: Amman
Languages: Arabic, English
understood

Kazakhstan
Area: 1,049,155 sq mi
(2,717,300 sq km)
Population: 14,998,000
Capital: Astana
Languages: Kazakh,
Russian (both official)

Korea, North
Area: 46,540 sq mi
(120,538 sq km)
Population: 22,776,000
Capital: Pyongyang
Language: Korean

Korea, South
Area: 38,321 sq mi
(99,250 sq km)
Population: 48,199,000
Capital: Seoul
Languages: Korean;
English widely taught

Kuwait
Area: 6,880 sq mi
(17,818 sq km)
Population: 2,493,000
Capital: Kuwait City
Languages: Arabic (official),
English

Kyrgyzstan
Area: 77,182 sq mi
(199,900 sq km)
Population: 5,064,000
Capital: Bishkek
Languages: Kyrgyz,
Russian (both official)

Laos
Area: 91,429 sq mi
(236,800 sq km)
Population: 5,787,000
Capital: Vientiane
Languages: Lao (official),
French, English, various
ethnic languages

Lebanon
Area: 4,036 sq mi
(10,452 sq km)
Population: 4,502,000
Capital: Beirut
Languages: Arabic (official),
French, English, Armenian

Malaysia
Area: 127,355 sq mi
(329,847 sq km)
Population: 25,581,000
Capital: Kuala Lumpur
Languages: Bahasa Melayu
(official), English, Chinese
dialects, other regional
dialects and indigenous
languages

Maldives
Area: 115 sq mi
(298 sq km)
Population: 298,000
Capital: Male
Languages: Maldivian
Dhivehi, English

Mongolia
Area: 603,909 sq mi
(1,564,116 sq km)
Population: 2,519,000
Capital: Ulaanbaatar
Languages: Khalkha
Mongol, Turkic, Russian

Myanmar
Area: 261,218 sq mi
(676,552 sq km)
Population: 50,101,000
Capital: Yangon (Rangoon)
Languages: Burmese,
minority ethnic languages

Nepal
Area: 56,827 sq mi
(147,181 sq km)
Population: 24,746,000
Capital: Kathmandu
Languages: Nepali (offi-
cial), English, many other
languages and dialects

Oman
Area: 119,500 sq mi
(309,500 sq km)
Population: 2,662,000
Capital: Muscat
Languages: Arabic (official),
English, Baluchi, Urdu,
Indian dialects

Pakistan
Area: 307,374 sq mi
(796,095 sq km)
Population: 159,196,000
Capital: Islamabad
Languages: Punjabi,
Sindhi, Siraiki, Pashtu,
Urdu, English

Philippines
Area: 115,831 sq mi
(300,000 sq km)
Population: 83,661,000
Capital: Manila
Languages: Filipino,
English (both official),
8 major dialects

Qatar
Area: 4,448 sq mi
(11,521 sq km)
Population: 743,000
Capital: Doha
Languages: Arabic (official),
English

Saudi Arabia
Area: 756,985 sq mi
(1,960,582 sq km)
Population: 25,131,000
Capital: Riyadh
Language: Arabic

Singapore
Area: 255 sq mi
(660 sq km)
Population: 4,199,000
Capital: Singapore
Languages: Chinese,
Malay, Tamil, English
(all official)

Sri Lanka
Area: 25,299 sq mi
(65,525 sq km)
Population: 19,569,000
Capital: Colombo
Languages: Sinhala
(official), Tamil, English

Syria
Area: 71,498 sq mi
(185,180 sq km)
Population: 17,954,000
Capital: Damascus
Languages: Arabic (official),
Kurdish, Armenian,
Aramaic, Circassian

Tajikistan
Area: 55,251 sq mi
(143,100 sq km)
Population: 6,615,000
Capital: Dushanbe
Languages: Tajik (official),
Russian

Thailand
Area: 198,115 sq mi
(513,115 sq km)
Population: 63,763,000
Capital: Bangkok
Languages: Thai, English,
ethnic and regional dialects

Turkey
Area: 300,948 sq mi
(779,452 sq km)
Population: 71,300,000
Capital: Ankara
Languages: Turkish (official),
Kurdish, Arabic, Armenian,
Greek

Turkmenistan
Area: 188,456 sq mi
(488,100 sq km)
Population: 5,719,000
Capital: Ashgabat
Languages: Turkmen,
Russian, Uzbek

United Arab Emirates
Area: 30,000 sq mi
(77,700 sq km)
Population: 4,193,000
Capital: Abu Dhabi
Languages: Arabic (official),
Persian, English, Hindi, Urdu

Uzbekistan
Area: 172,742 sq mi
(447,400 sq km)
Population: 26,359,000
Capital: Tashkent
Languages: Uzbek,
Russian, Tajik

Vietnam
Area: 127,844 sq mi
(331,114 sq km)
Population: 81,465,000
Capital: Hanoi
Languages: Vietnamese (offi-
cial), English, French, Chinese,
Khmer, tribal languages

Yemen
Area: 207,286 sq mi
(536,869 sq km)
Population: 20,025,000
Capital: Sanaa
Language: Arabic

AUSTRALIA & OCEANIA

Australia
Area: 2,969,906 sq mi
(7,692,024 sq km)
Population: 20,125,000
Capital: Canberra
Languages: English,
indigenous languages

Fiji Islands
Area: 7,095 sq mi
(18,376 sq km)
Population: 845,000
Capital: Suva
Languages: English (official),
Fijian, Hindustani

Kiribati
Area: 313 sq mi
(811 sq km)
Population: 90,000
Capital: Tarawa
Languages: English (official),
I-Kiribati

Marshall Islands
Area: 70 sq mi
(181 sq km)
Population: 57,000
Capital: Majuro
Languages: English, local
dialects, Japanese

Micronesia
Population: 271 sq mi
(702 sq km)
Population: 108,000
Capital: Palikir
Languages: English (official),
Trukese, Pohnpeian,
Yapese, Kosraean

Nauru
Area: 8 sq mi
(21 sq km)
Population: 12,000
Capital: Yaren
Languages: Nauruan
(official), English

New Zealand
Area: 104,454 sq mi
(270,534 sq km)
Population: 4,071,000
Capital: Wellington
Languages: English, Maori
(both official)

Palau
Area: 189 sq mi
(489 sq km)
Population: 21,000
Capital: Koror
Languages: English, Palaun,
Japanese, Sonsoralese,
Tobi, Angaur

Papua New Guinea
Area: 178,703 sq mi
(462,840 sq km)
Population: 5,680,000
Capital: Port Moresby
Languages: 715 indigenous
languages

Samoa
Area: 1,093 sq mi
(2,831 sq km)
Population: 183,000
Capital: Apia
Languages: Samoan
(Polynesian), English

Solomon Islands
Area: 10,954 sq mi
(28,370 sq km)
Population: 460,000
Capital: Honiara
Languages: Melanesian
pidgin, 120 indigenous
languages, English

Tonga
Area: 289 sq mi
(748 sq km)
Population: 102,000
Capital: Nuku'alofa
Languages: Tongan,
English

Tuvalu
Area: 10 sq mi
(26 sq km)
Population: 9,000
Capital: Funafuti
Languages: Tuvaluan,
English

Vanuatu
Area: 4,707 sq mi
(12,190 sq km)
Population: 216,000
Capital: Port-Vila
Languages: English,
French, pidgin (Bislama)
(all official)

 Web Link

Glossary

Note: Terms defined within the main body of the atlas text are not listed below.

Alkaline describes soil or natural body of water that has a high salt content; most often found in dry areas where soluble salts have not been washed away or where evaporation rates are high (p. 98)

Arid climate type of dry climate in which annual precipitation is often less than 10 inches (25 cm); experiences great daily variations in day-night temperatures (pp. 18–19)

Asylum a place where a person can go to find safety; to offer asylum means to offer protection in a safe country to people who fear being persecuted or who have been persecuted in their own country. (pp. 46–47)

Bandwidth in computers, the rate at which information can be transmitted along a communications line or device (p. 48)

Bathymetry measurement of depth at various places in the ocean or other body of water (p. 11)

Boreal forest *see northern coniferous forest*

Boundary line established by people to separate one political or mapped area from another; physical features, such as mountains and rivers, or latitude and longitude lines sometimes act as boundaries (p. 10)

Breadbasket a geographic region that is a principal source of grain (p. 64)

Brine solution containing a much higher concentration of salt than seawater (p. 98)

Canadian Shield region containing the oldest rock in North America; areas are exposed in much of eastern Canada and some bordering U.S. regions (pp. 56, 62)

Coastal plain any comparatively level land of low elevation that borders the ocean (p. 64)

Continental climate midlatitude climate zone occurring on large landmasses in the Northern Hemisphere and characterized by great variations of temperature, both seasonally and between day and night; **continental cool summer** climates are influenced by nearby colder subarctic climates; **continental warm summer** climates are influenced by nearby mild or dry climates (pp. 18–19)

Coordinated Universal Time (UTC) the basis for the current worldwide system of civil (versus military) time determined by highly precise atomic clocks; also known as Universal Time; formerly known as Greenwich Mean Time. (p. 53)

Culture hearth center from which major cultural traditions spread and are adopted by people in a wide geographic area (p. 100)

Cybercafe a café that has a collection of computers that customers can use to access the Internet (p. 50)

Degraded forest a forested area severely damaged by overharvesting, repeated fires, overgrazing, poor management practices, or other abuse that delays or prevents forest regrowth (p. 24)

Desert and dry shrub vegetation region with either hot or cold temperatures that annually receives 10 inches (25 cm) or less of precipitation (pp. 22–23)

Ecosystem term for classifying Earth's natural communities according to how all things in an environment, such as a forest or a coral reef, interact with each other (p. 10)

Fault break in Earth's crust along which movement up, down, or sideways occurs (pp. 14–15)

Flooded grassland wetland dominated by grasses and covered by water (pp. 22–23)

Fossil fuel a fuel, such as coal, petroleum, and natural gas, derived from the remains of ancient plants and animals (p. 42)

Geothermal energy heat energy generated within Earth (p. 43)

Gigabit the equivalent of roughly one billion information bits; a bit, which is short for "binary digit," is the smallest unit of information on a computer (p. 48)

Glacier large, slow-moving mass of ice that forms over time from snow (p. 54)

Global warming a theory about the increase of Earth's average global temperature due to a buildup of so-called greenhouse gases, such as carbon dioxide and methane, released by human activities (p. 25)

Globalization the purposeful spread of activities, technology, goods, and values throughout the world through the expansion of global links, such as trade, media, and the Internet (p. 48)

Gondwana name given to the southern part of the supercontinent Pangaea; made up of what we now call Africa, South America, Australia, Antarctica, and India (pp. 14, 98)

Greenwich Mean Time *see Coordinated Universal Time*

Groundwater water, primarily from rain or melted snow, that collects beneath Earth's surface, in saturated soil or in underground reservoirs, or aquifers, and that supplies springs and wells (p. 41)

Hemisphere one-half of the globe; the Equator divides Earth into Northern and Southern Hemispheres; the prime meridian and the 180 degree meridian divide it into Eastern and Western Hemispheres (p. 5)

Highland/upland climate region associated with mountains or plateaus that varies depending on elevation, latitude, continental location, and exposure to sun and wind; in general, temperature decreases and precipitation increases with elevation (pp. 18–19)

Host country the country where a refugee first goes to find asylum (p. 46)

Hot spot in geology, an extremely hot region beneath the lithosphere that tends to stay relatively stationary while plates of Earth's outer crust move over it; environmentally, an ecological trouble spot (pp. 15, 24)

Human rights basic universal civil, political, economic, social, and cultural rights of individuals based on the concept of personal dignity and value (p. 45)

Humid subtropical climate region characterized by hot summers, mild to cool winters, and year-round precipitation that is heaviest in summer; generally located on the southeastern margins of continents (pp. 18–19)

Ice cap climate one of two kinds of polar climate; summer temperatures rarely rise above freezing and what little precipitation occurs is mostly in the form of snow (pp. 18–19)

Indigenous native to or occurring naturally in a specific area or environment (p. 116)

Infiltration process that occurs in the water, or hydrologic, cycle when gravity causes surface water to seep down through the soil (p. 40)

Internally displaced person (IDP) a person who has fled his or her home to escape armed conflict, generalized violence, human rights abuses, or natural or man-made disasters; unlike a refugee, such a person has not crossed an international border but remains in his or her own country. (pp. 46, 47)

Internet a network of computers facilitating electronic communication across the globe by way of the World Wide Web (pp. 32, 36, 37, 48)

Internet host central computer in a network (p. 48)

Landform physical feature shaped by uplifting, weathering, and erosion; mountains, plateaus, hills, and plains are the four major types (p. 20)

Language family group of languages that share a common ancestry (pp. 32–33)

Latin America cultural region generally considered to include Mexico, Central America, South America, and the West Indies; Portuguese and Spanish are the principal languages (pp. 30–31)

Llanos extensive, mostly treeless grasslands in the Orinoco River basin of northern South America (p. 72)

Lowlands fairly level land at a lower elevation than surrounding areas (p. 12)

Mangrove vegetation tropical trees and shrubs with dense root systems that grow in tidal mud flats and extend coastlines by trapping soil (pp. 22–23)

Marine west coast type of mild climate common on the west coasts of continents in midlatitude regions; characterized by small variations in annual temperature range and wet, foggy winters (pp. 18–19)

Marginal land land that has little value for growing crops or for commercial or residential development (p. 24)

Median age midpoint of a population's age; half the population is older than this age; half is younger (p. 29)

Mediterranean climate type of mild climate common on the west coasts of continents, named for the dominant climate along the Mediterranean coast; characterized by mild, rainy winters and hot, dry summers (pp. 18–19)

Mediterranean shrub low-growing, mostly small-leaved evergreen vegetation, such as chaparral, that thrives in Mediterranean climate regions (pp. 22–23)

Melanesia one of three major island groups that make up Oceania; includes the Fiji Islands, New Guinea, Vanuatu, the Solomon Islands, and New Caledonia (pp. 112–113)

Melanesian indigenous to Melanesia (p. 116)

Microclimate climate of a very limited area that varies from the overall climate of the surrounding region (p. 20)

Micronesia one of three major island groups that make up Oceania; made up of some 2,000 mostly coral islands, including Guam, Kiribati, the Mariana Islands, Palau, and the Federated States of Micronesia (pp. 112–113)

Micronesian indigenous to Micronesia (p. 116)

Monsoon seasonal change in the direction of the prevailing winds, which causes wet and dry seasons in some tropical areas (p. 104)

Mountain grassland vegetation region characterized by clumps of long grass that grow beyond the limit of forests at high elevations (pp. 22–23)

Nonrenewable resources elements of the natural environment, such as metals, minerals, and fossil fuels, that form within Earth by geological processes over millions of years and thus cannot readily be replaced (pp. 42–43)

Northern coniferous forest vegetation region composed primarily of cone-bearing, needle-leafed or scale-leafed evergreen trees that grow in regions with long winters and moderate to high annual precipitation; also called boreal forest or taiga (pp. 22–23)

Oceania name for the widely scattered islands of Polynesia, Micronesia, and Melanesia; often includes Australia and New Zealand (pp. 110–121)

Pampas temperate grassland primarily in Argentina between the Andes and the Atlantic Ocean; one of the richest agricultural regions in the world (pp. 70, 72)

Patagonia cool, windy, arid plateau region primarily in southern Argentina between the Andes and the Atlantic Ocean (p. 72)

Plain large area of relatively flat land; one of the four major kinds of landforms (p. 16)

Plate tectonics study of the interaction of slabs of Earth's crust as molten rock within Earth causes them to slowly move across the surface (pp. 14–15)

Plateau large, relatively flat area that rises above the surrounding landscape; one of the four major kinds of landforms (pp. 16–17)

Polar climates climates that occur at very high latitudes; generally too cold to support tree growth; include tundra and ice cap (pp. 18–19)

Polynesia one of three major regions in Oceania made up mostly of volcanic and coral islands, including the Hawai'ian and the Society Islands, Samoa, and French Polynesia (pp. 112–113)

Polynesian indigenous to Polynesia (p. 116)

Predominant economy main type of work that most people do to meet their wants and needs in a particular country (pp. 36–37, 61, 77, 87, 97, 107, 117)

Province land governed as a political or administrative unit of a country or empire; Canadian provinces, like U.S. states, have substantial powers of self-government (p. 63)

Rain forest see *Tropical moist broadleaf forest*

Renewable fresh water water that is replenished naturally, but the supply of which can be endangered by overuse and pollution (p. 40)

River basin area drained by a single river and its tributaries (p. 72)

Rural pertaining to the countryside, where most of the economic activity centers on agriculture-related work (pp. 30–31)

Sahel in Africa the semi-arid region of short, tropical grassland that lies between the dry Sahara and the humid savanna and that is prone to frequent droughts (p. 92)

Savanna tropical tall grassland with scattered low trees (pp. 22–23)

Selva Portuguese word referring to tropical rain forests, especially in the Amazon Basin (p. 78)

Semiarid dry climate region that experiences great daily variation in day-night temperatures; receives enough rainfall to support grasslands (pp. 18–19)

Silt mineral particles that are larger than grains of clay but smaller than grains of sand (p. 79)

Sisal tropical plant with leaves made up of strong fibers that are used to make rope (p. 98)

Stateless people those who have no recognized country (p. 46)

Steppe Slavic word referring to relatively flat, mostly treeless, temperate grasslands that stretch across much of central Europe and central Asia (p. 102)

Subarctic climate region characterized by short, cool, sometimes freezing summers and long, bitter-cold winters; most precipitation falls in summer (pp. 18–19)

Subcontinent large landmass such as India that, although part of a continent, is considered a separate feature either geographically or politically (p. 98)

Subtropical climate region between tropical and continental climates characterized by distinct seasons but with milder temperatures than continental climates (pp. 18–19)

Suburb a residential area on the outskirts of a town or city (p. 30)

Sunbelt area of rapid population and economic growth south of the 37th parallel in the United States; its mild climate is attractive to retirees and a general absence of labor unions has drawn manufacturing to the region. (p. 60)

Taiga *see Northern coniferous forest*

Temperate broadleaf forest vegetation region with distinct seasons and dependable rainfall; predominant species include oak, maple, and beech, all of which lose their leaves in the cold season (pp. 22–23)

Temperate coniferous forest vegetation region that has mild winters with heavy precipitation; made up of mostly evergreen, needleleaf trees that bear seeds in cones (pp. 22–23)

Temperate grassland vegetation region where grasses are dominant and the climate is characterized by hot summers, cold winters, and moderate rainfall (pp. 22–23)

Territory land under the jurisdiction of a country but that is not a state or a province (p. 57)

Tropical coniferous forest vegetation region that occurs in a cooler climate than tropical rain forests; has distinct wet and dry seasons; made up of mostly evergreen trees with seed-bearing cones (pp. 22–23)

Tropical dry climate region characterized by year-round high temperatures and sufficient precipitation to support savannas (pp. 18–19)

Tropical dry forest vegetation region that has distinct wet and dry seasons and a cooler climate than tropical moist forests; has shorter trees than rain forests and many shed their leaves in the dry season (pp. 22–23)

Tropical grassland and savanna vegetation region characterized by scattered individual trees; occurs in warm or hot climates with annual rainfall of 20 to 50 inches (50–130 cm) (pp. 22–23)

Tropical moist broadleaf forest vegetation region occurring mostly in a belt between the Tropic of Cancer and the Tropic of Capricorn in areas that have at least 80 inches (200 cm) of rain annually and an average annual temperature of 80°F (20°C) (pp. 22–23)

Tropical wet climate region characterized by year-round warm temperatures and rainfall ranging from 60 to 150 inches (150–400 cm) annually (pp. 18–19)

Troposphere region of Earth's atmosphere closest to the surface; where weather occurs (p. 5)

Tundra vegetation region at high latitudes and high elevations characterized by cold temperatures, low vegetation, and a short growing season (pp. 22–23)

Tundra climate region with one or more months of temperatures slightly above freezing when the ground is free of snow (pp. 18–19)

Universalizing religion one that attempts to appeal to all people rather than to just those in a particular region or place (p. 34)

Upland climate *see Highland/upland climate*

Urban pertaining to a town or city, where most of the economic activity is not based on agriculture (pp. 30–31)

Urban agglomeration a group of several cities and/or towns and their suburbs (p. 31)

West Bank area bordering the west bank of the Jordan River that, according to a 1993 peace agreement between Israelis and Palestinians, has limited Palestinian autonomy; its future is subject to ongoing negotiations between these groups. (pp. 44, 47)

World Wide Web (www) a system of Internet servers that uses HTTP to transfer specially formatted documents that can be viewed on a computer using a Web browser; although many people think of the World Wide Web and the Internet as the same thing, the Web is actually only part of the Internet. (p. 48)

Web Sites (Web Link)

Activities and lessons using maps: http://www.nationalgeographic.com/xpeditions/
Antarctica: http://www.nsf.gov/div/index.jsp?div=ANT
Cultural Diffusion: http://www.geog.okstate.edu/users/lightfoot/lfoot.htm
Earth's Climates: http://www.worldclimate.com
Earth's Geologic History:
    Earthquakes: http://earthquake.usgs.gov/
    Tsunamis: http://www.noaa.gov/tsunamis.html
    Volcanoes: http://www.geo.mtu.edu/volcanoes/
Earth's Vegetation: http://www.earthobservatory.nasa.gov/Library/LandCover/
Environmental Hot Spots: http://earthtrends.wri.org/index.cfm
    Quiz for students: http://www.myfootprint.org/
Flags of the world: http://www.fotw.us/flags/index.html
Globalization: http://www.globalisationguide.org/
Map Projections: http://www.colorado.edu/geography/gcraft/notes/mapproj/mapproj.html
Political World: http://www.cia.gov/cia/publications/factbook/index.html
Predominant World Economies: http://www.wto.org/english/res_e/statis_e/statis_e.htm
Reading Maps: http://geodepot.statcan.ca/Diss/Reference/Tutorial/RM_tut1_e.cfm
Time Zones: http://tycho.usno.navy.mil/tzones.html
Types of Maps: http://erg.usgs.gov/isb/pubs/MapProjections/projections.html
World Cities: http://www.un.org/esa/population/publications/wup2003/WUP2003Report.pdf
World Conflicts: http://www.cnn.com/interactive/maps/world/fullpage.global.conflict/world.index.html
World Energy: http://www.bp.com/worldenergy/
World Food: http://www.cgiar.org/impact/research/index.html
World Languages: http://www.ethnologue.com/web.asp
    Interactive for students: http://www.ipl.org/div/kidspace/hello/
World Population: http://www.census.gov/ipc/www/idbnew.html
World Refugees: http://www.unrefugees.org
World Religions: http://www.adherents.com/
World Water: http://water.usgs.gov/

Thematic Index

Place-name Index

Staff for this book

Acknowledgments: We are grateful for the assistance of Richard W. Bullington, Jan D. Morris, Karla H. Tucker, and Alfred L. Zebarth of NG Maps; the National Geographic Image Collection; and Jo H. Tunstall, Robert W. Witt, and Lyle Rosbotham, NG Book Division

Illustrations Credits: Abbreviations for terms appearing below: (t) top; (b) bottom; (l) left; (r) right; (c) center; NGS: National Geographic Staff

Locator globes on pages 2–3 and in chapter openers created by Theophilus Britt Griswold

Graphs created by Stuart Armstrong

Continent chapter openers: NASA/JPL/California Institute of Technology/Advanced Very High Resolution Radiometer Project/Cartographic Applications Group

Front cover: NOAA satellite mosaic prepared for National Geographic Television by NASA/ JPL, color enhanced by Alfred L. Zebarth; background art digitally created by Slim Films; photos top to bottom: Ed George, NGS; Ed George, NGS; NOAA; George Grall, NGS

Back cover: (top) Radu Sigheti/Reuters/CORBIS; (bottom) CORBIS

About The Earth
4 (art) © NGS; 4–5 (t) Shusei Nagaska; (b) Earth Satellite Corporation; 5 (bl) Robert Hynes; 6–7 (art) Shusei Nagaska; 10 (l) Vlad Kharitonov NGS; 11 (t–b) NASA/GISS, NOAA/NESDIS/NGDC, NASA/GSFC, University of Miami; 14–15 (t) NASA/JPL/CalTech/CAG, (b) Christopher R. Scotese/PALEOMAP Project, U. of TX, Arlington; 16–17 (t) NOAA/NESDIS/NGDC; 22, (l–r), Des & Jen Bartlett; Raymond Gehman; Cosmo Condina /Getty Images; Walter M. Edwards; 23, (l–r), Tom Bean/Getty Images; Steve Jackson; Tim Laman; Medford Taylor/NGS Image Collection; 24, (l–r), Jeremy Horner/CORBIS; Joseph Sohm; ChromoSohm, Inc./CORBIS; Priit J. Vesilind/ NGS Image Collection; 25, Steve McCurry; 28, Stuart Franklin; 32, Les Stone/CORBIS SYGMA; 33, (l–r), Jeremy Horner/CORBIS; Ric Ergenbright/CORBIS; 34, (l–r), Annie Griffiths Belt/CORBIS; Lindsay Hebberd/CORBIS; 35, (l–r), Reuters/CORBIS; CORBIS; 36, (l–r), Martin Rogers; James P. Blair; Phil Schermeister; 37, (l–r), James L. Stanfield; Mark Thiessen, NGP; 38, (l–r), Steven L. Raymer; Sisse Brimberg; Steve St. John; 40, (l–r), Steve Winter; Annie Griffiths Belt; 41, (l–r), Herve Collart/CORBIS; Jim Brandenburg; 43, (tl), James A. Sugar/BLACK STAR; (c), Marc Moritsch; (b), Bob Krist; (r), Patrick Bennett/Getty Images; 44, (l–r), Spencer Platt/Getty Images; Antoine Gyori/Emmanuel Razavi/France Reportage/CORBIS; 45, (l–r), Ismail Danish/Reuters/ CORBIS; Malcolm Linton/Getty Images; 46, Patrick Barth/ Stringer/Getty Images; 47, (l–r), AFP/Stringer/Getty Images; Radu Sigheti/Reuters/CORBIS; 48, Joe Raedle/Newsmakers/Getty Images; 49, CORBIS; 50, Bojan Brecelj/CORBIS; 51, (l–r), Louise Gubb/CORBIS SABA; Spencer Platt/Getty Images; 52, (l–r), Bob Sacha; The Granger Collection, NY; 53, Shusei Nagaoka

North America
68, (tl–r), Roger Werth/Woodfin Camp & Associates; Ravi Miro Fry; 68, (b), Chris Stewart/ BLACK STAR

South America
79, (t), Bill Curtsinger; (c), Mattias Klum; (bl–r), Michael Nichols, NGP, both

Europe
88, Bert Blokhuis/Getty Images

Africa
98, (t), Chris Johns, NGP; (b), Paul Zahl

Asia
108, (t), James L. Stanfield; (b), Steve MCCurry; 109, (l–r), James P. Blair; Lynn Funkhouser

Australia
120, (l), Reuters/CORBIS; (tr), Gary Bell/Australian Picture Library/CORBIS; (br), Wolcott Henry; 121, (t), Wolcott Henry; (b), David Doubilet

Published by the National Geographic Society
1145 17th St. N.W.
Washington, D.C. 20036-4688
Copyright © 2001, 2005 National Geographic Society
All rights reserved. Reproduction of the whole or any part of the contents without written permission from the publisher is prohibited.

The Library of Congress has cataloged the 2001 edition as follows:

National Geographic Society (U.S.)
National Geographic student atlas of the world.
p. cm.
Includes index and glossary.
ISBN 0-7922-7221-8; 0-7922-7178-5 (pbk.)
ISBN 0-7922-7235-8; 0-7922-7168-8 (hc.)
ISBN 0-7922-7206-4 (library)
  1. Children's atlases. 2. Earth—remote-sensing images. 3. Physical geography—Maps for children. [1.Atlases.] I. Title: Student atlas of the world. II. Title.
G1021 .N42 2001
912–dc21
00-030006

Printed in the U.S.A.

World Facts

The Earth

AREA: 196,951,900 sq mi (510,066,000 sq km)

LAND: 57,313,000 sq mi (148,647,000 sq km)—29.1%

WATER: 139,638,900 sq mi (361,419,000 sq km)— 70.9%

POPULATION: 6,314,000,000 people

The Continents

	AREA (sq mi)	(sq km)	Percent of Earth's Land
Asia	17,213,300	44,579,000	30.0
Africa	11,609,000	30,065,000	20.2
North America	9,449,500	24,474,000	16.5
South America	6,880,500	17,819,000	12.0
Antarctica	5,100,400	13,209,000	8.9
Europe	3,837,400	9,938,000	6.7
Australia	2,968,000	7,687,000	5.2

Highest Point On Each Continent

	feet	meters
Everest, Asia	29,035	8,850
Aconcagua, South America	22,834	6,960
McKinley (Denali), N. America	20,320	6,194
Kilimanjaro, Africa	19,340	5,895
El'brus, Europe	18,510	5,642
Vinson Massif, Antarctica	16,067	4,897
Kosciuszko, Australia	7,310	2,228

Lowest Point On Each Continent

	feet	meters
Dead Sea, Asia	-1,365	-416
Lake Assal, Africa	-512	-156
Death Valley, N. America	-282	-86
Valdés Peninsula, S. America	-131	-40
Caspian Sea, Europe	-92	-28
Lake Eyre, Australia	-52	-16
Antarctica (ice covered)	-8,366	-2,550

Ten Longest Rivers

	LENGTH miles	kilometers
Nile, Africa	4,241	6,825
Amazon, South America	4,000	6,437
Chang Jiang (Yangtze), Asia	3,964	6,380
Mississippi-Missouri, N. America	3,710	5,971
Yenisey-Angara, Asia	3,440	5,536
Yellow (Huang), Asia	3,395	5,464
Ob-Irtysh, Asia	3,361	5,410
Amur, Asia	2,744	4,416
Lena, Asia	2,734	4,400
Congo, Africa	2,715	4,370

Ten Largest Lakes

	AREA (Sq mi)	(Sq km)	Greatest Depth (feet)	(meters)
Caspian Sea, Europe-Asia	143,254	371,000	3,363	1,025
Superior, N. America	31,701	82,100	1,332	406
Victoria, Africa	26,836	69,500	269	82
Huron, N. America	23,013	59,600	751	229
Michigan, N. America	22,318	57,800	922	281
Tanganyika, Africa	12,587	32,600	4,823	1,470
Baikal, Asia	12,163	31,500	5,371	1,637
Great Bear, N. America	12,086	31,300	1,463	446
Malawi, Africa	11,159	28,900	2,280	695
Great Slave, N. America	11,100	28,750	2,014	614

Ten Largest Islands

	AREA (Sq mi)	(Sq km)
Greenland	840,065	2,175,600
New Guinea	306,008	792,500
Borneo	280,137	725,500
Madagascar	226,658	587,000
Baffin	195,961	507,500
Sumatra	164,993	427,300
Honshu	87,806	227,400
Great Britain	84,215	218,100
Victoria	83,906	217,300
Ellesmere	75,759	196,200

The Oceans

	AREA (Sq mi)	(Sq km)	Percent of Earth's Water Area
Pacific	65,436,246	169,479,100	46.8
Atlantic	35,338,040	91,526,400	25.3
Indian	29,829,823	74,694,800	20.6
Arctic	5,390,024	13,960,100	3.9

Deepest Point In Each Ocean

	feet	meters
Challenger Deep, Mariana Trench, Pacific	35,827	10,920
Puerto Rico Trench, Atlantic	28,232	8,605
Java Trench, Indian	23,376	7,125
Molloy Hole, Arctic	18,599	5,669

Ten Largest Seas

	AREA (Sq mi)	(Sq km)	Average Depth (feet)	(meters)
Coral	1,615,262	4,183,510	8,106	2,471
South China	1,388,573	3,596,390	3,841	1,180
Caribbean	1,094,325	2,834,290	8,517	2,596
Bering	972,815	2,519,580	6,010	1,832
Mediterranean	953,324	2,469,100	5,147	1,572
Sea of Okhotsk	627,489	1,627,519	2,670	814
Gulf of Mexico	591,435	1,531,810	5,065	1,544
Norwegian	550,303	1,425,380	5,800	1,768
Greenland	447,048	1,157,850	4,734	1,443
Sea of Japan (East Sea)	389,291	1,008,260	5,403	1,647

Earth's Extremes

HOTTEST PLACE: Dalol, Denakil Depression, Ethiopia; annual average temperature— 93°F (34°C)

COLDEST PLACE: Plateau Station, Antarctica; annual average temperature— -134°F (-56.7°C)

WETTEST PLACE: Mawsynram, Assam, India; annual average rainfall— 467 in (1,187.3 cm)

DRIEST PLACE: Atacama Desert, Chile; rainfall barely measurable

HIGHEST WATERFALL: Angel, Venezuela— 3,212ft (979 m)

LARGEST DESERT: Sahara, Africa— 3,475,000 sq mi (9,000,000 sq km)

LARGEST CANYON: Grand Canyon, Colorado River, Arizona; 275 mi (443 km) long along river; 590 ft (180 m) to 18 mi (29 km) wide, about 1 mi (1.6 km) deep

LONGEST REEF: Great Barrier Reef, Australia— 1,429 mi (2,300 km)

GREATEST TIDES: Bay of Fundy, Nova Scotia— 55 ft (17 m)

ABBREVIATIONS

COUNTRY NAMES

ARM.	Armenia
AZERB.	Azerbaijan
B. & H.; BOSN. & HERZ.	Bosnia and Herzegovina
BELG.	Belgium
CRO.	Croatia
EST.	Estonia
HUNG.	Hungary
LATV.	Latvia
LIECH.	Liechtenstein
LITH.	Lithuania
LUX.	Luxembourg
MACED.	Macedonia
MOLD.	Moldova
N.Z.	New Zealand
NETH.	Netherlands
SERB. & MONT.	Serbia and Montenegro
SLOV.	Slovenia
SWITZ.	Switzerland
U.A.E.	United Arab Emirates
U.K.	United Kingdom
U.S.	United States

PHYSICAL FEATURES

I.-s.	Island-s
L.	Lake
Mt.-s.	Mont, Mount-ain-s
R.	River

OTHER

Eq.	Equatorial
Pop.	Population
Rep.	Republic
St.	Saint
&	and